Psychology, Race Equality and Working with Children

Psychology, Race Equality and Working with Children

edited by Jeune Guishard-Pine

tb

Trentham Books
Stoke on Trent, UK and Sterling, USA
Winner of the IPG DIVERSITY Award 2010

Trentham Books Limited
Westview House   22883 Quicksilver Drive
734 London Road   Sterling
Oakhill   VA 20166-2012
Stoke on Trent   USA
Staffordshire
England ST4 5NP

© 2010 Jeune Guishard-Pine

All rights reserved. No part of this publication may be reproduced or transmitted in any form or by any means, electronic or mechanical including photocopying, recording or any information storage or retrieval system, without prior permission in writing from the publishers.

First published 2010

British Library Cataloguing-in-Publication Data
A catalogue record for this book is available from the British Library

ISBN: 978 1 85856 474 6

Designed and typeset by Trentham Books Ltd and printed in Great Britain by Henry Ling Ltd, Dorchester

Contents

Acknowledgements • viii

Foreword • ix
Tony Cline

Chapter 1
Introduction – The other side of the coin • 1

Section 1
Training the professionals

Chapter 2
Race and culture in nurse education: learning through experience • 9
Christine Cork, Sarah Hawes and Clare Nichols

Chapter 3
Black expertise: can being black be a skill? • 19
Valerie Jackson

Chapter 4
Victim or criminal? The racialisation of the juvenile justice system • 29
Jeune Guishard-Pine

Chapter 5
Ensuring (E)quality of services: implications for Continuing Professional Development • 37
Hazel Sawyers and Jeune Guishard-Pine

Chapter 6
Education is for life: Further and Higher
Education for diverse Britain • 47
Olatayo Afuape

Section 2
Models of innovative work with specific ethnic groups

Chapter 7
Chinese pupils: the silent voices in British schools • 57
Karina Ng

Chapter 8
The psychology of identity:
the black refugee experience • 69
Randa Price

Chapter 9
Working with Pakistani Mothers in the community:
an early intervention child mental health service • 79
Alex Harborne

Chapter 10
The diagnosis of autism: the experiences of
West African parents • 89
Sarah Took

Chapter 11
Learning Difficulties: Distinguishing them
from issues of language • 101
Jan Carter and Jeune Guishard-Pine

Section 3
Theories and suggestions for ways forward

Chapter 12
Progressive African Caribbean masculinities
– a challenge to domination • 115
Taiwo Afuape

CONTENTS

Chapter 13
The Virgin Father: psychological research with black fathers in Britain • 125
Jeune Guishard-Pine

Chapter 14
Walking in Jung's shadow? Black Rage and domestic abuse • 135
Luke Daniels

Chapter 15
User engagement and African Caribbean experience in child and family care service • 145
Naomi Anna Watson

Chapter 16
Self-evaluation by primary school aged children: an existential intervention • 153
Yvonne Mills and Jeune Guishard-Pine

Section 4
Contextualisation and experiences of racism

Chapter 17
'Blank darkness': the invisibility of black women in the history curriculum • 165
Isis Guishard-Pine and Jeune Guishard-Pine

Chapter 18
Looking back at being black and gay in school • 183
Loyd Hamilton

Chapter 19
Conclusion • 191

List of contributors • 193

References • 197

Index • 217

*This book is dedicated to the memory
of Veronica Edmead*

Acknowledgements

My huge thanks firstly go to the authors who restored my trust and confidence in the creative rather than destructive power of the written word. I must also thank Professor Tony Cline for devoting his time and intellect to perusing the first manuscript and providing the Foreword. I must also thank Trentham's Gillian Klein for her solid support for this book and providing the opportunity for these ideas to be placed in the public arena. Most of this book would not have been produced if not for the generosity of the members of the various communities who put themselves forward to enable the research reported on here to be completed. Thanks are also extended to the various women and organisations that permitted the printing of photographs of historical significance. My final thanks goes to my family and especially my exceptional husband Professor Courtney Pine, CBE and our children for giving me the space to put together this book.

Foreword

Human service professions mirror the societies in which they develop and are often slow to change. In the United Kingdom these services became established when the country appeared for the most part to be culturally and ethnically homogeneous. Social and ethnic change stripped off this veneer after the Second World War, but it has taken most agencies and professions more than a generation to evolve a response to those changes. The knowledge base of disciplines such as psychology continued to rely on the established models long after their client populations had outgrown such norms. At the same time staff practices in settings such as schools and the juvenile justice system often continued to reflect an ethic of fair treatment based on one-size-fits-all. But slowly the confrontation of institutional racism in professional bodies and service providers led to a shift in expectations.

This book offers a celebration and an analysis of a new phase in service development. It moves beyond depicting what has been wrong to suggesting what could be done instead. Some of the authors examine the contribution their own personal involvement and commitment has made, in some cases painfully, to the evolution of their understanding of their theme. Moving between the personal and the 'professional' may not always be easy, but it usually enhances insight. The editor expresses faith in the value and power of research to help us avoid seeking simple answers to complex problems. This volume tries to address the complexities but also keeps the simple core value of action for equality firmly at the front of our attention.

Tony Cline
Co-Director of CPD Doctorate in Educational Psychology, University College London and Visiting Professor, Institute for Research in Education, University of Bedfordshire

1

Introduction –
The other side of the coin

Each one, teach one – African Proverb

I could fill a book with anecdotes about the racist assumptions made by professionals and educated people about children and families from black and Asian ethnic groups. I almost burnt myself out with my attempts to challenge these attitudes. Then in 2004, the British Psychological Society gave me an award for my dedication to the issues of marginalised groups throughout my career. Someone had noticed my efforts!

What's more, this acknowledgement gave a much needed boost to my endeavours to keep race on the British psychologists' agenda. This book is but one drive towards achieving this goal, but it would be arrogant to suggest that it gets even near to being a complete answer to race inequality in work with children. It is rather a step in the journey towards neutralising the racist beliefs and practices that have spanned several hundred years and travelled many thousands of miles. The *Every Child Matters* agenda has helped reignite the debates that can eventually lead to paradigmatic shifts in practice ... I hope.

Five generations after the *Windrush* brought its migrants to Britain, to be black and British has yet to be conceptualised so that significant stereotypes are on balance more positive than negative. Some say that other migrant groups have accessed self-employment, eg Jewish and South Asian people, and thus managed to change their position in society, whereas the lack of a rigorous black British business base contributes to ongoing social, economic and political disadvantage (Williams, 2006).

There is also the argument that where there is an integral class system of overt advantage and disadvantage, eg among some Indian groups, migrants to Britain whose families come from the professional classes are placed to set up businesses which thrive. However, other aspects of the various cultures of South Asian groups have been difficult to assimilate into British life, just as is the case for people from African and Caribbean backgrounds. If hard work were the answer, black people would be some of the richest in the world.

Tomlinson (1983) reported that black children were held back in school rather than promoted. She points out how they were entered for CSEs rather than GCE O levels and encouraged to go for low status jobs. I witnessed this practice myself. Many black students who were entered for CSEs when I was at school in the 70s now hold 1st and 2nd degrees and are running successful black-owned companies. Why aren't they getting attention from the mainstream and black press? Some say that it is because they are the exception and not the rule; the minority, not the majority. Yet that does not seem to prevent successful white people who are exceptional from receiving media attention.

All through my career I have carried out an exercise where I ask people to write down a list of facts, myths and stereotypes about various ethnic groups. The exercise quite often became contentious, but mostly it achieved the objective of raising the awareness that we each carry with us myths and stereotypes about ethnic minority groups rather than facts, and that these myths and stereotypes are pervasive and usually negative. I can never forget the time a group of educational psychologists produced just a single positive stereotype about black people: that they were good boxers. Neither can I forget the anger and tension amongst others because my focus and specialism was to be on the black experience rather than on class divisions or sexism or ethnicity. As Carter and McGoldrick (1999) argued, a focus on diversity similarly means that the specific histories of people of African origin in relation to white racist society is trivialised.

Over the years I have read many explanations for the persistent under achievement of black children in British schools. Some suggest that it is because of the racist, Eurocentric curriculum – but South Asian and Chinese children also have to endure this, yet they do well at GCSE. Others say it is because of the poor self image and low motivation in the black community – which in turn is attributed to their dysfunctional family life.

So just what is it that black people in Britain need to do to generate more positive images? What is black success? Some link black success to greater access to higher education; others to the stabilisation of the black family; more would link it to the financial growth and economic power of the black community; others to the penetration of black people at all strata of British society. My view is that without adequate research, we risk seeking simple answers to a complex problem.

What the research tells us

According to Myers, 'subjective and self-knowledge in the generation of knowledge ... reminds us that the psychogeneisis of knowledge occurs in a social context' (1991:3). Research conducted on black and ethnic minority children in Britain has gone in search of answers to issues within the communities and produced data such as poor educational outcomes, mental inferiority, family pathology, deviant language skills and, consequently, low teacher expectation of their academic prowess. The solution for all these problems was supposed to be multiracial and multicultural education.

In the 1970s there was a significant increase in publication of research into the life of black families in the United States. This was largely in response to the Moynihan Report (1965), which described African American families as pathological, culturally deviant, and in crisis. They asserted that the major problem confronting back people had to do with reorganising their families 'into a two-parent unit' (p 7).

Staples and Miranda (1980) observed that from the 1960s to the late 70s around 500 research reports on African Americans were published – five times more than in the previous 100 years.

In Britain, a teacher from the Caribbean working in London, Bernard Coard published a telling indictment in 1971, entitled *How the West Indian Child is made Educationally Subnormal by the British Education System*. In 1972 provision in social work was criticised by Cheetham, followed by Ahmed and Cheetham (1986). But it took until 1999 for the British Psychological Society to publish a special edition of *Educational and Child Psychology* which featured commentaries on the challenges of providing adequate child psychological services to ethnic minority children and their families (BPS, 1999). In 2006 Williams *et al* conducted a review of clinical psychology services and their ability to engage and serve ethnic minority service users.

The paucity of research into black children and their families in the UK cannot be overemphasised. Only four works in Britain (Finch and Mason, 1993; Guishard, 1992; Phoenix, 1987; Tizard and Phoenix, 1994) had been published which made any attempt to present a framework for developing the knowledge and understanding of black families and parenting in the British context. Reynolds (2006) is the most recent contributor to the field.

The ethnic minority intelligentsia in the UK have long been concerned that European models of family life cannot be applied to the whole range of ethnic groups: there are pronounced differences in philosophies, spirituality and culture.

Yet despite major differences, we continued to rely on European models to explain psychological phenomena in relation to ethnic groups from Africa, Asia and the Caribbean. This is mainly because, save for a distinguished few, the psychology establishment has been so slow to recognise black British psychology or even recommend readings in ethnic psychology as a compulsory module in psychology education. There is still no Division of the British Psychological Society dedicated to black and ethnic minority psychology.

Joseph White's book *Toward a Black Psychology* (1970) heralded the modern era of black and ethnic minority psychology in the US. A new perspective was created by the numerous ethnic minority psychologists and psychiatrists in the US. But in Britain, establishing an ethnic psychology discipline has been hindered by diversionary tactics such as obsession with defining and re-defining concepts such as 'race' and 'black'. Whilst the current perspective is that neither of these concepts exists in any true, scientific sense, the reality is that a significant body of research has successfully examined differences based on 'race' and much has been written about the black experience in the UK.

The black intelligentsia and professionals believe they have found a possible answer to the persistent problem of race inequality. The Equality and Human Rights Commission (EHRC) have not rescinded the view that: 'the growth of a strong ethnic minority business sector is of crucial importance to the attainment of racial equality' (CRE, 1984:1, cited in Williams, 2006). This book may not be directed at the business sector, but that sector would do well to heed it.

The eighteen chapters of *Race, Psychology and Working with Children* feature a diverse range of issues and ideas on how to enhance the work of child-focused practitioners with black and ethnic minority children. The authors are agreed that the development of culturally competent services, rooted in appropriate knowledge and skills, is the first step on a long journey towards achieving race equality.

The book has gone through many changes since it was first conceived in 2007, mainly due to the difficulty of finding British-based research that was theoretically or ethnomethodologically sound. What it offers is the thinking and action-research of some of the most fertile minds practicing in Britain today. Most of the contributors are dual-qualified in child and family-related practice. They are dedicated to imparting their knowledge of successful work with ethnic minority children and their families, much of which has been subjected to scientific evaluation. They present the other side of the coin.

The first section addresses the training of professionals working with children – nurses and psychologists, juvenile justice, further and higher education, continuing professional development. Five chapters describing innovative practice with specific ethnic groups make up the second section, focusing on Chinese children, refugees, Pakistani mothers, autism and West Africans, and how schools can – and must – differentiate between pupils' learning difficulties and their proficiency in the English language.

The first three chapters in Section 3 consider future development in three areas: Black fatherhood, combating domestic abuse and re-evaluating family care services, and ends with an example of self-evaluation among primary children. The final section is of two chapters which attempt to share innovative ideas that will enhance the understanding of practitioners about issues of race and equality and spur them to action: a review of the history curriculum shows the conspicuous absence of black women and the final chapter is a moving reflection on how it felt to be black and gay at school and society's implicit consent to the physical and psychological attacks on homosexuals in Britain.

The reader will notice that the phrase non-white is not used. The book is about the ethnic minority presence in Britain in terms of who we are, rather than what we are not. Comparisons are unavoidable and indeed necessary – an objective of this book is to examine the pervading psychological issues for various (but mainly black) ethnic groups, and the authors all strive to ensure that the reader witnesses ideas in action. This collaboration of writers has been a labour of love, and I sincerely hope that this is apparent. In the words of a Chinese proverb:

> *If there is righteousness in the heart, there will be beauty in character. If there is beauty in character, there will be harmony in the home. If there is harmony in the home, there will be order in the nation. If there is order in the nation, there will be peace in the world.*

Section 1
Training the professionals

2

Race and culture in nurse education: learning through experience

Christine Cork, Sarah Hawes and Clare Nichols

Introduction
Nurse training and nurse education

The way in which nursing is taught has changed dramatically over the years, progressing from training courses delivered in hospital to education programmes based in higher education colleges or universities.

In the 1970s, most student nurses undertook a predominantly skills-based 3 year training programme while working on hospital wards. Clinical tutors and more experienced nurses provided much of the day-to-day supervision and teaching. Procedure manuals provided guidance to ensure quality and consistency regarding nursing techniques. The final examination comprised both written (theoretical) and practical assessments in the host school of nursing. These assessments were validated externally but no academic accreditation was awarded.

The late 1970s saw the advent in Britain of university-based education for nurses. Nationally, only a small number of universities or higher education colleges provided a 4 year BSc or BN qualification in nursing. This change aroused much fear, suspicion and prejudice. However, a positive aspect of the undergraduate nurse programme was access to a month's elective period of study outside the British Isles, undertaken towards the end of the course. This exposure to a different culture may have been instrumental in developing an understanding of racial and cultural difference, and may have helped bring about a shift in thinking amongst undergraduate nurses towards the respectful curiosity which is so essential for working in an increasingly diverse UK population.

Successful trainees of both types of courses were eligible for registration with the body now known as the Nursing and Midwifery Council (NMC). The Council sets standards of education, training and conduct that nurses and midwives require so they can deliver high quality healthcare. The skills needed to meet the standards of proficiency for pre-registration nursing are identified (NMC, 2007). They include the requirement for nurses to demonstrate knowledge and understanding of the religious and cultural context of the patient in all areas of practice.

Towards the turn of the century, the Project 2000 nurse education programme moved all nursing into the domain of higher education institutions providing academic accreditation. This set the agenda for the existing and future needs of the profession and raised the professional status, credibility and autonomy for nurses alongside other professional courses. The curriculum became more concerned with encouraging the use of a body of robust nursing knowledge that included theoretical knowledge, professional craft and personal knowledge of self in relation to others (Wellard *et al*, 2007). It was argued that this type of education would better equip nurses to meet the increasing expectations of working in several settings and undertaking evidence-based practice.

As British trained nurses and health visitors, we consider how nurses have acquired competences and expertise in working with black and ethnic minority patients. Our experience of working in hospitals and community settings both in and outside the United Kingdom, as well as our current roles as Primary Mental Health Workers in a Child and Adolescent Mental Health Service, have enabled us to focus on our own experiences. But we have also spoken to nurse educators, school health nurses and some more recently trained post-graduate nurses. The reflections and suggestions here are intended to help readers consider how culture and diversity issues can be better incorporated into their individual practice and organisational structures. It is hoped that these ideas will generate a wider debate for improving service delivery.

Culture and difference in nurse education

Some might say that it is because of fear that difficulties arise in cultural and race relations. It might be fear of the unknown. It might be fear of change. It might be fear of loss of control. Fear may be expressed as prejudice.

A district nurse who graduated through the Project 2000 nurse education programme described how the issues of cultural and racial difference were addressed during the course. She recalled several occasions when examples of cultural and racial differences had been drawn to their attention. Attitudes towards death and dying and to childbirth were mentioned. The approach judged most helpful by the student nurses was being given a detailed description of how to manage patients from specific ethnic minorities in particular situations; but this was rarely forthcoming. Instead, nurses were encouraged to adopt a general position of respectfully letting patients deal with things in their own way. Teaching had become more psychosocial in response to a changing population and this highlighted the notion of promoting the patient as a person. However, the student nurses still regarded this as insufficient teaching. What they learnt during their working experience was judged to be more useful.

This rekindles the longstanding debate within nurse education as to whether nurses are better trained on the job or in higher education establishments. Some nurse educationalists consider that the prescriptive nature and current emphasis on care programmes and pathways continue to limit the essential development of the questioning and exploration skills needed to make professional clinical judgements.

So is it better for nurses to work to strictly prescribed rules and regulations or will they deliver better care if educated within a framework which develops motivation and the ability to think and problem solve?

A newly qualified nurse graduate described experiencing the ideas of culture, racial and religious difference 'from day one' under the general umbrella of ethics. It was emphasised that patients must be seen holistically, and not merely as people with certain conditions and symptoms. This nurse felt that the issues of race and culture had been neglected in the white middle class context in which she had studied. But while attempting to avoid stereotyping, the teaching programme had given nurses little opportunity to discuss the impact of race and culture on the process of delivering nursing care. This area of professional development was offered alongside other optional modules such as introduction to complementary therapies and ethics in health and social care practice and these were more appealing to the nurse students.

What are the processes that enable nurses to acquire the relevant knowledge about race and culture to pass on to trainees in placement? How do practitioners incorporate experience as knowledge?

Personal experience of working abroad

I was always warmly welcomed abroad where I was perceived as holding the cure for all their ailments. Being a young English nurse, I was revered as a 'doctor'. My recent qualification in nursing and midwifery in the UK however, hardly equipped me to meet all their expectations. Working within communities in West Africa and the Middle East I found that I needed to be open to the knowledge, experience and traditions of those communities. It was not useful to them if I tried to impose western ways that did not match their ideas of what was valuable. If I wanted to find out what service I could offer their community I needed to ask them and to listen to and respect their answers.

I remember being saddened and shocked when, seven days after a stillbirth, a bereaved family in the Middle East held a party, attended by the local village women and their children. I soon realised that the community were not seizing an insensitive excuse to party but were treating this mother the same as any woman who had recently given birth. Each visitor took turns to reach out her hand to the young mother, making contact with her and taking the opportunity to console her and establish her continued value to the community. How much better than the shy and embarrassed avoidance which might have happened in my own community?

The women were keen to learn from the village midwives – their mentors, and it was through their midwives that we learnt the local traditions and beliefs. After sharing and discussing ideas with them, we were able to help them to influence local families and to make useful changes in practice. One example was the importance of careful hygiene at the birth and ensuring that a clean blade and cord were used to cut and tie the umbilical cord.

Learning through experience

The changes to nurse training over the past 30 years also mirrored demographic changes in society. In the 1970s, traditional nurse training did not significantly address ways of thinking about issues related to race and culture. Nurses' training was colour blind: trainees were not made aware that they needed any more than a respect for individuals and a wish to offer the same standard of care irrespective of race, colour, creed or class. Nurses we spoke to had few memories of any specific training to raise their awareness of the differing experiences of the increasing immigrant population. Childhood and whole-life experiences together with an increasing political and public awareness appear to have had more powerfully influenced their racial and cultural understanding.

We talked to school health nurses working in the community who consider that they learn most from colleagues and their work experience. Importantly, colleagues from culturally diverse backgrounds enrich the bank of experience and knowledge. The vague memories and apparent irrelevance of specific cultural diversity training for nurses may indicate that their lived experience contributes more to their knowledge and understanding and is of more value to them than formal aspects from their training.

It is possible that the hands-on practical aspects of nurses' work encourages the use of non-verbal ways of communicating which may be more easily recognised and accepted by patients with whom they do not share language or culture. Malik and Krause (2005) describe this as an 'embodied' way of working.

[text obscured by receipt] visitors, school nurses and nursery nurses admit [...] confident when they use interpreters. Perhaps [...] ical connection with which they are at ease. The [...] tions in attending to the needs of their patients [...] a mother learns the needs of her infant (Brazel-[...]

[...] n (1991) contrasted learning about things with [...] of the self in the world, which he saw as a con-[...] ves. This has relevance to how nurses learn their [...] l the nursing and personal skills they have [...] ctual knowledge and a theoretical framework in [...] d culture are essential in any nurse education [...] e recognise the immense importance of nurses'

[...] ltural and gender groups might have different [...] s due to their different expectations of both the [...] t also (in the case of women) their different [...] r. This was borne out by community nurses we [...] or recognition of the differences between cul-[...] s and traditions.

[...] e of the interpreter in the facilitation of a three [...] intimate and less mechanistic than merely a [...] s. This reminds us again of the value of the felt [...] the importance of the process and skill of the [...] hly developed in an experienced nurse.

[...] need for adaptations of health programmes [...] us traditions. They recognised that working alongside link-workers and family support workers who shared a common ethnic origin with patients contributed significantly to the quality and efficacy of communication, not only through language but also through improved cultural acceptance and understanding.

Learning to listen to the ideas, skills and traditions of the community, developing and integrating services to accommodate these ideas rather than making assumptions of what is needed has proved to be a far more successful way of working. If professionals move too fast on their own agenda, the community quickly loses interest and trust. In Bedfordshire, specially trained workers from ethnic minorities have helped women to engage better with infant feeding and with parenting programmes.

It can sometimes be so difficult to accommodate differences that our ability to communicate is impeded. Nurses and patients were heard to say 'We can't understand him' when referring to a new Asian doctor although he spoke perfect English. Is it possible for the appearance of someone to mislead the ears of someone else? Can we listen effectively to someone if we can only see their differences from ourselves?

Changes in nurse education and methods of patient assessment have gradually become more holistic, as demonstrated in care planning and more recently, in the multi-agency use of the Common Assessment Framework. These assessment tools bring together a wider and hopefully more realistic picture of the strengths and needs of the individual. John Burnham's example of the social GRRAACCEESS (Gender, Race, Religion, Age, Ability, Class. Culture, Ethnicity, Education, Sexuality and Spirituality) reminds practitioners to investigate the wider complexities of people's lives (Burnham, 2008).

Our experience of working within a Child and Adolescent Mental Health Service has highlighted for us a way of working that includes the many points of view within a family. It embraces culture as a broader issue than either ethnic or religious difference. Within this setting, clinicians are encouraged to hear the story of each member of the family: to look for common story threads but also to accept differences as part of the fabric of family life. This kind of curiosity might present difficulties within cultures where the idea of allowing private family matters to be shared with strangers is frowned upon. Community nurses have found that they need to be sensitive to the splits within cultures and the dilemmas of young people who are inevitably influenced by the dominant culture but who also wish to remain part of their own culture. In this setting, as elsewhere, it remains of paramount importance not to make assumptions about what parents or children might think or feel, whatever their racial background – but particularly if it is different from one's own.

Beyond training to practical experience
Personal experience of working at home
While working as a clinical support manager in Children's Services, I saw a black doll undressed, lying on a table in a multi-purpose playroom that someone had

apparently forgotten to put away with the other toys. I removed the doll and wrote a polite note for the group leaders responsible for the sessions, stating that I felt it was potentially culturally insensitive to black children using the centre to come across the doll as I had.

My actions created a furore which lasted many months before being resolved. Being a multi-agency team, managers and staff from different agencies had become involved in the debate and most disagreed with my intervention. I learnt that it was considered inappropriate for me to touch property belonging to a different organisation. A number of health service managers were puzzled by my actions and laughed about it. Some informed me that they had consulted black friends and neighbours who had said they did not think their children would be offended by the naked black doll. I was asked to explain myself and made to feel that the problem resided in me, a black West Indian.

When I explained to people that the doll would reinforce a negative self-image due to the paucity of positive, affirming images of black children, I could see a visible change in their demeanour and in their understanding of the cultural issue. The consultant paediatrician wished to do something about it within the multi-disciplinary team. Some training or more open debate was suggested. The senior managers disagreed. Sensitivity towards inter-agency alliances and collaboration took precedence, despite the Children's Charter and service ethos. An apology was written to the organisation that raised the complaint against me and I was told to modify my behaviour.

This experience highlighted a number of issues:

- **Organisational culture**

  Training, while essential, is not enough to change attitudes or influence discriminatory practices. In order to negotiate satisfactory outcomes in the interest of the child it is essential that there is willingness by those in authority to be uncomfortable and to challenge organisational barriers without fear of alienation from their superiors.

  More recently, initiatives to improve the voice of black and ethnic minority staff and service users in the policy decisions of the organisation have improved. However, raising issues related to racial understanding is extremely sensitive for everyone. A challenge can be seen either as confrontational or as naïve. The black doll, regarded as insignificant, mirrored the organisation's unwillingness to value and to learn from the expertise of ethnic minority staff.

- **Understanding one's own identity, racial heritage and prejudices**
  When we raise issues of race, it makes us uncomfortable because we lack understanding and knowledge of the other. We do not wish to offend others, neither do we wish to confront our own ignorance. To be prepared to risk being misunderstood, it is first necessary to develop a feeling of ease and confidence in one's sense of self. A safe place is needed before these risks can be taken and it is an ongoing personal and organisational process.

  This process of exploration is important for everyone working in the health service. It is difficult, as it involves the emotive process of exploring aspects of ourselves that we may not wish to acknowledge. Staff need strong support to embark willingly on such a demanding undertaking. Regular discussions in team meetings about issues related to race and culture would facilitate the development of a culture that is willing to bear uncomfortable feelings and to embrace difference and learn from it.

Cultural awareness training needs to be provided for practitioners who wish to explore their own understanding of themselves in relation to working cross culturally. Preferably, it could be offered, as a course, over a number of days so that trust and safety can be established within the group. Mandatory day courses, common in many organisations, run the risk of being devalued by the unwilling or unmotivated attendance of some participants (see also Chapter 5).

Conclusion

In recent years there have been some positive changes in society's attitude to race and culture. Nurse education has attempted to encourage a broader acceptance of difference and has put greater emphasis on assessing the needs of patients in a psychosocial context.

Despite the move to higher education, nurse educationalists might do even more to promote the interpersonal quality of nursing care. Nursing could be influential in developing an understanding of the impact of issues of cultural, racial or religious difference on the patient's experience within the health care system, particularly in relation to the impact of power differentials. Student nurses need to be given the opportunity to discuss and reflect on their placement experiences in order to process any areas of personal difficulty they encounter in relation to race and culture. Nurse educators need to provide the setting in which such openness is regularly encouraged. Importantly, their own training needs have to be met before this can become a reality.

Roffe *et al* (1990) and Cline and Lunt (1990) emphasised the necessity for an increase in sound knowledge, information and facts about the culture and experiences of black and ethnic minority groups so as to change the underlying assumptions made about people of another race.

While seeking to understand cultural difference we also need to ensure that we do not compromise the understanding of the Universal Declaration of Human Rights (United Nations, 1948). Culture is not fixed but is continually evolving. Like families who adapt or struggle to adapt to the dominant culture, nurses need to engage in a similar process to achieve an understanding of the unique concerns and anxieties of their patients and to respond in ways that are helpful. There is always more to learn and we can never know it all.

It is vital that nurses working in the child and family sector learn about how ethnicity can mask socio-economic disadvantage, burying it amongst other disadvantages faced by many children particularly from inner-city areas. They need to understand how institutionalised racial discrimination manifests and, crucially, about the development of prejudice and racism in the early years. All nurses should be provided with information about a range of cultures: different ways of life, different care giving practices, different family structures and the roles within them. It is important that childcare nurses involve parents and carers and build good relationship with them.

Looking for common ground is seen as a good basis on which to build a healthy relationship between any two people, and perhaps particularly so between people from different cultural backgrounds. However, we also need to find the courage to understand and accept the differences. The quality of being curious and making a conscious effort not to judge differences would seem essential for any current nurse education. Experiences of working within different cultural contexts enhance the chance of developing a deeper understanding.

Key points for nurses engaging in work with ethnic minority patients and families:

- Create and confirm a meaningful framework for the piece of work
- Check that the patient agrees with the intentions of your care plan
- Be curious and ask how the patient understands what is happening for them and what might be helpful
- Go at a pace that is sensitive to the level of understanding of the patient.
- Openly acknowledge the strengths and resources of the patient or family and allow an element of choice

- Consider the multiple contexts and social structure in which the patient or family lives
- Develop an understanding of your own identity, beliefs and attitudes. Ask yourself: 'Why do I think that?' 'Why am I finding this difficult?'
- Accept the difference between what you might expect and what is expressed by the patients. Avoid judging the differences or making assumptions
- Listen to the ideas, traditions and resources of the patients. Be willing to challenge them and/or adapt what you have to offer
- Train and encourage the family workers and link workers with whom you work to understand the context of the work
- Keep yourself informed of the increasing research on the experiences of black and ethnic minority families and be willing to take the risk to develop new skills.

3

Black expertise: can being black be a skill?

Valerie Jackson

Introduction

> If white psychologists practice white psychology, then black psychologists practice _____ psychology.
>
> *What is the missing word?*

Baldwin (1989) sees explicit ways in which the black community can be served by the black psychologist. His controversial position is that black psychologists have functioned in the service of the continued enslavement and oppression of black people rather than in the service of the liberation of the black community from western oppression. He argues that black psychologists employ European models to explain black people's psychological reality or, by attempting to 'blacken' the same models, give the false appearance of being relevant to the needs of black people. Baldwin's position therefore invites the question: Do black psychologists add any value to a service to ethnically diverse communities?

Baldwin maintains that black psychologists commit a fundamental error in failing to use African history and the various philosophical and cultural models to give intellectual direction and inspiration to theoretical development. He is critical of the bulk of their research activities: in Baldwin's view, research on black people is rarely underpinned by any basic culturally relevant theoretical models.

Further, he suggests that the theoretical work of many researchers is devalued unless it is preceded by Eurocentric oriented empirical exercise. The Eurocentric training of black psychologists, Baldwin asserts, does not provide clearly defined models and so leaves them incapable of providing a truly culturally relevant service. Such is the lack of cultural competence in the training of black psychologists that, he believes, they have ended up treating black people as if they are 'white people in a black skin', with only the experience of European racism to distinguish them. The ultimate aim of this training process is to maintain the *status quo* and to discourage a black psychology developing that mainstream psychology believes will challenge rather than complement it. The poor image of educational psychology and its use to penalise black children, threatened to alienate black psychologists from the community they sought to serve (Association of Educational Psychologists (AEP, 1988).

> If white psychologists practice white psychology, then black psychologists practice WHITE psychology.

Black psychology

As well as being involved in educational psychology as practitioners, there is a role for black psychologists in increasing the knowledge base of black psychology. Horsford (1986) offers a critical appraisal from a black perspective, of the work of EPs. In his review of literature he found that the description of the phenomenon of 'black failure' was still being explained by theories of:

- cultural bias ie value judgements were made about the social organisation of the black family
- emotional disturbance ie no acknowledgement that living in a new country and having to cope with racism was taken into account by IQ tests
- low teacher expectation ie streaming and discipline of black children
- self-esteem ie one aspect of a complex personality structure which may differ for Asians/Africans/Europeans
- curriculum change ie a multicultural curriculum that is naively implemented whereas black perspectives need to be an integral accredited part of the whole curriculum (see Chapter 17).

Horsford (1986) believes that the work of the psychologist must acknowledge that some of the problems of black children are rooted in racism and that bicultural research has something to offer in understanding black psychology. He also reports on findings about the self-esteem of successful black children.

The AEP Working Party on Racism (1988) interviewed black EPs who outlined three areas of conflict in their professional role: school, EP service and community levels. At the school level, they found it difficult to accept psychopathology as an explanation for black children's behaviour because this ignores the system operated by teachers and peers that Coard (1971) has shown to be so influential. Schools were failing to address endemic racism; the damage caused by the education system in terms of underachievement and high exclusion rates was felt to be a response to cumulative negative attitudes which children had experienced earlier in their school careers. They found themselves in conflict when colleagues used tests and interpreted the results, while disregarding the effects of racism on the child. The use of poor self-image and poor motivation to explain the behaviour of black children were felt to be unacceptable within-child explanations. Lastly, they noted that relevant research from the USA was not readily available in Britain.

In redefining the role of the black psychologist, Baldwin takes the position that the European worldview is anti-black and has to be rejected and an African worldview adopted. Black psychology must be about developing basic models of the human psychological condition that are consistent with the African worldview and so begin to project a science of psychology which truly addresses the psychological needs of all people of African heritage. In other words, that black people are defined in relation to themselves, not as either a dominated or alien culture.

Jackson (1982), however, does not see black psychology as being racist or totally incompatible with Euro-American psychology. Rather, he is concerned with redefining existing psychological principles and concepts and developing additional models that reveal the strengths of black people (Sims, 1977 in Jackson). Jackson continues that 'the value of Black psychology ... lies more than its being slightly different from a western conceptualisation of psychology; its African base makes it a distinct outlook with immense possibilities ... while Black psychology is focused primarily upon Afro-Americans, it has a universal component' (p11).

Atkinson *et al* (1983) reflects Baldwin's view that an increased knowledge base, supported by bicultural research and the expertise of ethnic minority groups, is necessary for making psychology more pluralistic, but his emphasis is on the fact that this cannot occur without political power and influence which he locates firmly in the American Psychological Association (APA). The task for psychologists however, would be to identify several rather than a single solution as many ethnic group issues are conflicts in which one side has been dominant to the detriment of another.

Sue (1983) identifies several conflicts which have hindered the progress of ethnic minority groups:

1. **All humans are alike (etic) v valuing sociocultural differences (emic)**
   Psychology has traditionally opted for the etic perspective based on the Anglo model, not the emic.

2. **Assimilation vs pluralism**
   The superiority of the Anglo-Saxon culture was presumed and conformity expected. Functional arguments are used eg that bilingualism hinders learning so English is stressed. Here ethnic minorities are coerced in to the mainstream only to be denied access to other areas of society through discrimination and prejudice.

3. **Equality of opportunity vs equality of outcome**
   Equal opportunities run the risk of perpetuating unequal outcomes, while equal outcomes may entail discriminating by treating some groups differently eg positive discrimination.

4. **Modal personality vs individual differences**
   Stressing within group differences ignores cultural differences between groups while a between group approach ignores individual differences. Cultural patterns are usually described through the *modal personality*, and this can lead to stereotyped images of those differences.

5. **Presence vs absence of racism today**
   Despite improvements in race relations, discrimination continues. Overt racism has been largely replaced by more subtle forms; institutionalised racism has replaced direct expressions of anti-black sentiments.

Atkinson *et al* suggest one way forward would be through bicultural research where the emphasis is on understanding ethnic groups on their own terms, emphasising within group variations and individual differences. Contrasts between different cultural and ethnic groups frequently mask the degree of heterogeneity that manifest as differences in acculturation, assimilation, language proficiency, customs, values and perceptions of racism. Sue (1983) believes that genuine pluralism is only achieved when the diverse perspectives of ethnic groups are fully appreciated in research and practice.

Examples of work in this area in Britain include: Banks (1993); BPS (1999); Bryans (1988); BPS (2001); Guishard (1992); Kumar, (1988); Maximé (1993); McIntyre (1993); Tizard and Phoenix (1988).

> If white psychologists practice white psychology, then black psychologists practice BLACK psychology.

Teaching child-focused practitioners about psychology

Psychology as a field of study is integral to the training of child-focused practitioners. Tomlinson (1982) showed that racial beliefs amongst professionals contributed to the institutionalised practice of allowing West Indian pupils to be more readily processed than indigenous pupils to enter special education. Head teachers, in particular, suggested that West Indian pupils were low functioning, less keen on education, had additional behaviour problems as hyperactivity and an anti-authority stance, all of which were seen to be inherent to being black. Despite constructs such as that of racial prejudice and attitudes being psychological phenomena and therefore the province of psychology, psychology as a discipline was slow to respond formally to these findings.

Mainstream psychology in Britain has yet to show that it can incorporate black perspectives (Cline, 1986; Reed, 1999). The cultural milieu of western society has changed and psychology needs to absorb and reflect this transformation; it needs to acknowledge the influences of diverse ethnic groups. Most schools of psychology have given little attention to the transcultural implications of their theories. Their reluctance to take on such scientific enquiry seriously undermines the credibility of the profession. The working party into the teaching of social work for a multiracial society found it more difficult to obtain either texts or research studies that had ideas on psychology teaching for a multiracial society than did the disciplines of sociology and social policy (CCETSW in Cline, 1986).

The Standing Committee for Equal Opportunities Working Party made specific recommendations for explicit statements of intent on training courses for psychologists (BPS, 1988b). Davenhill *et al* (1989) recommended the urgent implementation of statements of intent to make adjustments that acknowledge the multicultural nature of British society and the possibility of racially discriminatory practices in the training clinical psychologists. Over 20 years ago, Cline (1987) pointed out that black voices were omitted from the work of psychological research and applied psychology. This led some to call for black psychology created by black scientists. Has anything changed?

Black psychologists in EP practice

A small survey looked at aspects of service delivery and the experiences of African, Asian and Caribbean EPs practicing in England. The main findings were that some psychologists were explicitly employed to deal with black issues while others were expected to do so when appointed to a generic post. Most services received requests specifically for black EP involvement. Some black EPs did not want to be singled out – they were psychologists who happened to be black – while others felt they had a particular role to play with ethnic minority groups. The expectations of white staff position black EPs so they have to provide the answers as well as to clarify the questions. Black EPs felt they had particular skills, knowledge and attributes to contribute to the work of the service but assumptions were made about these skills which led them to feel marginalised and discriminated against by school staff, other professionals, families and colleagues – a familiar outcome. Was the role of the black EP to be on the margins of a department but providing a more sensitive service to individual black people and groups, or was it more appropriately one of helping the department to rethink its mainstream services?

Some argue that white staff have a responsibility to use their existing skills just as they would with any other new area of work and that relying on black staff is yet another form of exploitation (Cawson in Connelly, 1989). The experiences of London black EPs were dissimilar to those in other metropolitan and county services. London services tended to address black issues as a whole service while other services leave it to the individual.

The Survey

Twenty-eight questionnaires were returned, representing a 55 per cent response rate. Ninety-six per cent were employed in education services and 4 per cent were employed in social services. Thirty-nine percent of the respondents described themselves as Asian; 39 per cent were Caribbean; 14 per cent African and 7 per cent from other ethnic minority groups. Half the respondents were female.

Results

The EPs believed they had specific skills, knowledge and attributes to contribute to their colleagues, the service and schools (Table 3.1 opposite).

The respondents had much to say, however, about how they were caught in their own daily reality of *micro-insults* and *micro-aggressions*. For example, several said that experiences in school varied from 'negative vibes' from teaching staff to racism from senior management, to direct antagonism and a lack of respect which showed itself when teachers questioned the respondents' authority, expertise and credentials, often after asking them whether they were a social worker. Black EPs may have to manipulate the superficial aspects of racism in an attempt to exert more control over the initial perceptions of themselves: '*I anticipate (or*

Table 3.1: Specific areas of knowledge that black EPs contribute to colleagues, the service and to schools

	Area of Knowledge/skills/attributes	Respondents %
1	Awareness of multicultural issues	22%
2	Issues relating to assessment	22%
3	Helping colleagues address their own attitudes	22%
4	Knowledge of language and culture	13%
5	Support and advice for working with black children and families	9%
6	Building bridges between black communities and professionals	9%
7	Own experiences	9%
8	Knowledge of black psychology	4%
9	Contribution to policy issues	27%
10	Prompting discussion on sensitive issues	23%
11	Knowledge and experience of multicultural issues	28%
12	Contribution to policy issues	9%
13	Prompting discussion on sensitive issues	5%
14	Knowledge and experience of multicultural issues	38%
15	Added credibility	19%
16	Contact with community groups	13%
17	Parental participation	19%
18	Contribution to SEN and equal opportunities policy development	13%
19	Improving pastoral systems	6%
20	Assessment/support for bilingual children	6%
21	Recruitment and deployment of staff	6%
22	Referrals to the service	35%

Area of Knowledge/skills/attributes	Respondents %
23　Role model	29%
24　Impact of the organisation on the individual	18%
25　Cultural issues across the curriculum	12%
26　Advice on language development	6%
27　Appropriate materials and resources	6%
28　Bilingual assessment	6%
29　Racism/stereotyping of children	28%
30　Cultural expectations	23%
31　Cultural and language issues across the curriculum	11%
32　Antiracism awareness/equal opportunities	6%
33　Child development	6%
34　Black identity work	6%
35　Managing challenging behaviour	6%
36　Counselling	20%
37　Interviewing for staff eg support assistants	25%
38　Professional and personal experience	15%
39　Challenge staff assumptions/aware of own influence	25%
40　Consultation/advising/counselling	5%
41　Help address staff anxieties	
42　Awareness training	
43　Personal experience and community links	

try to) possible marginalisation and discrimination and take action eg generally I power dress and remain assertive. I am rarely aggressive but occasionally functionally passive'. One respondent felt that teachers were sensitive about a black EP being involved with a black child as they feared collusion between the EP and the family.

One respondent felt that their contribution as a black EP was underestimated by colleagues and were recognised *'only when it suits them, otherwise skills are denied or disregarded.'*

Another felt the opposite: that there was *'always an expectation to some extent, ie a more subtle expectation to be an 'expert' in this area.'*

Can being black be a skill?

> '*I identified it (being black) as an area of skill, knowledge and interest [and] offered it as a personal selling point in my interview for the job*'.

Some black EPs do not want any attention brought to the fact of their race. But due to an assumption by black clients of shared experience(s), there was often an expectation that they would provide a receptive ear for grievances, be an 'ambassador' for their race and build bridges between the EPS and the community. The complaint is often expressed that if black teachers and other professionals are not part of the solution they are part of the problem; an abdication of responsibility to promote and better explain some of the specific difficulties of the black population creates mistrust among the black community and the black EP becomes tokenistic in their presence and in their impact.

Many respondents reported that they were consulted by white colleagues on race-related issues which concern schools, parents and pupils such as: teachers' perceptions, attitudes and responses to pupils with difficulties, cultural practices and etiquette, racism, racist bullying, constructive rules to offset the oppression of black children, antiracist practices and procedures and disproportionate exclusions of black boys from school.

> **If white psychologists practice white psychology, then black psychologists practice APPLIED psychology.**

Where we are now

It is Government intervention that has prompted educational psychology to reconsider its role in promoting racial equality (Division of Education and Child Psychology (DECP), 2001). Nevertheless, the evidence suggests that there has been little change over the last 20 years, with action manifesting mainly through audits and writing activities rather than any practice beyond recruitment. The employment of black EPs can raise alternative issues about the way services may be operating. Black EPs can be seen as a threat – they are needed because there is something that is deficient about the service provided by white EPs. The flawed logic would be that if this is true for white EPs, it would mean that black EPs have nothing to offer families that are not black. On a practical level, once a black EP is employed, the quality of their supervision may be poorer because they are too often supervised by someone whose practice is neither refined nor sophisticated enough to work with families from communities that are not indigenous to the British Isles.

Conclusion

If black expertise is a skill, can it be taught to every trainee? And can it be developed in practicing EPs? Can professionals truly *know* about a racial group with whom they have no contact other than through the conditions of their employment? Carroll and Leyden (1988) and later Lunt (1993) reported on how training courses involved ethnic minority people who were not directly connected with the course in designing and planning it and in preparing the course material or the materials sent to prospective applicants. The community cohesion agenda has for the moment passed educational psychology by. The black community, via black teachers and black parents groups, needs to be actively engaged to assist with designing the initial and ongoing training courses so they are made relevant to the communities served by EPs.

4

Victim or criminal? The racialisation of the juvenile justice system

Jeune Guishard-Pine

'Right through the system, from a stop on the street to the type of sentence and prison allocation, ethnic minority people are affected by racial bias'. From 'Creating Criminals' Institute of Race Relations website (2005)

Introduction

Racism is a form of psychological violence. Bulhan (1985) defines violence as: 'any relation, process or condition by which an individual or group violates the physical, social and/or psychological integrity of another person or group' (p135). Much of the racism of the psychologist occurs in their day to day work, in settings which span the entire discipline (Howitt and Owusu-Bempah, 1994). The treatment of people from black and ethnic minority groups by public services was criticised in the Stephen Lawrence Inquiry (Macpherson, 1999). Reports on the criminalisation of black people in the UK are seen as the end product of a series of racist practices beginning with the police. Fuller descriptions of these practices are usually confined to police relations and to the processes of the court systems (Gordon, 1983).

Compared with the adult service, there is a dearth of research in to the fate of youngsters from the visible minority groups in the UK (Feltzer and Hood, 2004). What exists paints the picture of young black and Asian offenders ending up in court on flimsier evidence than white offenders (Barclay and Mhlanga, 2000); being more likely to be imprisoned for a first offence; receiving harsher sentences and more often being refused bail or probation (IRR, 2005). These processes also affect youngsters of mixed parentage (Youth Justice Board (YJB), 2004). Such outcomes occur, notwithstanding that research shows that white youngsters commit more crimes than black and Asian youngsters (Armstrong *et al*, 2005) or at the very least a similar level of crime (Smith, 2003).

In the court arena, discourse analysis of transcripts reveals racial bias in the assumptions and assertions made by the professionals involved (Harrison, 1987). As Smith (2003) so succinctly puts it: *The evidence of overrepresentation of young black people at each stage of the youth justice system ... produces an overall picture of progressively intensified discriminatory practices* (p120). Following arrest, their grievances are rarely upheld even when they complain of racism (Wilson and Moore, 2003). So what is the role of the forensic psychologist in these processes and how might they influence the changes to create a fairer system?

Psychology is believed to be concerned with the well-being of humanity, yet practitioners violate and oppress others on racial grounds (Howitt and Owusu-Bempah, 1994). The forensic psychologist is an advocate of both the court and the client (Gray-Little and Kaplan, 1998), yet is clearly working in an environment – the court – that has been proven not to be colour-blind in its practices. As an advocate for the client however, true solidarity with the oppressed would mean fighting at their side to alter their reality (Freire, 1972). The assessments of diverse cultural groups by forensic psychologists have not been extensively explored in Britain (Home Office, 2004). If their work is not culturally sensitive and therefore ethically defensible this is likely to indicate racist practice.

Scientific racism

Psychology and its predecessors in medicine, philosophy and eugenics has a history of over 300 years of active scientific racism. Oppressive and racist epistemologies pervade psychological research (see Brown, 1995; Guthrie, 1976; and Howitt and Owusu-Bempah, 1994 for reviews; see also Henwood, 1994). Psychology is criticised as being monocultural at its root in the way that it has foregrounded research with white samples, to the point that a black radical psychologist exclaimed about the stereotypical work of the experimental psychologist that '...even the rat was white!' (Guthrie, 1976). Psychology is also seen as 'ghettocentric' in the way it uses studies of black people seeking help (usually those living in poverty) and generalises pejorative characteristics to all people of African descent (Myers *et al*, 2003).

The pervading negative stereotypes constructed by white society that are embedded within inappropriate assessments include an assumption that people of African descent are anti-intellectual; and that young black people are anti-authority (Antonopoulos, 2003). Strickland *et al* (1988) found a tendency for black people to be assessed as less verbally skilled than whites even when they followed an identical script to a white person. They are also portrayed as being incapable of abstract reasoning and deep thought (eg Eysenck, 1971; Jensen, 1969; Lopez and Hernandez, 1986). In addition they are seen as lazy and lacking motivation (Seymour, 1997); prone to violence and aggression (Bolton, 1984) and riddled with repressed hostility so they 'have a chip on their shoulder' (Reicher, 1999). People of African heritage in particular have a history of being defined in psychology as insane or otherwise psychopathological, of being less than human and of having no rights (Myers *et al*, 2003). Black youth are stereotyped as being dangerous and disruptive (Connolly, 1995; Wright, 1992). Henwood (1994) criticised social psychology's research tradition of presenting socially undesirable characteristics of certain groups as objective reflections of reality – as if it were a fact. She observed that other approaches within social psychology would call this phenomenon *blaming the victim*.

Most African Caribbean people enter the psychiatric system through the courts (Gordon, 1996). Pavkov *et al* (1989) found race to be a significant predictor of diagnosis. It has been found that white psychiatrists either over- or under-estimate symptoms in black people (Loring and Powell, 1988). Taking this together, it is not surprising that assessment, diagnosis and treatment of culturally diverse populations invite closer scrutiny, as the determination of 'normality' and 'abnormality' is often culture-bound (Sue, 2003).

Culturally competent assessments

Howitt and Owusu-Bempah (1994) list five forms in which racist practices are integrated:

- *Denial* – where there is a rejection of the existence of institutionalised racism and reframed as personal prejudice
- Being *colour-blind* – where the psychologist professes that all clients are treated the same
- *Patronising*: where 'lip service' is given to issues with the ultimate aim of ensuring the status quo
- *Decontextualising*: where there is an acknowledgement that racism exists but a denial that it exists within one's own belief system and organisation
- *Avoidance*: where there is an acceptance that racism exists but the psychologist tells themselves they are powerless to oppose it

In the US, psychologists began to question whether the profession could make fair and accurate assessments and the concept of 'cultural competence' was introduced (Atkinson *et al*, 1983). Forensic psychologists are expected to examine the role of culture and cultural differences in testing and assessment practices, and to take account of their reality. A change in their professional attitude may incline them to gather different or more information using a higher level of skill and insight into the social history of the client (Festinger, 1956).

Delivering this higher level may require them to be flexible in their engagement with clients and to take on many helping roles, eg advocate, consultant and facilitator of access to appropriate therapeutic approaches, and also be willing to take a systemic perspective in interventions (Atkinson *et al*, 2003). Culturally competent approaches require the psychologist to be active in making a *counter-stereotypical* response to the client's culture in assessment practices and to resist the temptation to make assumptions based on their notions of culture and thus avoid 'base-rate errors' (Finn and Camphuis, 1995). Base-rate errors occur when comparisons are made between black clients and white where the behaviour of the white person is seen as the norm.

In the US, Lewis *et al* (1979) conducted epidemiological studies of young offenders and found differential interventions for the clients according to their race. They found that 15 per cent of the white youths were diagnosed with psychiatric symptoms compared to 26 per cent of the black youth. Further, 70 per cent of the white youths diagnosed with psychiatric symptoms were referred for help, compared to just 18 per cent of the black youths. In the UK, Bolton (1984) found that there were differential outcomes for black criminals and white detained under the Mental Health Act. More black people were recommended for high security units despite having been assessed as having a similar profile to a white prisoner who was recommended to be placed on an open unit. The decisions were made based on negative stereotypes of black people as potentially more aggressive and explosive. The situation is of greater concern in relation to black women, who are also over-represented in British prisons (Home Office, 2004), but the research evidence on this group is sparse (Sender *et al*, 2006).

Research has shown that diagnoses are racialised; white offenders are more likely to be diagnosed with depression or 'personality disorder' while black people are more likely to be diagnosed as psychotic (Gray-Little and Kaplan, 1998) or as having a severe mental illness (Myers *et al*, 2003).

Researchers suggest that such stereotypes are formed because the majority of forensic professionals have no social contact with black people (Gray-Little, 1995; Lopez, 1989; Rosenfeld, 1984). For example, Rastafarianism is seen as deviant in psychological terms (Gordon, 1996). The lack of social contact may also make it more difficult to establish rapport with black clients, and risks producing an assessment interview that is fuelled by stereotypes. Concern also persists about the link between juvenile delinquency amongst black youth and family life (Guishard-Pine, 2006; Home Office, 2007). This point is particularly relevant for actuarial assessments as there is potential danger that each client is treated as though they were a 'cultural caricature' (Cooper, 1973). It is important therefore that the black client's cultural background is seen as the canvas and their life story or narrative as the detail that makes up the real picture.

Butcher and Pope (1993) argue that knowledge of diversity issues in forensic work is essential, because the forensic specialist has a *unique* understanding of a black defendant's capacity to stand trial, by examining factors such as the length of trial and the availability of other witnesses, or the psychological impact of an all-white jury.

Only 50 per cent of professionals associated with the criminal justice system believe that tests are central in recommending fitness for trial. Gray-Little and Kaplan (1998) recognised the potential advantage of an 'Interdisciplinary Fitness Interview' which assesses psychological functioning and understanding of the defendant, through a discussion conducted by a lawyer and a forensic psychologist with the aim of counterbalancing potential biases in their individual perceptions.

Psychologists argue that the use of tests allows for a more objective assessment of a client. In the US, 'The Competency to Stand Trial' assessment instrument has thirteen functions. It incorporates factors such as the defendant's understanding of the courts; whether they have a history of unmanageable behaviour; and their capacity to testify. However, given what is well-documented about the validity of many tests in relation to black clients, one could ask – do we need another test?

The paradox of testing

One of the persistent challenges for practicing psychologists is whether psychological tests distil bias? The dominant view is that tests potentially provide valid and unbiased information on the testee. However, estimating test validity for a single group is challenging enough and cannot be accurate for a diverse group. Radical psychologists argue that tests were essentially designed for research (Hiliard, 1994), and that if a test is (ab)used to make life-transforming decisions on a vulnerable individual it is tantamount to using a refrigerator to make ice. Myers *et al* (2003) argue that mental health care overall is antagonistic towards black clients, who often feel invalidated, abused, misunderstood and oppressed by professionals. What the psychologist regards as helping, such as a specific type of assessment or therapy, may differ considerably from the traditions and expectations of the client.

Researchers have also asserted that many test instruments are simply not robust enough to pick up on cultural issues or to distinguish between psychopathology and a genuine unfamiliarity with being tested, or the type of test (Gray-Little and Kaplan, 1998). They found that as much as a 43-point difference can be found for people who understand the test and those who do not, even when applied to people from similar ethnicity to the defendant .

There are also issues about the validity of the trait being measured. Self concept, for example, has been criticised by radical black psychologists as being a Eurocentric construct that can be misapplied to people of African descent, as high self-concept scores could in many African cultures be seen as tantamount to boasting (Nobles, 1973). Self-acceptance is a more Afrocentric construct (Guishard, 1983).

Supporters of culturally-competent psychological practice recommend that tests should be embedded in the wider assessment and, if used at all, the psychologist should facilitate optimum performance by examinees and only use tests that are psychologically sound instruments for that cultural group. However, Frisby (1998) warns against throwing the proverbial baby out with the bathwater, proposing that competent psychologists will know if a test has a 'health warning' with regards to cultural insensitivities and should make recommendations accordingly. The challenge for the forensic psychologist is how to apply a creative interpretation of the numbers, whilst maintaining the belief in the objectivity of a test. The alternative is a failure to discern how prejudice and stereotyping skew interpretation and can build up an assessment on information that is fundamentally flawed.

Ethical concerns

The British Psychological Society draft Code of Conduct states that psychologists must:

> ...value the dignity and worth of all persons, with sensitivity to the dynamics of perceived authority or influence over clients, and with particular regard to human rights, including those of privacy, autonomy, and self determination ... psychologists should respect individual, cultural and role differences ... and ... avoid practices that are unfair, biased or discriminatory... (p5)

It is difficult for practitioners in our society not to encounter clients and client groups who differ from them in terms of race, ethnicity or culture. The logical conclusion of that assertion is that the worldviews of a culturally diverse population are likely to be quite different from those of the forensic psychologist. Forensic psychologists are in a powerful position, as recommendations of clinical assessment have been found to influence the judge in child custody cases in a remarkable 92 per cent of the time (Gray-Little, 1995).

The Council of National Psychological Associations for the Advancement of Ethnic Minority Interests (2003) in the US recommend that cultural competence in the delivery of services is absolutely essential to the psychological and physical well-being of culturally diverse groups. Their assumption is that no individual psychologist is immune from inheriting the prejudicial attitudes, biases and stereotypes of the larger society. They make clear suggestions about how practitioners can equip themselves with the personal resources to provide ethically and scientifically defensible assessments. They recommend a range of activities that can reduce bias in forensic assessments, such as consulting with the wider community to obtain an idea of the customs and traditions of cultural groups – for example, kin networks are common amongst ethnic minority families (McGoldrick *et al*, 1996; Rubin 1992). It is also important for the psychologist to explain as fully as possible what the nature of their assessment is, whilst at the same time acknowledging that testing can underestimate performance and ability.

Conclusion

> The illusion that racism is somewhere out there, expressed by people that we ought not to be mixing with anyway, means that the rest need not see the locus of responsibility as much in their thinking and actions as elsewhere. (Howitt and Owusu-Bempah, 1994:61)

The British Psychological Society draft Code of Conduct states that the practicing psychologist should be 'honest and accurate in conveying professional conclusions, opinions and research findings, and in acknowledging potential limitations' (p13).

This advice can be taken quite literally by establishing systems and measures that safeguard the integrity of both the practitioner and the client. For example: reports could carry a 'health warning' to explain the limitations of the assessment; references can be provided as appropriate. It is imperative that such reports should not convey any certainty and make it clear that tests can underestimate and should be seen as no more than a snapshot taken through a keyhole.

A system of organisational support is required, involving a manager who will read the report and look at any questions that arise before it is submitted. Alternatively, support can be provided through peer supervision or support where peers are required to discuss each other's assessments to check whether anything was missed or misconstrued, in the way one might defend one's thesis in a *viva voce*.

Frisby (1998) points out that symbols such as the Confederate flag (or, equally, the Union flag) have different meanings to different cultural groups due to their associations with fascism. It is important to be aware of how discrimination operates at community level, and of research findings about the bully-victim cycle that show black and Asian people of all ages as the most frequent victims of crime and victims of racially-motivated crime (IRR, 2005) and acknowledge that youngsters may defend themselves or retaliate aggressively. Boyd-Franklin (1989) speaks of the specific economic and social issues of black people as the 'ecostructural context' and asserts that a life of poverty in an urban area under the intense scrutiny of police and racial harassment may alter the choices a person makes to ensure their survival. Such evidence should be taken into account in actuarial assessments.

Boyd-Franklin's ecostructural context can also be evident when the stressors that lead to emotional problems, such as anxiety and depressive disorders and physical health problems, come into play. New immigrants may have come from a country at war, and may show signs of acute psychological distress. In Chapter 8, Price points out that how refugees express distress will vary and this needs to be taken into account as a sign of humanity rather than a sign of abnormality. It is vital that both the cultural and the sociological factors affecting the life experience of black people are fully understood.

5
Ensuring (E)quality of services: implications for Continuing Professional Development

Hazel Sawyers and Jeune Guishard-Pine

Introduction

This chapter argues that practitioners need to be prepared to think outside the box about their continuing professional development and take more personal responsibility for their everyday learning about race equality. We suggest two methods practitioners might want to adopt to help further their understanding of race equality and how it can be applied to their work and we consider Race Equality Impact Assessments as a process for furthering service development.

How do we understand the concepts of race and equality?

Our understanding of all forms of knowledge is rooted in the dominant society's concepts and value systems. We can see that the idea of equality is notoriously difficult to define and ultimately to experience if we accept that all humans are organised into an indefinite number of overlapping social groupings. The current debate in psychology is that race is a socially constructed idea and has no biological validity. Recent scientific research has revealed that the oldest human skeleton indicates (at the moment) that humankind has its origins in Africa. And, geneticists have found that the human race shares over 95 per cent of the gene pool. In contrast existential thinking has the idea that equality is inconsistent with the core concept of uniqueness. These views suggest that from the perspectives of both logic and reality, it may be a simpler task in practice to dissect how inequality works rather than to search for true equalities.

In the realm of child and family work however, the idea of race as colour is a 'fact' (McGoldrick *et al*, 1996) and the idea of racial difference is defined largely by skin colour and culture. This notion goes on to shape how work with families is organised. Systemic theory would acknowledge that child and family work does not involve a one-way channel of communication; differences of, for instance, ethnicity and class between the family and the worker also shape the families' responses to the practitioner. Child and family workers must therefore evolve by transforming the process of applying their skills and knowledge to their practice.

How practitioners can apply their knowledge and skills to practice

Experienced and self-reflexive practitioners may use the early stages of work with families to pursue a joint understanding of the problems from the ecostructural context that overlays race. People from visible minority groups generally live within a different economic structure from white, middle class practitioners; their economic structure tends to be under-resourced, and they are actively excluded from full participation by the dominant society. Contemporary child and family practice would dictate that the practitioner should allow the family to drive the problem-solving process, as the family may not accept that their ecostructural context influences their perceived difficulties in any way. To gain a more complete understanding of the family the practitioner should strive to notice areas of sameness as well as difference .

To illustrate this point: families of African origin throughout the diaspora have a dominant feature of extended families. These are not multi-generational households as in many South Asian cultures, but multiple households that appear to be nuclear. In their classic work on the black extended family, Martin and Martin (1978) called this a sub-extended family. In their view, white practitioners often had a distorted view of black family life as dysfunctional because of the amount of time spent at the household of the grandparents – the base household. This level of involvement was seen as a weakness of the black family whereas, as black practitioners and researchers know, this family structure is a strength. So questions for assessments that pivot on the structure and role of various members of the kin network and how they enact that role would be useful. Thus working with families that are ethnically different from the practitioner may require additional training and supervision.

How legislation influences race equality in child and family work

Both strategic and operational developments flow from the anti-discriminatory legislation. The law now requires child and family workers within statutory services to prevent and address racism in their practices. The Race Relations (Amendment) Act 2000 (RR(A)A) places a specific duty on public bodies to provide evidence that they are working to eliminate race discrimination and to promote equality of opportunity and to promote good relations between people of different ethnic groups. The RR(A)A sets out detailed guidance to ensure compliance with the legislation, which is monitored in the Race Equality Impact Assessment (REQUIA) [See Box A].

Beware that a negative attitude can develop in which REQUIAs are seen as extra and non-essential paperwork. Within all public sectors, work on race equality is often under-resourced in terms of staff, time and money, or left to Human Resources departments, many of which have little experience or understanding about race equality in frontline service delivery.

Box A

The REQUIA is like a risk audit. The policy or function is assessed to find out whether it is likely to have a positive, adverse or neutral effect on race equality. It seems an obvious action to take when developing services but, like ethnic monitoring, there is always the risk that REQUIAs may become a tick box exercise and exacerbate race relations rather than improve them. When carried out correctly, the REQUIA should help to improve the overall service being provided. Since the first 3-year Race Equality Schemes were written and implemented in 2002, there have been very few examples of good REQUIAs. Even the Commission for Racial Equality and the Government have not always carried out REQUIAs on policies and functions they have introduced themselves. REQUIAs are obligatory within the legislation so staff need to be trained and supported to carry them out. Each organisation will need to decide the best method to teach their staff about REQUIAs. Methods can range from face to face teaching in groups, e-learning and in-house training, or specialist organisations can be commissioned to provide training. Multi-disciplinary groups or training staff from different agencies might provide enough diversity of opinion to get good results from the training. Follow-up sessions can be commissioned or supported by a line manager with the relevant knowledge, skills and training. You can find a template at www.cehr.org

---

How the training needs of the practitioner can be met

In child and family work, practitioners should be equipped to evaluate the outcomes of their work from a race equality perspective. Two methods for ensuring the best outcomes for achieving excellence in race equality practice are discussed here: the *MePLC* approach and the race equality SWOT analysis which includes the PESTLE analysis.

There are many methods to choose from to enhance your understanding of race equality. The MePLC method focuses on personal responsibility and leadership and does not rely on major financial or personnel resources; it can be used by all staff regardless of seniority. Similarly, the race equality SWOT (Strengths, Weaknesses, Opportunities and Threats) and PESTLE (political, economic, social, legal and environmental) analyses are methods used in organisational development: both are adapted here to improve personal effectiveness.

The MePLC approach

This approach is based on how individuals can take responsibility for their behaviour and actions. MePLC (Sawyers, 2007) uses the acronym FOCUS to look at five key aspects of personal leadership: being fearless, optimistic, creative, unique and a storyteller. Hazel has used this approach when running workshops on race equality in the health sector.

Fearless

Many people fear race equality training; they worry about causing offence and being seen as racist; others are afraid lest they appear stupid or ignorant because they do not know much about different races or cultures. But fear cannot be allowed to prevent action. Facing one's fears can initiate and stimulate an examination of where these fears stem from and identifying actions to alleviate or manage them. It is essential to teach child and family workers about racism that manifests as: stereotypes and myths about family life of ethnic minority groups; how these create misjudgements about families and might even lead to splitting up healthy families. Parallel teaching examples of where equality exists helps practitioners to understand discrimination and its harmful consequences. Health and Social Care workers need to get to know and understand people from a range of ethnic groups. Participants must be prepared to ask questions and truly listen to the answers.

Optimistic

Pessimism permeates education, health and social care. This is due to the way the statutory services are portrayed in the media. Optimism entails being both positive and realistic. Being open to ideas about self-improvement is a natural antidote to pessimism. In race equality terms this promotes the idea of surveying the diversity in the people who surround you and considering what they can contribute to your personal development. Do not discount anyone's contribution.

Creative
There is plenty of evidence from both child development and personality psychology to show that being stimulated promotes growth. Being prepared to take risks to promote one's growth is a significant issue for professionals. Being innovative is about being prepared to try new things, use new ideas, practice new skills or constantly improve on the ones you already have. If trying to achieve your personal or professional goals proved unsuccessful, you may need to come out of your comfort zone – take the risk of something new. If you usually conform to rules and procedures become more rebellious to attain your goals, or *vice versa*.

Unique
Being unique is about knowing and valuing yourself in relation to how you work best through teamwork or independently, your learning style, the personalities that complement or antagonise you, understanding what motivates you, and why others see you as they do. Knowing your uniqueness allows you to work with it to achieve your goals.

Storyteller
As part of continuing professional development, practitioners will have stories to tell about their experiences; their learning and development; their skills and knowledge. Sharing stories is a way of making an oral history of the work you do: it is what defines you as a practitioner. With respect to race it is important that these stories are documented and shared so that others in the profession can learn from your experiences. This is particularly relevant for health and social care professionals, as many of the stories presented in the media focus on negative outcomes. Practitioners should be encouraged to share examples of good practice. Telling your own stories gives practitioners a chance to be in charge of what information about their work is communicated. Excellent practice and progress in race equality within health and social care should be rewarded and publicised so that others may learn from the experience.

Initiating the transition from knowledge and skills to practice
Guided discussion can help to ensure that all staff learn about race equality. Guided discussions encourage the use of personal knowledge and experience to explore and act on the barriers to race equality. These are most effective when the groups are diverse. The facilitator can pose a leading question or statement such as '*Has the race agenda gone too far?*' or '*Racism is about the promotion of white supremacy across the world*'. The diverse responses can bring out issues such as the perceived unfair advantages that race equality legislation gives to particular ethnic groups or the exclusion of white people, women and the working class

from the race equality agenda. The debate should assist the clarification of definitions of direct and indirect discrimination, positive action and positive discrimination. The group can define these terms and decide which terms are lawful.

Race Equality SWOT Analysis

When assessing yourself or your organisation's race equality work, a race equality SWOT analysis can be useful. This allows you to look at your professional strengths and weaknesses and the opportunities and threats to your development from a race equality perspective. Use a PESTLE analysis to help identify the opportunities and threats.

Table 5.1 (opposite) suggests some questions to use in your race equality SWOT analysis.

How can organisational infrastructures ensure the implementation of race equality practice?

Deliberate and concerted action can be pursued at organisational and interpersonal levels. One idea, which straddles the organisational and the interpersonal, is the sponsorship of action research conducted by practitioners. McGoldrick (1994) and Barnes (1991) suggest that individual practitioners from diverse ethnic groups need to take the initiative to conduct research on their group in order to advance knowledge. The difficulty is that it is still the white, middle-class establishment that holds the key to accessing the forums in which the findings of this research are disseminated in the mainstream.

A first step is to develop the sophistication of organisations to reflect the ethnic diversity of their workforce through analysing data. Effective use of data focuses attention and resources on organisational issues. The line management and appraisal systems can assist with setting personal objectives, prioritising developmental areas of work and implementing action plans to monitor and evaluate outcomes.

Since the RR(A)A 2000 came into force in 2002, there is a plethora of training methods, tools and devices to provide training in how to reduce racial inequalities. These include formal learning, one day courses, online learning, coaching and mentoring, shadowing, secondment, learning from peers, joining a community of practice or interest group, intranet and the internet. There must also be a commitment to invest in boosting resources and information and allowing practitioners to use networks that help them carry out their work. However, practitioners should never underestimate what they can learn from their colleagues while working in an ethnically diverse environment.

Table 5.1 Questions to support a race equality SWOT analysis

STRENGTHS	What is going well at the moment with the children and families who are racially different from me?
	How are my personal thoughts and actions affecting the children and families who are racially different from me?
	What evidence is there of any positive impact on children and families who are racially different from me?
	Which plans or programmes positively affect the children and families who are racially different from me?
WEAKNESSES	Which objectives have not been achieved with respect to families that are racially different from me?
	Which areas of work need more attention to ensure that race is appropriately foreground in my work?
	How can the relationships be strengthened with the racial groups whose voices and opinions are not privileged in shaping service developments?
	Do I have difficulty understanding race equality because I have no experience of racism or of being a member of an ethnic group that is discriminated against?
OPPORTUNITIES	Are there any political, economic, social, technological, legal, environmental issues that can meet the needs of children and families who are racially different from me?
THREATS	Are there any political, economic, social, technological, legal or environmental issues could obstruct various objectives in relation to children and families who are racially different from me?

Are there any particular lessons for schools?

Schools were among the first organisations to attempt to implement race equality practice in a transparent way, mainly through the inclusion agenda (Ofsted, 2002).

Relative success was achieved through: the analysis of data to create a picture of how each racial group is being privileged within the school system as evidenced by inclusion and achievement; evidencing the school's response to the RR(A)A to remove barriers to achievement, particularly the use of REQUIAs of the curriculum; the application of measurable targets for the school; the provision and access for teaching and non-teaching staff to high quality training to increase confidence and competence in meeting the needs of children from diverse ethnic groups.

Schools and other organisations involved with the health and social care of children can also adopt the two approaches outlined above.

The FOCUS approach might be:

> **Fearless**: Schools need to risk initiating open debate with parents and the wider community about what they consider to be the barriers to achievement and on the attitudes towards race equality across the school community – that is, everyone involved with helping a school to function. These discussions are potentially incendiary and many schools avoid this approach for fear of making things worse
>
> **Optimism**: However, the hope is that the RR(A)A can countermand that risk. The law now requires explicit practices to be set up to eliminate barriers to achievement and to promote good race relations
>
> **Creativity**: A guided discussion can be initiated to encourage thinking outside the box, asking questions such as 'How does the school community understand the dimensions of race, gender, culture, religion and class?'
>
> **Unique**: Individual schools will generate a unique constellation of ideas about the responses that can be made to address discrimination and also which strategies are likely to bring lasting change
>
> **Storytelling**: It is hugely important that schools can tell the story of their progress towards reducing racial inequalities. Successful schools have spoken of their signposts that illustrate good practice in meeting the educational needs of their ethnically diverse school populations (Ofsted, 2002)

When a PESTLE analysis was performed, these schools recognised that the political landscape was crucial to embedding the practice that needed to develop. Schools have to join up with other local services to ensure that the social inclusion agenda is prioritised. There is little evidence of sustained, successful interagency work across the country, in relation to the race equality agenda. However, Chapter 9 describes achievements in Luton with the Pakistani community.

How will I know that the (e)quality of my work has improved?

The use of skilled supervision is a non-negotiable essential in tracking progress in relation to race equality strategies and whether they have made real and lasting changes to the way you approach your work. But you must be self-motivated and dedicated to looking for areas that can be improved.

Conclusion

In the initial training of child-focused practitioners, a case study that focuses exclusively on race and culture as proxy measures of 'power' should arguably be compulsory in the first term of training, so that it begins to become part of the consciousness of practitioners at once, rather than waiting until learning is advanced. Wherever one is placed in the statutory sector, the perpetual questions are: *Do I know how my work fits into the race equality plans of my organisation? What race equality targets are my department working to achieve? What targets have been set for me and my team?* And above all: *What are my personal needs and goals?*

6

Education is for life: Further and Higher Education for diverse Britain

Olatayo Afuape

'Education is not preparation for life; it is life itself'
(Dewey in Hickman and Alexander,1998)

Introduction

'You can steal the fruits but not the roots' – Jamaican saying

Imagination and creativity, the forerunners of cognition and conceptualisation, drive our instinctive desire to be curious, explore and to understand ourselves, others and our surroundings. When we dream and play we flex our cognitive muscles, making our hearts and minds fit for learning. We are motivated and inspired to learn in order to grow, relate, interact, change, adapt and compete. Our cultural context, norms, and values determine the manner in which we perceive and process our learning experience and the diversity of our learning context and experience determines the length and breadth of one's development.

Philosopher and psychologist John Dewey's defining and impassioned description of education sets the scene for this chapter. Dewey asserted that education is about others as well as self, about instinctive knowledge as well as acquired learning, about common interest as much as personal gain and the conflict between lifelong fulfillment and immediate gratification. This is essentially a humanistic, utilitarian position which focuses on the common good and a society's collective consciousness and sets the scene for the educational conditions under which meaningful change can and must occur in the world.

As a member of the Yoruba tribe, my connections with Dewey's mantra are immediate; African elders impart life's lessons through their camp-side parables. My belief that the seat of understanding of life's lessons and the personal transformation and growth associated with it that rests with many tribal societies, has been cultivated by what my father would preach to me when I was an impetuous child: *'Eyin omod e e fojusi eko nyin nitoripe elegi ni ngoni di eni nla ni eyin ola,'* which means 'child be serious with your studies because it is the gateway to you becoming a responsible and educated adult.' I recall this scolding with fondness and appreciation of education as his lifelong legacy to me.

This chapter contributes to a body of theoretical and researched work about cultural diversity and education in the UK. It offers insights and reflections based on personal experiences of life learning in the context of family, the community and formal institutes of further and higher education, keeping in view the conflicts and challenges that one has to face and overcome. I propose that 'life learning' should be the essence of all educational programmes, from home to school and from nursery to university. It is essential for life and living, since it instructs our understanding of self, others, culture, society and our environment.

The student's overall experience of learning and teaching is underestimated by society and its institutions and this works to the detriment of a diverse Britain which is striving to be inclusive. An academic ethos which has life learning principles at its core would seek to promote learning outcomes which impact on others and the local and global context and would incorporate diversity in learning and teaching as a fundamental characteristic of its inclusive culture. In this chapter I evaluate the difference that higher education made to me – the system in which I trained as a teacher, psychologist and psychoanalytic psychotherapist. I offer some insights and reflections on the integration and inclusion process from my perspective as both learner and teacher in the post-16 sector.

'We were born to learn' – the basics of teaching and learning for life

About being a teacher, Albert Einstein proposes that 'setting an example is not the main means of influencing others; it is the only means.' But the psychotherapist in me would add that the most effective teacher not only leads by example but also identifies with the learner-self in each of his students. Learning is both instinctive and acquired, as demonstrated by our propensity to learn as babies without being instructed; instinctive learning enables us to develop socio-linguistic skills vital for our survival. These are some of the primary signs of the osmotic, continuous process we call life learning; we wittingly or unwittingly experience the strangeness and joy of learning something new from the day we are born until the day we die.

Over twenty years ago when I was teaching in Further Education (FE) there was little emphasis on using teaching methods which draw on the instinctive and informal ways we use to learn. As a psychologist and psychotherapist I came to understand more about how babies and children use their instinct and senses like little scientists to observe, imitate, problem solve, explore, experiment and, most importantly, experience (Piaget, 1923). Adults do this too. The creativity expressed during leisure not only brings out our natural, innate desire to learn and communicate but also our urge to imagine, create, and harness our environment as adults.

The traditional chalk and talk practices generally employ a limited range of visual and language intensive strategies. It treats the mind of the learner as a vessel to be filled rather than as a seed to be planted, cultivated and groomed. The Jamaican saying at the beginning of the chapter reminds us of the principle underpinning life learning that knowledge that is deep rooted is never lost and cultivates the seeds for new ideas and understanding. Today chalk and talk methods have been replaced by electronic white-boards, libraries, computers, internet and electronic mailing systems. Although these teaching and learning aids facilitate the fluent acquisition of information from world wide sources, they are decontextualised and this means they impede the conversion of information to knowledge and understanding. The age old practices of life learning as delivered via teaching from peers and elders or through experiential learning, ie self teaching, although more commonly mediated in primary schools, are rarely encouraged in places of higher learning.

As a psychoanalytical psychotherapist, I grow more and more anxious over an educational system which seems driven by what Freud (1920) calls our *Nirvana* principle – *Thanatos*, the death instinct, contradicts the very essence of life learning. A fundamental flaw in the pedagogy of the further and higher educational systems is that it seems more Thanatos-led and this elicits urges to control, suppress and dominate. An educational process that is attuned to *Eros*, our life instinct, appeals to the desire to be creative and consequently fills teaching and learning with energy. Knowledge is more likely to be retained when it is engaging, purposeful and context sensitive. Although Freud proposes that the interplay between Eros and Thanatos is both an inevitable and a crucial dynamic, he also warns that a system, organism or institution driven by Thanatos disintegrates and eventually perishes.

The present higher and further educational system cultivates a fiercely competitive but conformist learning environment by being prescribed and performance driven. The learning agenda, teaching methods and assessment procedures are tailored to a culturally homogeneous and elite group who, although rarely stretched to their full potential, are at least familiar with the performance demands and elaborate linguistic code. Geneticists believe that intelligence is innate rather than acquired, that intellectual superiority is preordained through race and gender, and that physical, social or learning environments ultimately have little bearing on educational achievements. Institutes of higher and further education that favour such racial bias and follow a conservative, educational agenda rather than cultural diversity and life learning stunt the growth of all learners.

The impact of culture on learning to learn – the psychology and significance of the other

Ethnicity is derived from *ethnicus* which is Latin for 'heathen, strange, inferior group or the other' (*Oxford English Dictionary*). The predominant use of this term in education in pursuit of political correctness is consistent with a society which is institutionally racist. It seems ironic that a term introduced to acknowledge and accommodate difference actually highlights an institutional and societal psyche so defended against difference that it has established structures and systems designed to alienate and exclude. Sociologist professor Michael Rustin captures this paradox when he describes race as: '*both an empty category and one of the most destructive and powerful forms of social categorization*' (Morrison, 1993:xi).

In institutes of higher and further education, sociologists and educationalists would refute the validity of the category race and argue that one's phenotype does not always denote one's genotype. They would dismiss it as nothing but a social construct made up by those wishing to justify their subjugation of 'other' groups. However western classifications of race, culture and their associations with inferior/superior, bad/good, ugly/beautiful have affected the identity of many people of African origin. The Thanatos-led, destructive construct of race continues to impact on teaching and learning practices within education. I felt this especially during my training as an educational psychologist.

It was the first year that not one but four black women won places on this very competitive, prestigious course. I constantly experienced myself as a foreign body which created such irritation, conflict and fragmentation within the host system that the threat of expulsion felt ever present. This was so overwhelming and uncontained that a black fellow trainee was, in unprecedented fashion, asked to leave one term before the end of the course because her credentials and experience were deemed insufficient for her to qualify. This made me question why I had even embarked on the training. On reflection I think I wanted to position myself to challenge these practices.

Conversations between my Nigerian heritage and my British culture

To be Yoruba

My father is a Nigerian immigrant who, like many Africans, had intended to study in England and then return home. He would proudly relate stories of his ten mile return journey to a missionary school in Nigeria, where he acquired a passion for Shakespeare, Burns, Hardy and John Bunyan. I recall reading *Pilgrim's Progress* with him at the ripe old age of ten. Learning was my release from a very structured and disciplined upbringing; it also secured eagerly awaited quality time with my father. He taught me the use of Literature as a way of both understanding one's social condition and escaping from it. Despite the enjoyment of learning with my father and the colourful stories he told of his school days, he also imparted a serious message that education was a privilege that came with great responsibility to one's community as well as to one's self; making a difference to others was the ultimate fulfillment.

For the Yoruba people, children are synonymous with education as they are seen as the *summum bonum* – the highest good – and as an active and physical embodiment of life learning. In traditional Yoruba religion the various parts of the soul can continue the good life eternally in a cycle of three states: the living, the ancestors, and the unborn awaiting reincarnation. We believe that children reincarnate ancestors of their own lineage and that language, culture, tradition and knowledge are passed on spiritually through this lineage. The Yoruba circle of life, which is evident in many pagan and tribal societies, is derived from Man's study of Nature's life cycles. Yoruba customs, traditions and practices are communicated through verbal nuances, social interplay and with demonstration and modelling where children are instinctive participants expected to learn by studying and experiencing life and their environment. Inherent in the concept of lineage structure or the natural order of things, is the system of seniority which establishes a single hierarchy of reciprocal obligations (Aronson, 1980:93-94). Traditionally, any senior had a right to unquestioned service, deference, and submissiveness from any junior (Lloyd, 1974:35-36). It is considered insolent and a sign of bad upbringing to make decisions, ask a direct question, make direct eye contact or show familiarity towards an elder (which could include an older child as well as an adult).

To be British

I was fortunate that I was able to read before I went to school so my reticence over doing any of these things, even when asked to by a teacher, was put down to shyness rather than defiance or stupidity. What I loved about learning was the experience of the self transformation and adaptation that came with exploration and discovery. Although the insights that appeased my curiosity about my peers, teachers and educational context were my motivation and reward, to my teachers I appeared too passive and socially reticent.

Britain's demand for cultural homogeneity means that immigrants are, coerced both implicitly and explicitly, into losing their identity. It is endemic to all institutions: the judiciary, employment, mental health and social welfare systems. My parents and their friends experienced discrimination when looking for work and accommodation. It was six times more likely for black men to be prosecuted or sectioned, and this has not changed. My teachers felt it appropriate to train me to behave and think as though I were a white child, whereas my parents wanted me to do well at school whilst also embracing the traditions of my cultural heritage. The negative depictions of Africans in history, science and, most literature disappointingly, contradicted and undermined my experience of a sophisticated culture whose traditions were embedded with symbolism and meaning. For some time during adolescence I felt culturally confused and conflicted.

Too often during my educational history as a learner and teacher I have experienced interactions that were intended to make me feel inferior and insignificant, as though my difference was contaminating and disruptive rather than enriching and healthy. At primary and secondary school I recognised that black children were problems: labelled disturbed if they were challenging or learning disabled if they were too quiet or passive. Being one who was engaged with the learning process rather than schooling, I avoided the imprisoning effect of this labelling process. Both intuitively and consciously, I perceived learning as an adventure, an essential part of my evolution and a crucial component of my induction into community culture, be it Yoruba or British.

Life learning and diversity for adaptive change

Knowledge expires and evolves, trends in the Arts are orchestrated by our social, political and economic circumstances; our habits, morals and laws are revised in the wake of personal tragedies, global events and ecological and climate changes. Culture, like life learning, is a fluid and ever changing experience influenced not only by time and space but also by the interaction and experience of others. This is not to dismiss the importance of difference but to highlight the impact diversity and culture, especially African culture, has had and is still having on the western world and *vice versa*.

Living to learn

If one accepts that life learning is a continuous acquiring and applying of knowledge and skills in the context of authentic, self-directed problems, solutions and goals, then as Dewey muses it is life, and these lessons offer the best opportunity for holistic growth, development and change. This makes the context of today's further and higher education system, where learning and teaching is for academic and professional gain, seem redundant and regressive.

When Barack Obama was newly inaugurated as the United States' first visibly African President, with a mixture of apprehension and anticipation I awaited the hour when his African American family took up residency in the White House. His intellectual and oratory prowess was acknowledged by Black Americans and White, young and old, whose votes secured him a landslide victory. His mantra, 'a change we can believe in' capitalised on world recession, domestic and global conflict, moral and financial decline, but it also proposed an ideal inspired by Martin Luther King Jr and Mahatma Gandhi that the United States as a nation of diverse cultures could lead by means of peace and collaboration rather than aggression and destruction.

Obama's election has penetrated America's psyche and challenged its institutional resistance to difference. Like his mentors King and Gandhi, Obama believes that real change will only occur when the diverse parts of America's culturally fragmented psyche become integrated and whole. Obama must move the rest of the world to change through example. This is also a challenge for contemporary Britain.

In order to become more progressive and competitive Britain must create a stratified educational system where diversity and 'life' learning are interconnected, where integrated themes run throughout all the phases of education. This will open the minds of learners, educators, politicians, employers and policymakers to a universal understanding of the role of life learning as integral to the holistic development of a world society where knowledge and information essential for advancement is defined and determined by many diverse, technologically superior or environmentally enlightened cultures. It is both ironic and just that this competitiveness or survival of the fittest will depend on cooperation and collaboration (*Eros*) rather than domination and aggression (*Thanatos*).

The western world has to undergo an extreme cultural makeover, potentially taking its cue from diverse tribal societies whose interpretation of life learning centres on the ecology of self in relation to others and the environment. Life learning (which includes unlearning and relearning) has a role in addressing the global and local concerns which impact on us now and in the future. As we see, the United States and Europe's economic and social crises have global implications. Both ancient and present tribes have long understood and heeded the 'butterfly effect', yet life learning has only catapulted on the national and international stage within the last ten years.

The European Year of Lifelong Learning (1996), the UNESCO including 'Lifetime Education', a key issue in its planning, and the G7 group of countries naming Lifelong Learning the main strategy in the fight against unemployment, taken altogether indicate the critical nature of lifelong learning at last being grasped; but even here its intrinsic and pervasive application seems diminished.

Conclusion

My final reflection is upon the original teacher/student relationship. It is that of mother and child. Psychoanalytic psychotherapists expect there to exist an indulgent relationship between mother and child, described by Winnicott (1958) as the 'primary maternal preoccupation'. It enables the mother to respond reflexively to the baby's psychological needs, so providing the baby with a safe and stimulating space that enables them to strive to develop basic socio-linguistic or life skills. There is an immeasurable reciprocity between mother and child. The mother is dependent on the child's emotional cues, the smiles and cries and the child is dependent on the mother for understanding and containment. Bion (1970) stressed that containing is both an active and dynamic relationship.

Our earliest processes of teaching and learning should inspire further and higher educational institutions to nurture the emotional and intellectual needs of all involved in an educative process. Within this ethos diversity has a rightful place: the mother, however experienced, has to deal with the idiosyncratic and diverse needs of each of her babies. So too does the tutor for her or his students.

An effective, progressive and resilient further and higher educational system in Britain must reconceptualise learning and teaching so that it embraces diverse experience, skills and knowledge in both teachers and students. Accreditation, negotiated contracts of learning, self assessment, group evaluation, peer and elder teaching, self teaching, experiential and context related teaching should be the core features of a fluid system designed to ensure the successful adaptation to an organic environment. For change to become adaptive we must have sustainable life knowledge of our environment and our unique and collective selves that will enable us to deal with the opportunities and challenges that we will inevitably face now and in the future.

Section 2
Models of innovative work with specific ethnic groups

7
Chinese pupils: the silent voices in British schools

Karina Ng

Introduction

British Chinese pupils stand out as a high achieving group in the British education system. *The Independent on Sunday* (16.2.07) reported that over 65.9 per cent of Chinese pupils gained five or more GCSE A*-C passes in comparison to 44.3 per cent of white and 59.1 per cent of Indian pupils. In A levels too Chinese pupils outperform other ethnic groups. A study by the Royal Society of Chemistry and Institute of Physics (Elias *et al*, 2006) revealed that Chinese students were 3-4 times as likely to achieve three or more science A levels as white students.

Recent studies look at the perceptions and educational experiences of various ethnic minority pupils in the UK (eg Archer, 2003; Basit, 1997; Gillborn and Gipps, 1996; Mirza, 1992; Sewell, 1997) but Chinese pupils receive little attention. It appears that educational bodies, researchers and policy makers have failed to keep pace with their educational performance (Archer and Francis, 2005b). Where Chinese pupils do appear in the literature, the focus tends to be on their academic success (Archer and Francis, 2005; Chen, 2007; Woodrow and Sham, 2001). Chinese pupils are rarely positioned as educationally or socially problematic. Their academic success has led many researchers to label and simplistically present them as a 'success story' (Chau and Yu, 2001; Parker, 1998; Parker, 2000).

This upbeat stereotypical image has homogenised the diverse educational experiences of Chinese pupils and masked the difficulties that Chinese children encounter in education. Whilst the media are happy to report that Chinese are the ethnic group most likely to have university degrees they fail to say that Chinese are the third largest ethnic group with no qualifications. Twenty per cent of Chinese pupils leave school without gaining any qualification compared with 15 per cent of white British pupils (DfES, 2004). By portraying Chinese pupils as uniformly clever, hardworking and obedient, stories of those who experience difficulties in school never surface.

The invisibility of Chinese pupils

Over thirty years ago, Anne Garvey highlighted the dilemmas for Chinese pupils in Britain: 'They're not black so they can't be in our gang. And they're certainly not white now, are they?' (*Times Educational Supplement*, 4.10.74). Other writers (Cheung, 1986; Roper, 1987) attributed the lack of interest in Chinese pupils to their dispersal in British schools; it is rare for any school to have even 5 per cent of Chinese pupils. It is not uncommon to find solitary Chinese children in schools which have little or no experience of dealing with Chinese children and parents. Because there are so few, their problems are given no attention. The acute needs of some Chinese pupils and the concerns of their parents are seldom a priority and are largely ignored.

Special educational needs and Chinese children

The definition of 'special educational needs' was defined in the 1996 Education Act (as amended by the Special Educational Needs and Disability Act – SENDA, 2001). Children have special educational needs (SEN) if they have a learning difficulty which calls for special educational provision to be made for them. English as an additional language, giftedness and high ability are not included within the definition of SEN. In my study, I tried to ascertain the number of ethnic minority pupils with SEN in certain South London boroughs, but the data was not available. Nor could I obtain data regarding the number of Chinese pupils with SEN on School Action and School Action Plus levels of the SEN Code of Practice (2001).

Lindsay *et al* (2006) conducted a large-scale British study into the attainment and progress of ethnic minority children and the prevalence of SEN among pupils in maintained schools. They found that Chinese pupils were less likely than white pupils to be identified as having Behaviour and Emotional Difficulties, Moderate Learning Difficulties, Specific Learning Difficulties or Autistic Spectrum Disorder. They recommended that an investigation into whether these children's needs were being appropriately identified and assessed be called for and asked whether their English – which is an Additional Language (EAL) had led professionals to underestimate the nature and severity of their cognitive and language needs. One may conjecture that the low incidence of Chinese children with specific SEN is due to the positive image of Chinese children in UK schools. Archer and Francis (2005a) reported a Chinese parent being told at a parents' evening at her daughter's school: *'You shouldn't need to worry too much about (daughter's name) ... and another thing is your race: you're Chinese and generally speaking Chinese people seem to do well in education.'*

Chinese pupils often present an image of self-sufficiency. They are often thought to have fewer problems in school. Due to their respect for authority, they appear to be quieter than children from other ethnic groups and they adopt a low profile to avoid trouble. Such assumed passivity may have masked the special educational needs of some Chinese children. Similarly, the neat handwriting of Chinese children can lead teachers to overlook the problem that some simply copy without understanding the words. Is it really true that Chinese children are doing much better than other ethnic groups or are their special educational needs underestimated, as Lindsay *et al* (2006) suggest?

The aims of this study

Chinese parents, irrespective of their social class and gender, place great value on their children's education, (Archer and Francis, 2005c; Taylor, 1987). They send their children to supplementary schools and many hire private tutors. Yet, like many ethnic minority parents, Chinese parents rarely go to schools to discuss concerns about their children or participate in school functions (Ng, 1992). What causes this seeming apathy? Are all the parents who have concerns about their children's learning and development given a voice? How can schools facilitate a mutually supportive relationship? Both the *Education Act 1996* and the 2001 SEN Code of Practice emphasise the importance of a home-school partnership in the assessment, intervention and statementing of pupils with SEN. Partnership denotes mutual respect, shared objectives and equality of power as well as knowledge and skill. Does this reflect the real life encounters of Chinese parents? How do the parents of a Chinese SEN pupil perceive their role and involvement in their child's education?

Although Lindsay *et al* (2006) cite parental or cultural belief as a plausible reason for the under-representation of specific groups of pupils in certain categories of SEN, little research has been done in the UK on parental perspectives (see Chapter 9). My study sought to elicit the views of Chinese parents about building and maintaining trusting home-school relationships. In my attempt to highlight the concerns, feelings and perspectives of Chinese parents, I examined the processes that encourage or discourage constructive dialogue with schools. This involved looking not only at the experiences and expectations of parents of children with SEN but also at their construct of SEN.

Method
Materials
A bilingual semi-structured questionnaire with open-ended and five-point rating items (1 is low) was used to interview the participants. It comprised five different sections:

- Family information
- How do you think your child is doing in school?
- The educational needs of your child
- Home-school relationship
- Special educational needs

The parental interview transcripts were analysed using a qualitative methodology.

The participants
Twenty parents (19 mothers and one father) were recruited from a local supplementary school in South London where children attend every Saturday for Chinese lessons. Eighteen parents spoke Cantonese and two Mandarin. Unlike other ethnic groups such as African-Caribbeans whose major migration was during a defined time, migration amongst Chinese people continues as a steady stream. This means that there are many Chinese parents who have yet to acquire fluent English. Their English language proficiency and occupations vary markedly, as shown in Tables 7.1, 7.2, 7.3 and 7.4.

Table 7.1. Proficiency in English (N=20)

Language proficiency	%
Fluent English	10
Fairly Fluent English	15
Some English	35
No English	40

Table 7.2: Occupations of participants

Occupation	%
Catering	60
Professional	25
Housewife	15

Over half the parents (60%) were educated to primary level. Others had received education up to secondary or university level. Four parents (20%) reported having a child with SEN (See Table 7.3).

Table 7.3: SEN of children

SEN	Number
Severe learning difficulties (statemented)	1
Hearing impairment	1
Autistic spectrum disorder	1
Awaiting diagnosis by an EP	1

Results
The parents' concerns
Sixty per cent of the parents in the study thought that their children got on well with their teachers and peers. Thirty per cent believed that their child should receive additional help. The three most common areas of concern were numeracy, speech and language and emotional development. These findings differed from those in 1992 where the parents main areas of concern were over language difficulties, lack of motivation and behavioural problems.

The concern about numeracy was somewhat unexpected. A number of parents felt that their children were not given sufficiently challenging work. Some parents were also concerned that the teaching methods and slow pace of teaching hindered their child's progress. This may be a reflection of dissatisfaction with both the content and pedagogy of the numeracy strategy.

The parents' concerns about speech development are consistent with the findings of Lindsay et al (2006), which showed that Chinese pupils were more likely than other groups to have SEN in relation to speech and language. But caution is needed as the interpretation of what constitutes a speech and language problem varies widely. It was unclear whether the concern raised was associated with having English as an Additional Language (EAL) or if it indicated language delay or disorder.

The concern about emotional development is also surprising as it challenges the assumption that *'because a Chinese child is quiet, troubleless and obedient, they are less prone to racial harassment and bullying from other children.'* (parent A). Thirty per cent of the parents in this study reported concerns about their child being bullied or isolated in school. It may be that their quiet disposition, their EAL status and racism in schools make them targets for bullying.

What the parents said about home-school relationships

Sixty five percent of the parents in this study gave a ranking of 1 or 2 out of 5 when asked to rate their relationship with schools, indicating that it was very detached. Half gave *'the lack of a common language'* as the cause. This confirms the findings by Ng (1992) that communication difficulties may have challenged the Chinese parents who did not feel confident to converse with teachers.

There are also subtle difficulties arising from cultural beliefs and parental attitudes which impact negatively on the home-school partnership. One parent in the study observed: *'I'm only a minority.'* The experience of being an ethnic minority in predominantly white society apparently left this parent feeling impotent and explained her unwillingness to participate in after-school activities. Culture also plays a prominent part in influencing attitudes and behaviour. For a start, in Chinese society, teachers are held in the highest esteem. If the parents' and the school's opinions are at variance, they would not challenge the school. Two parents said that this reverence for teachers had prevented them from approaching the school to discuss concerns about their children; they worried that they would be seen as troublemakers. Secondly, the idiom, 'Seek yourself rather than seeking others' means that parents are reluctant to discuss concerns with someone outside their family or to seek help unless it is absolutely necessary. One parent felt ignored by the teacher when she raised her concerns about her child's slow progress in literacy. In the end she had to find her child a private tutor as she had lost faith in the teacher. Such experience only served to reinforce the cultural belief that one relies on oneself rather than seeking help from others.

Parents' views about ways to improve communication with schools

All the parents were asked to suggest ways to build and maintain a positive relationship with schools. Five of the twenty parents chose not to respond and four said they felt powerless to effect change:

> 'Nothing can be done because the school system is too complex to understand.'
>
> 'Impossible because my English is so poor.'
>
> 'What can be done? Very little. Everything depends on teachers' attitude.'
>
> 'If school does not change its policies and discriminatory practice, we as parents can do nothing.'

Although a number of parents expressed feelings of negativity, others were more positive and made some suggestions, such as ensuring that letters and newsletters home be translated into Chinese and an interpreter be used to facilitate parental involvement. A parent whose child has a Statement of SEN was very appreciative when an effort was made to find her an interpreter in meetings with the school staff and other professionals. The availability of an interpreter in annual reviews of the Statement had made matters easier for her as there was at least somebody who had some knowledge of her language and she could communicate her view via the interpreter. Although she had to rely on school, the EP and the paediatrician to suggest what was best for her child, she felt she had been included in the discussions and consulted over her child's education.

The parents' understanding of 'special educational needs'

Forty per cent of parents in this study defined SEN as children with physical disabilities or sensory, visual or hearing impairment. Four parents equated SEN with children who had very low IQ and required total care from their parents/carers. Two parents mentioned '*slow learning*' as a criterion for SEN. Another mentioned disorders like Autistic Spectrum Disorder. Interestingly, 25 per cent of parents indicated that they had no idea how SEN is defined in the UK and did not give a response. All this shows that there is a very narrow understanding amongst Chinese parents of SEN as restricted mainly to conspicuous physical or sensory difficulties. The limited knowledge of special education was most apparent when parents were asked how and where children with SEN were educated. Sixty five per cent thought that these children were educated in special schools. Thirty five per cent remarked that the child should follow a differentiated curriculum. Only two parents mentioned '*inclusion*' and educating such children in an ordinary school. Both were parents whose children had SEN, one a hearing impairment and one Autistic Spectrum Disorder (ASD).

Table 7.4: Responses of participants

	Parent of a child due to be assessed by an Educational Psychologist	Parent of a child with hearing impairment	Parent of a child with ASD	Parent of a child with a Statement of SEN
Do you know who the Special Educational Needs Co-ordinator (SENCO) is in your child's school?	No, don't know what a SENCO does.	No, I have never heard of the term SENCO.	Yes	Yes
Do you know where your child is on the SEN Code of Practice?	No, never heard of school action or school action plus	Yes, school action	Yes, school action plus	No
Have you seen or read SEN – a *Guide for Parents or Carers*?	Yes, school gave me one but it is difficult to understand the English and the terminology.	No	Yes, I was given one by school	No, I have never seen one
Have you heard of the Parent Partnership Service which provides information, advice and support to parents of children with SEN?	No	No	No	No

Clearly then, most Chinese parents still harbour the idea of *segregated* education for children with SEN and know little about the government's inclusion policy. Their ignorance reflects how ill informed Chinese parents are about the British education system and about developments in special education, although this is likely to be true of other parents whose children do not have SEN.

An unexpected finding of this study was that although 30 per cent of the parents believed that their child required additional support, including extra time in examinations, only 10 per cent considered that their child had SEN. The parent whose child had a diagnosis of ASD (Parent B) said that she wanted her child to attend a mainstream school because of the stigma associated with children attending special schools. Her perception was that children with SEN were alienated and discriminated against. Although their children were being supported under the SEN Code of Practice or awaiting an EP assessment, three parents did not accept that their children had SEN. Like many parents, Parent B was hoping that her child's difficulties were short-term. Overall, 90 per cent of parents did not believe that their child had SEN. Again, this is not unique to Chinese parents but the cultural perspective that there is a stigma concerning SEN may make them reluctant to accept such a label.

Awareness of the special educational needs process

Although four parents had children with identified SEN, none were aware that a process exists for identifying and assessing children with special educational needs. Their reported experiences of the SEN process gave cause for concern.

Table 7.4 shows how poorly informed the parents were of the special educational needs procedures and of their roles and rights in supporting their children with SEN. Neither had they been made aware of the existence of organisations or support groups that offered advice and information. Although the SEN booklet for parents and carers is available in different community languages including Chinese, none of the parents had received it in Chinese.

Discussion

Can it be that 'partnership' with families of Chinese children with SEN is no more than rhetoric? The study suggests that it does not reflect real life. Although only twenty parents were involved in this study, the implications for home-school partnerships and supporting the SEN of Chinese pupils cannot be underestimated. Effective parent-teacher communication has been shown to underpin positive educational outcomes (Adam and Christenson, 2000). There is evidence in this study to suggest that parents are not always provided by schools with information which enables them to participate fully in discussions with teachers, other educational professionals and local authorities. This goes against the ethos of the Education Act 1996 which strongly emphasises the importance of partnership with families of children with SEN. This problem may have been compounded by their lack of proficiency in English. Given the multiracial and multicultural characteristics of our schools, it is imperative that schools review their procedures for involving parents whose first language is not English, especially when there are concerns about a child's SEN.

The data also revealed the general reluctance of Chinese parents to engage with schools. A constellation of reasons has been identified: the language barrier, parents' long working hours, the cultural respect for authority and the fear of recrimination have all been cited as obstructions. School-related factors have also been highlighted, including the attitude of individual teachers and the lack of literature in Chinese to keep them informed. The negative comments or lack of response when Chinese parents were asked how ways to improve communication with schools could be improved revealed their feelings of aversion.

A way forward

What can be done to overcome this *impasse*? Here are some suggestions:

- Schools can consider conducting a multilingual survey and consult parents on alternative systems of communication that take into account the needs of parents whose first language is not English.

- Written communication such as letters and newsletters should be available in Chinese so that parents are kept informed of what is happening in their child's school. A community psychology approach may be useful in which parents who are more fluent in English can be empowered to form a bridge between their community and the school.

- In some schools, the availability of Chinese speaking home-school liaison workers has proved effective in supporting communication between Chinese families and the school. Parents will arguably be more interested in attending school activities if an interpreter is available; at least parents will not feel embarrassed that they are the only ethnic minority parents who cannot understand and communicate in English.

- The use of an interpreter in meetings with parents may go some way towards encouraging parents to express their views and opinions. Some parents may feel uneasy about using a stranger as an interpreter due to considerations of confidentiality – as the Chinese saying goes: '*Keep family trouble under the roof. Don't tell your neighbours.*' Schools need to check with parents before booking an interpreter.

- Teachers need to be aware of the prejudices and stereotypes they may harbour about Chinese children and how these might affect the perception of their educational needs. This may be addressed via peer observation and whole school in-service training.

- To safeguard the emotional health and well-being of pupils from a range of ethnic backgrounds, it is imperative that schools revisit and evaluate their anti-bullying policies and strategies. *Bullying around racism, religion and culture* issued by the Department for Education and Skills (DfES, 2006) and the Safe to Learn (DCSF, 2007) provide specialist advice to schools on tackling bullying related to race and culture and bullying which involves children with SEN and disabilities.

Conclusion

Local authorities provide guidance to schools and should lead by example on how to integrate different ethnic groups in the local community. When considering the needs of Chinese children, local authorities should contemplate collaborating with Chinese community organisations to inform parents of the latest changes in education. Local authorities can help establish parent support groups to provide information and advice for Chinese parents of children with SEN. They should also consider a more vigorous use of PLASC[1] data to identify patterns of over-representation or under-representation of different categories of SEN and to scrutinise the SEN-ethnicity data to identify issues.

As the Chinese are the least vocal and the most 'invisible' ethnic group in the British education system I hope that this study will go some way to allow the parents' voices to be heard and the needs of Chinese children to be acknowledged and effectively addressed in schools.

Note

1 PLASC stands for the Pupil Level Annual School Census. PLASC returns are a statutory requirement on schools under section 537A of the Education Act 1996 and include data on gender, date of birth, Unique Pupil Number (UPN), surname, first name, ethnic group, date of admission to school, first language and home postcode. They form the basis of the Local Authority and National Pupil Database and are used in publications such as the PANDAs.

8

The psychology of identity: the black refugee experience

Randa Price

Introduction

Identity is a diverse and complex construct to define and to work with. Many disciplines, such as sociology have contributed to its development through research and academic writing (Archer, 2002; Mac Innes, 2004). Psychology's contribution remains unique because of its distinctive emphasis on how identity emerges through childhood experiences and continues to develop throughout our lives (Erikson, 1950; Marcia, 1966). Psychologists agree that identity is the unique collection of thoughts, emotions and behaviour that defines a particular person or group. The agreement extends to include the view that identity is dynamic, personal and open to social and environmental influences. Arguably these theoretical ideas are too diffuse to inform the research needed to test their usefulness.

Several psychological orientations focus on aspects of identity to guide research and psychological understanding. Psychodynamic thinking considers personality characteristics as a biological blueprint; they are collectively known as the Id. As we develop, our personalities are chiselled through interaction with significant others, represented by the *superego*. The *ego* or the 'person' emerges as an outcome of this continual dramatic process (Louvinger, 1976; Moore *et al*, 1989; Stafford- Clark, 1965). Guided by this thinking, psychoanalytic research draws on individual case studies to understand the dynamic process of growth (Kaechele *et al*, 2008; Sandler *et al*, 2000).

Social psychology, on the other hand, studies membership of groups such as the family, friendship and work groups and their shared behaviours (Gilovich *et al*, 2006). On the other hand, self psychology looks into aspects such as self image, self esteem and locus of control (Branden, 2001; Heider, 1958; Jenkins, 2008). Recently, cognitive behaviour therapy (CBT), offered a unified approach that can incorporate these different aspects of personality (Dobson and Dobson, 2009). For the purpose of this Chapter, CBT is defined as an umbrella term that covers a number of therapeutic interventions which challenge flaws in our thinking with the aim of modifying maladaptive behaviour and emotional distress. CBT thinking emphasises the part thoughts, emotions and behaviour play in shaping personality. It suggests that a person or group selects and interprets what they see. Their interpretations are influenced by what they have learnt from life experiences. Take for example colour. Colours can evoke thoughts such as disdain or admiration, which can convert to feelings of hate or love which lead to either seeking or avoidant behaviour. Another example may be how a group of adolescents talking loudly at a bus stop can be seen: are they threatening or are they just youngsters enjoying the end of the school day? How we act is shaped by our understanding of the situation. We may feel apprehensive and cross the road, or we may think that the youths remind us of how we were, enjoy their exuberance and wait with them for the bus.

Diagram 8.1 shows this process, as adapted from an exercise described by Neenan and Dryden (2002) as a tool to modify thoughts about the self.

Diagram 8.1: An example of how CBT works
Situation: Waiting at the bus stop

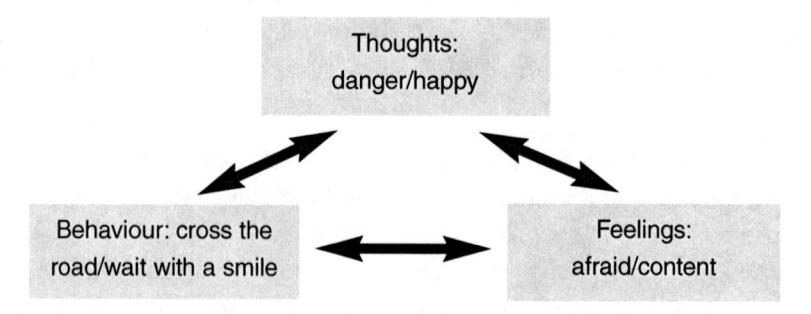

Thoughts: danger/happy

Behaviour: cross the road/wait with a smile

Feelings: afraid/content

A CBT view of how personality is developed within a specific environment is shown in Diagram 8.2.

The Environment

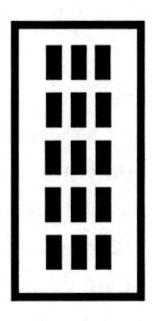

Diagram 8.2: A CBT view of personality

The big I is the contour of the self, the whole person. All its diverse qualities such as gender, race, age and group memberships are represented by the small I's contained within. This hypothetical person does not exist in vacuum, but is located in a complex and diverse ecological setting, identified as the environment in the diagram. The setting is made of intricate and influential networks: biological, geographical, socio-economic to name but a few. This model is an interactive one, with room for new I's and potential for consolidation of others as we grow older or move to new settings. The formation of the self is greatly influenced by the environment, as the context in which we operate highlights the small relevant I's. In a school, the pupil identity is the most significant; as an adult a woman can be a mother at home and a doctor at work.

Groups work in a similar way. Its members highlight certain characteristics and erase others before drawing a boundary to exclude yet others. One of the most significant and enduring ideas in the history of western psychology is contained in the small I's of race, with colour as its marker. Black psychology evolved as a challenge to the dominant group's idea of inherent inferiority (Du Bois, 1903). Black thinkers, informed by Fanon (1967), engaged in a psycho-social discourse as a way to liberate academic thinking from the confines of such long held beliefs. The story continues and race and ethnicity are still given as reasons for differential outcomes, despite research firmly pointing towards inequality as the prime factor (Department of Health, 2009; Harris, 2001).

The social challenge of race

The most central idea in personality development, I believe, is that of social challenges. Erikson, a neo Freudian, described social challenges in 1950, using the social model of identity development put forward by Freud (Freud and Strachey, 1962; Stafford-Clark, 1965). Through his work with clients, Erikson observed the pivotal role of managing social tasks in identity formation. In this model, life is seen as a social journey to wisdom and maturity and our identity strength comes from the successful resolution of a series of developmental or age related social challenges.

The idea of linking colour to achievement was, and still is, used in education. The question of individual differences is put as 'Why do some children do better than others when they share similar environmental conditions?' All children are seen as having access to free and universal education, career advice and health care in Britain and yet black children are over represented on negative indices for educational achievement, health, and employment (Haas *et al*, 2003). Individual differences in patterns of achievement become negative group attributes through psychologically informed studies (Hatchschild *et al*, 2004; Lane, 1998). These studies play their part in perpetuating disadvantage, as their findings affect both the educators and the educated.

The psychological reason for their longevity can be found in Diagram 8.2 too. The small I of colour/race becomes the big I. This black container holds all the most problematic, enduring, intransigent characteristics. These are the attributes that nobody in the dominant group wants and which are safely kept in the black container. Eventually, these qualities solidify into explanations for poor performance and delinquency (Deaton, 2004; Heilbrun *et al*, 2005; Olivier *et al*, 2002), through the recognised psychological process of projection (Kieser, 1948). Taking this route has the advantage of reducing the anxiety of those who use it. Dominant group members do not have to worry about their intelligence because they are not black and their dominance is protected and reinforced.

There is currently a trend in black thinking to dismiss pre existing psychological theories because they have evolved in a racist context, and continue to reinforce racism (Baldwin, 1970). In my view, certain psychological observations call for throwing out the bath water and keeping the metaphorical baby.

This Chapter puts forward the view that we may all meet challenges as we negotiate our path through life but that challenges are not equally distributed across the population (Griffin, 2002; Pantzer *et al*, 2000). The challenges are particularly difficult for black children in general, and even more so for those from a black refugee background. This is due to the multiple rejections and hardship they face through their own social journey.

The Black refugee experience in Britain
Refugees have always been an integral part of the social history of Britain. There is a mosque in Brick Lane in East London that was first built as a Huguenot church and later became a synagogue. It reflects the transitions of refugees in

Tower Hamlets. Generations came and triumphed despite hardship; they later settled and became accepted as part of the general population. This ongoing cycle of movement and settlement continues today and is part of our social experience, as new waves of people come to Britain for work or for refuge. Not only is the idea of seeking refuge socially familiar, but it is part of our personal experience.

Those of us who are settled occasionally experience the need for refuge, whether from work or family tensions. This can happen at different times in our lives. Our need may be in response to less life threatening circumstances than fleeing from torture but it argues for a universal perspective on the need for a safe haven. Yet, to date, the refugee is seen as a stand alone category. The concept of refugee is useful but it comes at a high cost. On the one hand, it serves to remind the host population of the extreme and brutal experiences people suffer, and allow those so labelled to remain in Britain by right. On the other, it demands great psychological and social sacrifice from the refugees. The refugee big I serves to keep those who belong to this group as the 'Other', always alien, with differences that take the experience of its members beyond what is possible to comprehend (Said, 1975). They remain forever the 'outsider inside' (Dockar-Drysdale, 1968) and become the repository for difficult feelings and states of being.

The British Congolese community

One of the recent refugee groups in Britain are the Congolese. They carry a number of markers predisposing them to be seen as alien: they are black, and few speak English when they arrive. They faced traumatic experiences that still echo through the news from the Democratic Republic of the Congo (DRC). Their painful, destructive and life threatening experiences are re-enacted through their lives within the societies they have joined. The narrow lens is used by professionals to examine the Congolese experience in Britain and presents the refugee as 'alien or different'. This lens does not show other facets, such as the group's resilience, ability and hardiness despite their experiences. The lens blocks the development of necessary protective links with other mainstream black and newly settled communities. The two salient I's the Congolese carry are the refugee and the African ones, both predisposing this group to the status of the Other (Said, *ibid*).

Said's description of the Orient being seen as untouchable, static, separate, eccentric, backward, passive, and despotic is similar to the west's view of Africa. By being African, the Congolese community are the new representatives of this unflattering Other.

Professionals find the Congolese experience hard to understand and the Congolese themselves difficult to engage (Price, 2006). Their newness is emphasised although there is a historic connection between Britain and the DRC when it was known as the Congo. When author Marcel Lloyd published pictures in Britain of the atrocities committed during the reign of King Leopold of Belgium, the publicity resulted in the Congo Reform Association being set up, which famous authors such as Sir Arthur Conan Doyle and Mark Twain joined (Gondola, 2002).

In spite of the past connection between the two countries, there is little evidence of this in the history taught at schools (see Chapter 17). This is also the case with the Somalis, whose presence in Britain in the form of settled seamen and their families dates back to 19th century . Evidence exists that Somali initiatives helped ease the settlement of new arrivals from Somaliland (Northern Somalia) (Price, 1990). The recent migration from the DRC to the UK started in 1990. Britain received 25 per cent of the 14,000 applications made to western European countries, but only 1 per cent were admitted (*The Guardian*, 29.9.9).

Like other black refugees, the Congolese are, in the main, highly educated and resourceful but their qualifications are not recognised in Britain and they face the triad of dislocation, lack of resources and harassment about the legality of their status in the UK (*ibid*). Another identified factor they share with other refugees is the experience of humiliation, which affects their psychological health (Price, 2007). As the British Congolese community emerges from the initial phase of settlement, this is a critical factor influencing the family, the socialisation of their children, and their achievement in school (Papadopoulos, 1999).

The formation of the Congolese identity in Britain

The most influential environments that help shape identity formation are the family and the school. During the early stages in a child's life, they also mediate the effects of other societal institutions (Carter, 1995; Dagitcibasi, 2007).

The British Congolese family negotiates its way through the continual challenges arising from living in a hostile environment in much the same way as the Somalis, Moroccans, and other older communities in Britain. Like many black men before them, some British Congolese, transfer the effects of the pressure and anxieties of being in the line of fire to the women and children in their homes (Laubschov, 2005). My work as a community relations officer often involved resolving incidents of domestic violence and child protection resulting from the environmental stresses on refugee family life (Price, 1990). Some children brought their troubles to school, manifest as anxious behaviour, concentration difficulties and an inability to learn (Timisui, 2005). Reports submitted to a commissioning London borough linked their problems to within-child deficits rather than making a more valid interpretation as a manifestation of the effect of ongoing difficulties faced by British Congolese families because of racism.

Most British Congolese families feel ambivalent about the homes they left behind because of their tough and often brutal experiences prior to departure (Price, 2006). Many are at the stage of idealising the country they have decided to join (Papadopoulos, 1999). In my experience, the dialogue the families have with professionals has not yet covered the effects of institutional racism. Research shows that recognition of racism is an important protective factor used by black families to prepare their children for life outside the home (Colt, 2006; Guishard-Pine, 2005). Recently, the British Congolese have started to form relationships with other black organisations (Congolese community organisations conference, 2006), and such encounters may deal with racism in Britain, how to survive its impact and its effects on the health of the black family.

The school case study

The following exploration was completed in 2007 in an inner city school. Concerns were expressed about the overrepresentation of pupils from a Congolese background on the borough's special educational needs register and their overall pattern of underachievement. Two previous studies were commissioned: the first documented the pattern of underachievement and the other raised issues related to language and communication.

Educationalists and researchers were aware of the pioneering work done by writers such as Coard (1971) and Stone (1981) and more recent work (Richardson, 2005). Before its dissolution the Inner London Education Authority published a report on its language units. The report documented the over representation of children from West African communities in these units as did the 1987 report about the overrepresentation of black children in its special schools. Without knowledge of these earlier documents, the needs of the British Congolese community appear unique (McGonigal, 2007). Yet my study highlighted the similarities between the needs of children from the British Congolese community and their peers (Pace and Hemmings, 2006). All pupils benefit from clarity and structure and from a variety of teaching and learning experiences, whether or not they are Congolese.

Like most children, the children from the British Congolese community are sensitive to the way their parents and their culture are seen by their school. At the time the research was conducted, the only sign of Congolese culture was an after school language club – and this was invisible to their peers. Other ways for the school community to demonstrate their respect and appreciation of the children's home culture were suggested, eg welcome books for parents in their mother tongue; art displays on the walls and the appointment of a Congolese learning support assistant. I recommended the 'exceptions' idea from solution focused approaches ie learning from examples of success (Price, 2007). Such ideas were previously excluded from the thinking and dialogue around the research.

Recognition of various refugee groups along the lines mentioned had been implemented for years and had had successful outcomes, but this was not the case for the British Congolese partly due to the artificial distinctions that set their children apart. Experience shows that old lessons have to be re-learned with the arrival of each new refugee group as the small distinctive I of being new arrivals is recreated as the big I of unmanageable difference.

The development of a black refugee identity

One interesting finding from my study was that the children were reluctant to see themselves as either African or black. Black identity was seen as exclusively African-Caribbean and with little to commend it. Congelese children were creatively exploring and constructing their big I and excluded every aspect they saw portrayed as negative in the environment around them. Some black models that chart the development of a black identity recognise this behaviour as an early stage on the 'route to roots' (Griffiths, 1994).

As the first generation of British Congolese children to be born in Britain, their construct is not surprising. Their parents' formative experience was mainly in Africa. Black may be a political concept that has a special meaning in a predominantly white society, but it does not retain its significance in a black one. Instead, its value as a social marker is diluted. The parents of the children in the study are exploring new ways to transfer their considerable survival skills to tackle the challenges of life in a black community that is subject to racism. Established families of African Caribbean heritage, on the other hand, have lived for a long time with the alienating experience of racism and pass on their coping strategies to their children (Guishard-Pine, 2005). It is an ongoing journey for all and the route is signposted by American research (Scottham *et al*, 2008).

Black psychology charts the development of a healthy African American identity in young adults using inventories and self report methods. Their validity was tested on other ethnic groups (Johnson *et al*, 2005), but the inventories were not developed with children in mind and do not take sufficient account of the refugee experience. Besides forming a black identity, Black refugee children need to find their unique way to retain the idea of a home country while making a new home in another. This route was explored by earlier communities. British Somalis have told me about of the importance of establishing a pan-European Somali identity to prevent fragmentation (Price, 2008), while other groups have used faith, such as the Jewish Diaspora and the Islamic Umma.

Diagram 8.3 below represents the journey of the black refugee child towards social maturity and fulfilment.

Diagram 8.3: The development of a black refugee identity

The social challenges these children face may be best viewed as two interacting I's. One represents the journey to a robust black heritage linked to its diversity and richness. The other I is the path towards becoming a member of a settled, acknowledged and respected community in Britain, with healthy links to their country of origin. Both I's, along with other I's, are hopefully to be contained within the Big I of social maturity and fulfilment.

9

Working with Pakistani Mothers in the community: an early intervention child mental health service

Alex Harborne

Introduction

This chapter describes our work with Pakistani mothers accessing an early intervention and prevention (EIP) child mental health service through a small number of primary schools where the majority of pupils are from Pakistani backgrounds. The service is now delivered through local primary and high schools and has drawn on a community psychology model of intervention with particular reference to two elements: empowering communities to care for themselves; and promoting well-being in communities (see Orford, 1992). The overall aims of the service are to promote emotional and psychological well-being in children and families and to address potential risk factors for the development of mental health difficulties in adolescence and adulthood.

Background

The early intervention and prevention service (EIPs) originally developed as part of a multi-disciplinary, multi-award winning *On Track* community initiative. It aimed to address risk factors for youth offending, and also health inequalities by improving awareness of, and access to, services provided by health, education and social care systems via a small number of schools. This initiative came about after a Rowntree Foundation report on the South Asian communities in Luton, Bedfordshire by Qureshi *et al* (2000).

The team currently employs around 15 staff to provide a universal service to schools. The theory and practice of Community Psychology (Orford, 1992) underpins the framework and philosophy for our way of working. Research looking at engagement between Pakistani mothers and education (Crozier and Davies, 2007) and health systems (Stein *et al*, 2003) has informed recent practice.

Culture and religion

Within the *On-Track* schools, the majority of pupils and a significant proportion of staff were from Pakistani backgrounds. The schools supported the cultural and religious traditions of the Muslim faith, acknowledging Ramadan and Eid and reflecting the community's Muslim identity in the dress code. Urdu and Pahari enhanced communication between school staff and families. The Headteachers of the schools were generally white British. The political drivers that influenced the school's culture can become projected onto children and the local community. For example, the Islamophobia that has flared up in society since the 7/7 bomb attacks is taken into account in understanding the anxiety and difficulties experienced by some members of the community.

Community Psychology

Community Psychology has its roots in psychology, sociology and social justice (Orford, 1992). Community Psychology focuses on promoting well-being and quality of life through understanding (1) the relationship between the individual and their community, and (2) the position of the community in relation to wider society. Kelly (1966) outlined four important principles for understanding people's behaviour within communities:

- **Adaptation**: that a person's behaviour within a community is adaptive to the context in which they live and work
- **Succession**: each community functions according to its unique history
- **Cycling of resources**: each community has its own resources, skills and strengths which need to be harnessed and utilised, rather than imposing external mechanisms for change
- **Interdependence**: the different settings within communities are interdependent systems and so changes in one area will inevitably lead to changes in others.

Community psychology focuses on preventing problems before they start by sharing the skills, resources and experience that exist within communities, not imposing ideas from outside. This contrasts with traditional medical approaches to mental health, which respond to individualised problems that already exist.

The effect of social and economic arrangements and resources of power on generating distress is recognised as an important area for change. The focus of practice is on changing these wider issues rather than working at an individual level.

This approach was adopted because of its applicability to the Pakistani community which had been considered 'hard to reach' by mainstream services. The marginalised position of the community and particularly mothers and children, made a community psychology approach particularly appropriate. Many of the women who accessed the service were immigrants and were not fluent in English. Many were homemakers with no personal income and few had high educational qualifications. They had limited power in their households, compared to their husband and his parents; and little power in most domains of their life (Hagan and Smail, 1997). The support structures already in place in the community, such as schools, adult learning centres and community centres provided essential resources for the service to engage directly with mothers and those working with them.

Engagement with schools and health services

Crozier and Davies (2007) discuss how the education system has become impenetrable to lower class, ethnic minority parents. Although Pakistani parents had come to be viewed as 'hard to reach' by the educational system, I would argue that it is the schools which have become hard to access. Ofsted (2004) used the term 'cultural differences' to explain the suggested lack of involvement by Pakistani parents in their children's education (cited in Crozier and Davies, 2007). In Luton the Local Authority took the bold step of investing in support services for families from disadvantaged and hard to reach communities, giving schools the resources to fund Family Worker posts to enable them to become more 'family facing'.

In mental health contexts, the term 'hard to reach' has been applied with equal weight to clients from most of the visible ethnic minority groups. Attendance rates at child and adolescent mental health (CAMH) clinics are traditionally much lower, and engagement shorter for families from visible ethnic minorities than for white British service users. Stein *et al* (2003) looked at factors affecting attendance at CAMH clinics in Luton and Bedfordshire and found that Pakistani mothers were more likely to address mild to moderate problems within the family than to seek support from outside agencies. Factors thought to increase the likelihood of attendance at clinics included the availability of culturally and gender matched therapists and better access to translation facilities.

Empowering communities to care for themselves: the role of the Family Worker (FW)

A key objective of the community psychology approach, and indeed one of the main successes of the *On-Track* project, was the utilisation of skills already present in the Pakistani community: the development of the FW as school-based employees of the local authority. FWs were mainly young women whose strengths were their unique understanding of the cultural, linguistic and social issues which affect the community. They were usually the first point of contact for families needing support or guidance, and were familiar with the stresses experienced by the community, as well as the attitudes and belief systems which make up part of it. The FWs came from diverse professional backgrounds, with a wide range of experience in child-care practice.

The main role of the FW was to encourage the community to engage with local services, and to promote the emotional well-being of families by providing practical, emotional and social support. They run classes for parents such as exercise classes, cookery classes, sewing classes, and stay-and-play sessions; they mentor mothers to build and develop their own personal resources by helping them learn English and how to budget; they offer support and guidance on housing, benefits and legal matters; they contact social services or the local authority, or attend court with a parent at their request; they offer a sympathetic ear for a parent to share concerns or worries; and they provide interpreting services in a co-worker role to support children's education.

Resourcing the EIPS

FWs have played a crucial role in the success of some of the interventions offered. They have been particularly important in the delivery of the Incredible Years parenting programme (Webster-Stratton, 2000), where they acted as co-facilitators as well as interpreters. FWs advised EIP service clinicians on how to engage parents who appeared uncertain of the service and have given direct support by accompanying mothers to sessions, translating material and supporting mothers at home with putting ideas into practice. Mothers reported that they felt confident attending the group because they had developed trusting relationships with the FWs. The service was acceptable to the extended family because it was seen as coming from within the community, as illustrated in the chart opposite.

Personnel	Service Delivered	Target Group
Family Workers	Parent Training Plan programme of school-based activities Advice surgeries Advocacy Interpreting Mentoring	Pakistani mothers
Primary Child Mental Health Workers (PCMHWs)	Training Consultation	Family Workers
Health Support Workers	Health Promotion	Families
Clinical Psychologists	Service Design Training Supervision	Commissioners Family Workers PCMHWs SENCos

Development of the FW role

The EIP service has contributed to the professional development of FWs by creating a bespoke training package, and through regular consultation meetings. Due to their position within the community, FWs have reported that they found it difficult at times to sustain a professional distance in their work with the mothers.

The training was delivered in two main phases:

- focusing on helping FWs learn about systemic theory and practice and
- monthly consultation groups to think about their needs

The groups use training techniques such as role-play of scenarios such as exploring the difficulties of engaging a family which has complex problems. Staff consultation groups are a well-established problem-solving forum in education settings (Guishard-Pine, 2000; Hanko, 1987, 1990). They provide a space for FWs to receive and give support and guidance in ways of promoting child mental health, or on how to use a reflecting team (Andersen, 1987) where appropriate. During both phases FWs are encouraged to keep a reflective journal of their thoughts and observations about themselves, their work and their relationship with other professionals.

Direct work with families

The EIP provided little direct work with families except occasional sessions with families with complex or longstanding issues, mainly issues of social disadvantage and the social care needs of the family. FWs had a vital role in facilitating direct clinical work with families that would enhance emotional health within the Pakistani community. Without FWs, engagement between the EIP service and the Pakistani community would have been more difficult, to the point where some families would simply not access the service at all.

Promoting wellbeing in the school context

Consultation meetings with school staff were held twice every term. They proved to be vitally important to:

- discuss children who were presenting with difficulties in regulating their emotions or managing their behaviour, and families with relationship problems
- share ideas about emotional wellbeing with the school staff who were implementing SEAL (social and emotional aspects of learning) initiatives
- discussing the interaction of the school culture and the community

The systemic thinking that guided these meetings enabled an understanding of the child and family in context, and of how certain meanings are ascribed to children's behaviour.

The Webster-Stratton Incredible Years parenting programme is a well validated and highly successful group intervention for parents seeking to learn ways of managing children's behaviour (Webster-Stratton, 2000). FWs were able to adapt the programme to make it more culturally acceptable, for instance avoiding offensive terms like a 'piggy' bank. An additional session was developed to involve the extended family in the work, and other materials were added to encourage the dissemination of ideas to the extended family eg using place mats as well as fridge notes to attract the father or mother-in-law's attention. Although Orford (2008) argues that parenting interventions are not truly reflective of a community psychology ethos, we found that the group work enabled discussions about the psychological wellbeing of parents and children, and about the ability of the whole household to address any family difficulties.

Health promotion

Health support workers (HSWs) played a crucial role in supporting families with their physical health needs. Their linguistic and cultural understanding of the community equipped them to facilitate access to health services. HSWs jointly facilitated highly successful workshops with the EIPs for groups of mothers seeking advice around mental health promotion and about how to understand presenting symptoms. We learnt that although the language barrier is often assumed to be the main problem in engagement, anecdotal evidence suggested that it is the *meaning ascribed to symptoms* which can be more problematic. The workshops incorporated both spiritual and psychological elements, including which recommendations from the local imam to follow, such as prayers and holy water.

Workshops with mothers revealed that they tended to adopt a deficit model of wellbeing. Parents talked about their child's mental ill health and believed that psychological distress should be understood and treated at the level of the individual, rather than the community. For example, when they discussed depression in children they emphasised treating children with medication or counselling, rather than addressing the underlying causes. The role of the EIP service was to enable the families to start thinking about the broader social and economic factors that affected depression. The workshops were also used to think about how service providers might better understand the religious and spiritual meanings ascribed to mental ill health, such as being possessed by a *jinn*.

Work discussion groups

Work discussion groups (Jackson, 2008) provided a regular space within the schools for staff to consider their concerns about their work. The groups were intended to allow staff to reflect on their roles as teachers and mentors, to think about the personal impact of working with very complicated or stressed families, and the stress of working with children who were experiencing issues of loss. One key reason for the success of the work discussion groups is that they provided a forum for staff to support and learn from one another. They were able to share experiences and difficulties about a wider range of issues than they would personally experience, and to think together about how to make sense of a difficult situation. The role of the EIP service was to validate and encourage the use of resources that already exist within the school community. The staff took the benefits of the group process into the wider school community, which then filtered through to the parents and children.

Outcome

The range of activities the EIP offered in its efforts to promote psychological wellbeing within the Pakistani community could not have been accomplished were it not for the successful relationships developed with FWs, HWs and school staff. It is these which have enabled a sharing of ideas, experiences, and mutual learning, as well as harnessing the resources and strengths of the community to deal with emotional health.

The EIP service used various quantitative and qualitative measures to evaluate the benefits of this work at both individual and systems levels.

Qualitative
School staff report they found the consultation meetings:

- reduced the stress and anxiety they felt about case work
- helped them to feel supported in carrying out their roles
- served as a form of training in mental health work
- allowed early multi-agency working and partnership

Feedback from the training of FWs indicated that the training had enabled them to take a different position in relation to families, and allowed them to move to a more facilitative and reflective role with the parents they work with. They also felt more confident about their ability to understand the systemic nature of difficulties encountered within particular communities.

Quantitative
After the parents' programme ended, parents reported lower levels of stress and greater understanding of factors which promote emotional well-being in children. Evaluation measures are therefore demonstrating that the work of the EIP service is useful and beneficial. But we need to be cautious about assuming that this way of working will be directly appropriate to all the schools we work with. The service has recently secured funding for the development of a 0-4s service, which will work predominantly through Children's Centres. It will be important to consider how this way of working can be adapted to staff and to more ethnically diverse families with young children.

Limitations to our way of working
Clinical psychology has been criticised for a lack of vision in providing services to ethnic minority clients (Williams *et al*, 2006). Although we attempted to apply the theories of community psychology to our work, we became aware of a number of ways in which our model of working has yet to really embrace the realities of this framework. Professional training in mental health often biases clinicians towards considering mental illness as a discrete, value-free idea and assumes shared understanding across the individuals and communities concerned. In our clinical work, we inevitably draw on our own experiences and beliefs about what makes good or poor mental health. Our definitions are created within the context of a National Health Service; our theory and practice is guided by research generated within monocultural contexts. For example, 'parenting' work implies a deficit in

parenting skills and that these need to be taught or learnt from a certain (western) perspective.

Our engagement with schools has worked well but we have been less successful in engaging other influential community groups such as local mosques, community organisations and voluntary agencies. Our work has focused mainly on mothers and we need to be mindful that this approach may reinforce the position of women within the community by failing to work with fathers and the extended family. Community psychology focuses on empowerment, liberation and social justice, but we recognise that such aspirations may contradict cultural and social norms. The demographics of our team do not reflect the populations we work with. Service users and workers who reflect the Pakistani community need to be recruited so they can act as consultants for further development of the service.

10

The diagnosis of autism: the experiences of West African parents

Sarah Took

Background

> Just as painters need both techniques and vision to bring their novel images to life on canvas, analysts needs techniques to help them see beyond the ordinary. (Strauss and Corbin, 1998:8)

The family is believed to be the most significant social institution in determining the quality of daily life experience and parents are central to its functioning (White and Woolett, 1992). Although parents' experiences are generally considered important when early intervention is made for children, there is scant research into autism that positions parents as the focus for understanding and supporting autistic children. Even less of the available literature on the parental experience of autism in the UK makes direct or explicit reference to culture or ethnicity. A review of the *Journal of Autism and Developmental Disorders* revealed no articles before 2000 pertaining to cultural variables in the UK. The inference is perhaps, that parenting an autistic child is a shared experience despite families being diverse in terms of structure, culture and values (Dale, 1996). This belief may obscure the importance and impact of different cultural beliefs. An awareness of the individual experiences of parents seems central; while similarities are apparent, differences are also clear. The specific issues for children with Autistic Spectrum Disorder (ASD) have been highlighted relatively recently by the National Autistic Society in the UK (Corbett and Perepa, 2007).

A review of the literature shows that most of the research had been done in the US. Most studies on culture and parenting compared parents' coping styles (eg

Magana, 2006; Elder *et al*, 2003). Gray (1993) concluded that no single method of coping with autism could be guaranteed to be successful, as different families employ individual coping strategies. As many of the professionals represent the majority culture, parents from ethnic minority groups may feel less confident about developing their own strategies, fearing that their culture may not be valued.

A London borough which made routine audits of pre-schoolers with special educational needs (SEN) over a number of years identified that West African families were overrepresented as having social communication difficulties. This group of parents often disagreed with the diagnosis, and thus prevented them from accessing services provided. My research emerged to explore these phenomena. The overall findings in the US are that children from ethnic minority groups are generally under identified (Begeer *et al*, 2009; Mandell *et al* 2009), but children of African origin have higher rates of diagnosis than other ethnic minority groups (Morrier *et al*, 2008; Yeargin-Allsop *et al*, 2003). Due to the paucity of research in the area, the primary aim of my research was to explore the process and impact of the child being diagnosed as having autism on parents of West African origin.

Autism: diagnosis and intervention

Thinking has converged about the defining characteristics and diagnosis of autism, as exemplified in the unified descriptor of DSM-IV – American Psychiatric Association (1994) and ICD-10 – World Health Organisation (1992). In the UK, the prevailing understanding of autism is as a medical condition or neurological disorder which requires specialist intervention (Wing, 1996). This model defines the disorder as fixed and constant (Trevarthen *et al*, 1996), however, Alvarez and Reid (1999) offer a different perspective, identifying autism as a mutable condition that is responsive to intervention. This view was echoed by Jordan (1999) who described the role of education as central to remediating the effects of autism.

The main approach to diagnosing autism is based on a 'triad' of impairments (Wing and Gould, 1979), namely:

- socialisation
- verbal and non-verbal communication
- imagination

Although the recognition of diversity is implicit in the concept of an autistic spectrum, it has generally been a deficit approach that has dominated research, with a specific focus on looking for common defining abnormalities that may be explained by biological theories of the nature of autism (Rutter, 1999; Trevarthen *et al*, 1996). Given this approach, diagnosis of autism may impact on the parent and how it does so is a part of how individual children with a diagnosis can be supported.

Parental involvement

The accurate diagnosis of autism relies purely on the judgements of clinicians. There is always a delay between the parental report of concerns and the diagnosis. Therefore the diagnosis should not in itself be regarded as a guide to provide support to families and individuals. Dawson and Osterling (1997) highlighted family involvement as a common element in successful interventions; empowering and understanding the family's experiences is therefore essential. Carpenter (1997) suggests that to promote genuine partnership, parents may consider offering training about their children to professionals. He seeks to develop a new way of thinking about the role of parents and the potential of their position in progressive research.

Conceptualising culture

> Culture is one of the two or three most complicated words in the English language. (Williams, 1983:87)

O'Hagan (1999) describes culture as being derived from the physical environment of birth, language, institutions, family and social relationships, child rearing, education, systems of belief, religion, morals, customs, dress and diet. All or some of these may be regarded as culturally significant to individuals and families. Cultural identity issues are complex and have wide reaching implications for both consumers and providers of services. The examination of cultural bias places the emphasis on discovering each group's unique explanation of the meaning behind behaviour.

Ethics

This research aimed to produce a meaningful account that held together the multiplicity and complexity of parents' experience. I used a qualitative research paradigm. A distinctive feature of qualitative research is the notion of reflexivity, which acknowledges the central role of the researcher and their effect on the research process. Denscombe (2007) suggests that it is difficult to avoid a personal relationship with the research process, particularly when interpreting the findings; our own cultural backgrounds and beliefs influence us all in our thinking. To monitor this aspect of the research I kept a reflective diary.

Theoretical perspectives

The telling of a story may be enhanced by the individuality of the teller and their own beliefs and understanding. Research is a process influenced by different theoretical views and perspectives so it is useful to consider the systemic and psychodynamic perspectives.

A systemic perspective

This perspective promotes the exploration of the family's philosophy of living and life cycle (Barratt *et al*, 1999). The impact of acculturation and adaptation or the loss of social and wider family networks may be significant for families. Cultural constructs of spirituality and religion, emotion and illness are pertinent to this study. It also acknowledges that autism is defined as within the child and also in terms of the child's relationships with others in the system, thus moving away from the belief that children can be treated without changes being made in the social and professional systems of which the child is part. Further, it allows professionals to consider their impact on the family and the child.

A psychodynamic perspective

Culture may be seen as operating at many different levels and involve both conscious and unconscious processes. Minsky (1998) suggests that culture and cultural change cannot be thought about adequately if we use only the language of consciousness and rationality. An inner world is a psychoanalytic concept, making it possible to think about human behaviour as it is affected by different mental states. Menzies-Lyth's work (1959), shows how patients' feelings of, for example, helplessness can be re-experienced through relationships with others. If we apply this to the parents of children diagnosed with autism, we see the possibility that positive and negative projections may exist between parents and professionals.

A loud silence

Young (1994) explored the issue of racism in the context of training and made me realise the importance of acknowledging my perspective as a white researcher who grew up in Africa and the Caribbean. I do not recall defining myself as white until I returned to the UK, where I found that colour and cultural differences were regarded with a degree of anxiety. I had no shared understanding with British people of the stereotypes presented to me when I entered education in the UK. During my conversations with families during the process of this project, recognition and reflection of difference contributed to breaking the silence.

Transcultural difference

As Markus and Kitayama (1991) note, the motivation for behaviour in Western cultures is individualist and independent, whilst motivation for behaviour in African cultures is more collectivist and interdependent. Sue (1999, 2003) questioned whether findings from research that is not based on ethnic minority populations can be applied to all racial groups and whether an intervention has the same phenomenological meaning for different cultural groups. Torrey (1986) suggested that in Nigeria interpersonal relationships are more important objectives than rational thinking symptom removal and improved when people are confronted with illness. A focus of my research was to determine how a medical model that identifies deficits in the diagnosis of autism fits with West African beliefs.

West Africa: Background information

West Africa is a major geographical region of the continent, extending to some 6.2 million square kilometres. The three major religions are: Islam, Christianity, and traditional beliefs (Else *et al*, 1999), with ancestry in West Africa encompassing a great diversity of cultural values (Nsameng, 1987).

West African families

Lee *et al* (1992) found that two models of helping seemed to pervade in the seven non-western countries he investigated: Barbados, Korea, Nigeria, Pakistan, Singapore, Sudan and Zambia – kinship systems and spiritualism-religion. In West Africa, there are *kinship networks* that comprise both nuclear and extended family and close friends and are maintained across wide geographic areas, (see also Chapter 13). The socialisation of the young and psychological security are the responsibility of the kinship network (Nsamenang, 1987; Nwadiora, 1996). Kamya (1994) described how the absence of family and friends as support takes its toll on parents who are struggling to cope with the stresses of raising a family. For West African families the feeling of being isolated from one's kin is comparable to a kind of death. According to Nsamenang (1987), the concept of marriage includes parenthood, and parenthood is rated as the most crucial aspect of the relationship. In Nigerian culture, children are seen as representing the wealth of the future as well as ancestors from the past. Children are discouraged generally from seeking attention from adults (Tuakli-Williams, 1997).

Diagram 10.1 represents an overview of researcher themes based on parental interviews.

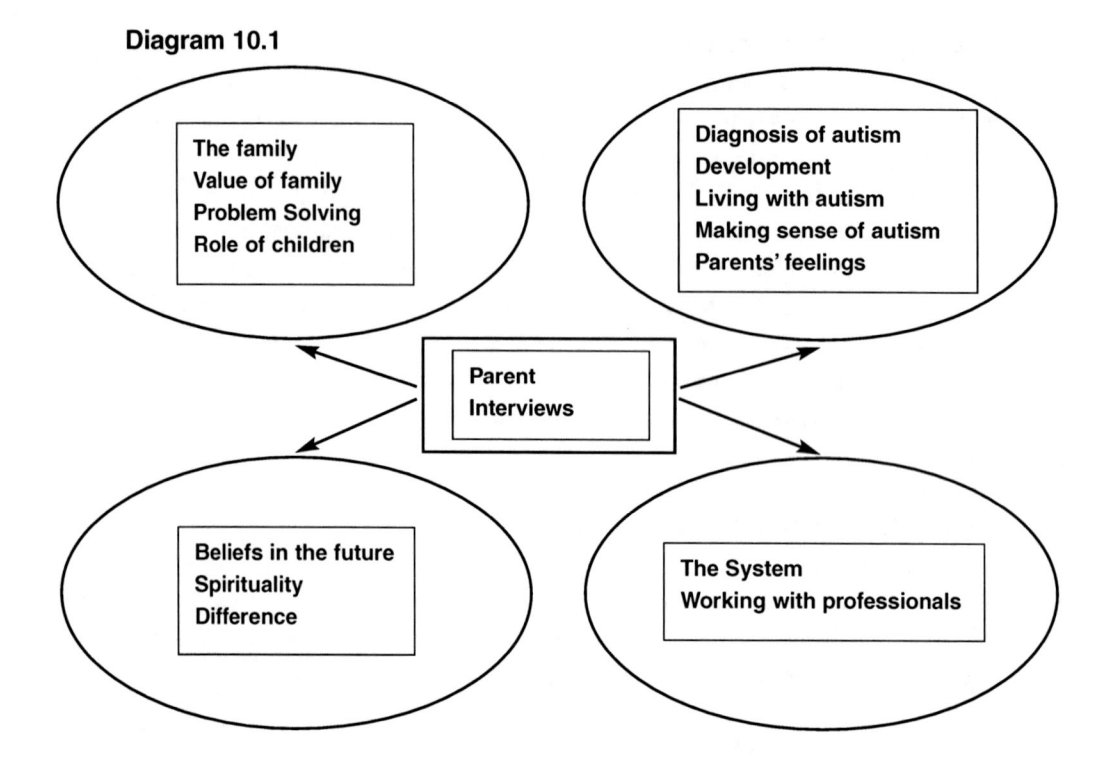

Diagram 10.1

- The family
  - Value of family
  - Problem Solving
  - Role of children

- Diagnosis of autism
  - Development
  - Living with autism
  - Making sense of autism
  - Parents' feelings

- Parent Interviews

- Beliefs in the future
  - Spirituality
  - Difference

- The System
  - Working with professionals

Qualitative analysis

Grounded theory allows a focus on theory through systematic analysis of data. When eliciting themes I consulted the views of Charmaz (1995): the researcher is encouraged to model self-reflexivity. This ensures that they look at participants' understanding of their own experiences, and this enables them to consider perspectives that differ from their own.

What parents said

When asked to reflect on a time when they faced a difficulty or problem and how they had found a way forward, all the participants said they turned to their family. Two subcategories were defined: the strengths of family and valuing all children.

Family

> We do not have a problem because my family are close by; the family is very important.

The family was described by parents in terms of support during difficult times:

> It was my family (who was supportive during the process of diagnosis) ...I mean we were all worried about him we were all hoping for a change my mum she was com-

ing here often... My mum is with my sister supporting her at the moment because she has breast cancer....

For one parent, family were not geographically close and she told me:

> I wish I could close my eyes and be at home with my family that the support I could have. At least they would tell me not to cry and they would be there to support and help me ... Being on my own here now I would like to put my head on someone's shoulder ... I find it very difficult and sometimes I say to myself what am I doing here, it really gets me down, sometimes I won't use the word sometime, most of the time it really gets me down because I have no family here ...

How children are valued in West African families

Children were described as important within the context of family. One parent stated that:

> ... regularly the family will get together and see all the children ...The kids are a blessing. There are things that I want to do but the children come first ... The children are my family ... It is a joy to have them around ...That children have their own roles and responsibilities we should accept the child regardless and try and help ... Also that children carry the family name ... You have to do your best and look after them ...

One parent said that: 'In West Africa things are very different.... In Nigeria children grow at different rates and children learn to speak at different ages: is it something you see a lot of back home'.

Having a child with autism

During the interview, parents were asked when they first became concerned about their son or daughter. A number of parents compared their child's development to that of others. One parent recalled:

> I thought there was something funny you know. The older boys, it was different because they were in the Ivory Coast...

Other parents also described differences they experienced:

> Nobody else there seemed to be like him, he just wanted to sit around... and she was not like other children you know like some friends I have we have the same age group...

Some parents regarded differences between children as usual in their home country:

> In Nigeria, children develop at different rates some fast some slow... He just needs time.

Explaining autism

Parents' understanding about autism ranged from sophisticated to wholly uninformed. Some parents were unclear about what the term autism meant:

> I didn't understand it and I still don't know exactly what it is...

Parents formulated an explanation for the siblings:

> They (siblings) asked why she is like this, she wants an explanation why she shouts 'leave me' or hitting her which any other girl can help, I explain to her the way it was explained to me that you may be matured but your brain might not be matured...

Other parents echoed this:

> Maybe it is something in his brain... I think it involves the brain.

Parents also expressed reassurance:

> In my family we all have the same concerns but we are confident that he will continue to make progress...

One parent described:

> She'll get better, autism isn't an issue for me...

In two interviews the parents cried as they spoke about their feelings. One mother described her shock at hearing the diagnosis:

> I was shocked when I found out it was autism...

A mother who had been informed by letter told me:

> It hits you like a bridge when you get a letter like that...

And another parent described their feelings, and had also observed this in other parents:

> It is very worrying when your child is not right.

Working with professionals

Parents described their difficulties in the following ways:

> I feel the system is very messy...
> It was such a hassle (process of diagnosis)
> I think they're a bit OTT overreacting so early on...
> I would have asked for more limits to professional involvement...
> and Classic autism, I mean what is classic about it? Obviously there are problems but they should check themselves before they diagnose autism, they are diagnosing it too quickly...

Parents presented a picture of inner resources and strength:

> Well they (professionals) have their own ideas and expect you to follow then, but I think it comes down to what you think is right.

> ... you have to make them understand what you want...

Some parents reported that they felt that the professionals they met listen to them:

> They listened at the centre...

> Yes they (professionals) listened to us.

> ...People would come back and say that that we were wrong. When they had worked with T after a while they began to understand T better ...

One parent described the support provided for her emotionally by a professional:

> ... They console, they try to help, they try to console, they try to understand my feelings...

Another found the process of diagnosis to be handled unhelpfully:

> I think that when a situation like this arises they (professionals) should think more of the parent. They used all these big words, you look lost, that is how I felt very lost and confused. If they say they are going to do this for the child, they have to explain and give you time to take it in. It feels like you're rushed everyone is coming at you with different things to say and do it is all very stressful they should give you time and if they give you any advice, explain it so you understand.

Beliefs about the future

One father explained how as he saw it:

> Where there is hope there is life, for example, if you have cancer even if you have no hair and you may be very sick, when you wake up in the morning, there is hope.

A number of parents described changes in their child which led them to believe, as one said:

> In time things would be OK, we had to believe in ourselves and our child as well. We exposed him to lots of children to play with so we know there was nothing wrong, so we had to believe in ourselves that he would be OK eventually. Change over time was described. Yes, in the reception class I told his teachers there was nothing wrong with him, he just couldn't talk so we were leaving him to mix with the other children and he was transformed...

These views about change were echoed by other families:

> He is a bit better now since he started nursery... He tells me his friends names, before nursery, he wouldn't speak about his friends... Once upon a time he wouldn't be able to sit playing like he is now...
>
> I think that she is ok now...
>
> He will continue to make good progress because there is nothing wrong...
>
> He just needs time... A delay soon he'll be ok... and all I do know is that he couldn't do a lot that his peer group or age group could but now he can.... He is even ahead in some things.

Spirituality

The majority of parents attended church and described religious beliefs – especially faith and hope – as important. It was thought to be 'supportive, I think especially for the family ...' Their religious beliefs gave some parents a different way of regarding the world:

> Who am I to challenge God and ask why do you do this? All I am asking him is for the strength, and the courage, to be patient and to accept everything day by day as the time goes...
>
> Because we are Christian we always have faith that you can get through this... My mother says that we should all pray for her...

Conclusion

The acceptance and adaptation that emerged was characterised by three interlinking strands; the child, family life and the future. Parents in this study felt that acceptance of their child's condition was of paramount importance. The parents' acceptance resulted in what they described as 'valuing their child as an individual' and a more optimistic view of the future than previously. Parents did not express a need for the input of professionals, and this may indicate low expectations of their own communication skills and whether professional advice is useful to them or their child. Some believe that their child will change over time, or have ideas about the place of children within the family. All these issues indicate that a professional should avoid assuming that the parents all have the same beliefs or attitudes or that their views are static and unchanging.

Although it is important to become informed about ethnic and cultural difference, diversity within a group needs to be recognised and responded to. A family and their values, beliefs and practices can only be understood through learning directly from the family itself. Listening to parents and consulting their views are the most valuable ways of finding out information and understanding people's feelings and experiences: the quality of the relationship between professionals and parents is as vital as the need to establish cultural and ethnic similarities. Sensitivity to cultural variations should be considered within the training and professional development of those who work with families.

Implications for professionals

- The tools professionals use for assessment and interventions need to be carefully evaluated in terms of cultural and linguistic validity
- Culturally competent staff must offer an assessment that seeks out the child's strengths and works out how to utilise them to promote learning for each child as they function in their unique family context
- Psychologists are ideally placed to act as an information conduit between parents, support groups and local departments
- During the process of diagnosis, consulting significant family members named by parents may help in supporting families to share important family beliefs
- Professionals are in a position to reinforce family competence and ensure that parents/families can make choices based on up-to-date information about the resources and interventions available
- Each family's experience of the process of diagnosis may reflect their personal experiences of loss eg through migration
- The psychological adaptations made by individuals when they move between cultures are a process of acculturation. Professionals need to be mindful of the stress that is a consequence of acculturation

Reflections

Keeping my reflexive journal allowed me to examine the structures and operations underlying the study, to use and develop ways of addressing bias, and to redress power inequality between the researcher and the participant. Critical reflection has allowed me to consider the interviewing process from different positions – though it is likely that a researcher from a West African background could add a different dynamic to the work (see Chapter 8). Social, cultural and environmental forces shape who we are and how well we function in the everyday world. The increasing multiculturalism of our nation offers both challenge and opportunity to professionals working with children and their families.

11

Learning Difficulties: Distinguishing them from issues of language

Jan Carter and Jeune Guishard-Pine

The children's linguistic adjustment relates in many ways to their educational progress... (Bullock Report, DES 1975:20.1)

The Bullock Report made the important point that the academic progress of children from overseas may be disadvantaged in their learning of English 'in the areas of oral comprehension, spoken intelligibility, reading, writing and spelling' (DES, 1975:20.7). It made recommendations on how to advance these children's learning in mainstream settings. However, our thinking has advanced with the knowledge that special educational needs and bilingualism are separate concepts and separate issues. This chapter examines the challenges in providing learning support to children who straddle both groups – those who have various special educational needs (SEN) and are bilingual or multilingual. It goes on to indicate what constitutes best practice for these children in primary schools.

Introduction

One of the most intriguing things about inclusion is the way it is being presented as though it were a novel concept. One could argue that due to perilously poor resources many societies around the world have always tried to educate all their children as best as they can, whilst others offer education to the elite few. In the UK the concept of inclusion was enshrined in law in the Education Act of 1981. This made the proviso that children with Learning Difficulties and Disabilities (LDD) must be included only if it is consistent with the education of the other children with whom they will be educated, and the efficient use of resources. Ofsted, however, described inclusion as the diversity of provision and outcomes to meet the needs of pupils with learning difficulties and disabilities – what used to be described as special educational needs (SEN) (2006) so as to establish a common language across the statutory services.

The primary objective of schools is to develop children into responsible citizens, as defined most recently in the *Every Child Matters* (DCSF, 2004) agenda. This has heightened the awareness that there has to be more synthesis between the aims of educational and other statutory bodies, families and schools if the pupil is to feel truly valued and respected – a condition for fulfilling their educational potential. Schools which alienate, disempower or suppress the development of high self-esteem will provoke disaffection in their pupils (See ILEA, 1985; Rampton Report, 1981 and Swann Report, 1985).

From the Commonwealth to the UK

> Schools are largely middle class institutions in terms of their ethos, values, assumptions and teaching force. Books reflect middle class norms and lifestyles, regional dialects and accents are less valued and standard English is the rewarded goal. Leicester (2008:26).

As early as 1963, the Department of Education proposed intensive English language courses for migrants, but only for those whose first language was not English. Consequently the language issues for those from the Caribbean were ignored.

The earliest systematic attempt to support the needs of learners with English as an Additional Language (EAL) came through Section 11 of the 1966 Local Government Act. Principally it supported Asian pupils, most of whom were fluent in their mother tongue, in learning to speak and use English. Willey (1984) documented how some teachers resisted mother-tongue teaching or maintenance, or of EAL teachers working in mainstream schools. Linguistic theory indicated that children would learn English best if they did so in the context of the playground and the curriculum rather than withdrawing them. Gradually local education authorities (LEAs) closed down their English language centres and redirected support to the mainstream classrooms. The special educational needs of EAL pupils were examined in the Fish Report, *Educational opportunities for all?*, commissioned by the Inner London Education Authority (ILEA, 1985) to look at the equality of opportunities in education for pupils from migrant families. The reference to the special educational needs of pupils for whom English was an additional language indicated a shift in thinking as this group had not been recognised in the Warnock report (1978) or the consequent legislation of 1981.

From underachievement to achievement

> Inclusion is important because exclusive practices damage children and their learning while inclusion removes unfair barriers and promotes respect. (Leicester, 2008: 29)

There are clear racial patterns to the identification of LDD (Mabey, 1981). In their research into the special educational needs of bilingual pupils, Lindsay *et al* (2006) found, for example, that compared to English, Scottish and Welsh white children: Bangladeshi pupils had nearly twice the levels of hearing impairment and that although Pakistani pupils had lower recognised levels of LDD overall, they had over twice the levels of Profound and Multiple Learning Difficulties (PMLD), Visual Impairment, Hearing Impairment or Multi-sensory Impairment. However Indian and Chinese pupils had lower levels of Moderate Learning Difficulties (MLD), Specific Learning Difficulties (SpLD) and Autistic Spectrum Disorder (ASD) and Indian, Bangladeshi and Chinese pupils had lower recognised levels of LDD overall.

Studies suggest that these phenomena might be linked to the persistent difficulties in extricating learning difficulties from issues associated with proficiency in English (Cline and Shamsi, 1999; Usmani, 1999). These findings informed the *Primary National EAL Strategy* launched in 2004. However, there were calls for research to establish whether pupils with EAL are receiving culturally-competent services to assess and meet their needs. An example of one action research project that looked at children in the early years is described below. Concern was also expressed about the psychological well-being of multilingual pupils and their families (German, 2008) and Lindsay *et al* (2006) commented on the low levels of access such children had to meeting their health needs. Systems and processes, rather than techniques designed to close this gap are described in Chapter 9.

Children with diverse language backgrounds have much to gain from mixed-ability, mainstream teaching. Apart from the linguistic advantages (see Conteh, 2005) opportunities to share their language, to show empathy for and generally take an interest in differences within and across and cultures are enriching. Children come to the pre-school setting with prejudices and racist attitudes already formed (Lane, 2009).

One area that has spearheaded positive action to create a more equal society, has been the inclusion of children with LDD in mainstream education. Inclusion in the school context requires teachers, parents and children to negotiate preventable barriers to their learning. In multicultural schools the needs of multilingual pupils must be considered. Nowadays the Bullock recommendations (DES, 1975) are unchallenged: it is no longer expected that a child completely loses their cultural identity in order to achieve in school. The school community must together explore, reflect and decide how it can support every child. Leicester (2008) suggests that multicultural schools are more effective if their staff reflect the ethnic makeup of the pupil population so that children have role models among their teachers, who can also connect well with parents or take a home-school liaison role.

From school as institution to school as community resource

Each school has its own individuality, based on its physical and social environment, its legal status, the governance arrangements, the senior management, the staff, pupils and their families and all the diversity that they bring to the school in its governance. The school can include families who speak other languages by eliciting their opinions using the appropriate community languages. The SENCo role (Special Educational Needs Co-ordinator) in the multicultural school must fit with the structures that support the language development of the bilingual pupils. A model of the role is indicated in Diagram 11.1 opposite.

The SENCo must be able to see the bigger picture at all times: that is they must have a perspective on the issues and concerns of the entire school community. The amplification process relates to the ability, role and function of the SENCo to listen and to hear the limitless concerns that will emerge from the problem-identifiers found within any school community. It is vitally important that those expressing concerns feel that the SENCo is turning up the volume on what they are saying rather than minimising or dismissing any difficulties identified.

In Diagram 10.1 opposite, the magnification process relates to taking a microscopic view of the problems raised by the problem-identifiers. This will require a data collection process that may include evidence from both quantitative assessments such as testing, assessment-through-intervention, dynamic assessment, round-robin analyses, and observation schedules and also qualitative assessments, such as team-teaching, open observations, running records and interviews. The magnification process may also involve collating the views of other professionals the SENCo consults for advice, as well as the parents' and carers' perspectives. Where large groups of children are being identified within one class year group, the SENCo must also provide direct support such as mentoring or team-teaching, to the class teachers. The magnification process ostensibly aims to refine and define the problem more accurately so that there is a better fit between the intervention and the key agents of change – the problem-solvers.

The skill of the SENCo is most appreciated in the simplification process, as the SENCo is the chief investigator and can explain and justify the intervention to be

LEARNING DIFFICULTIES: DISTINGUISHING THEM FROM ISSUES OF LANGUAGE

Diagram 11.1. The role of the SENCo in a multilingual school

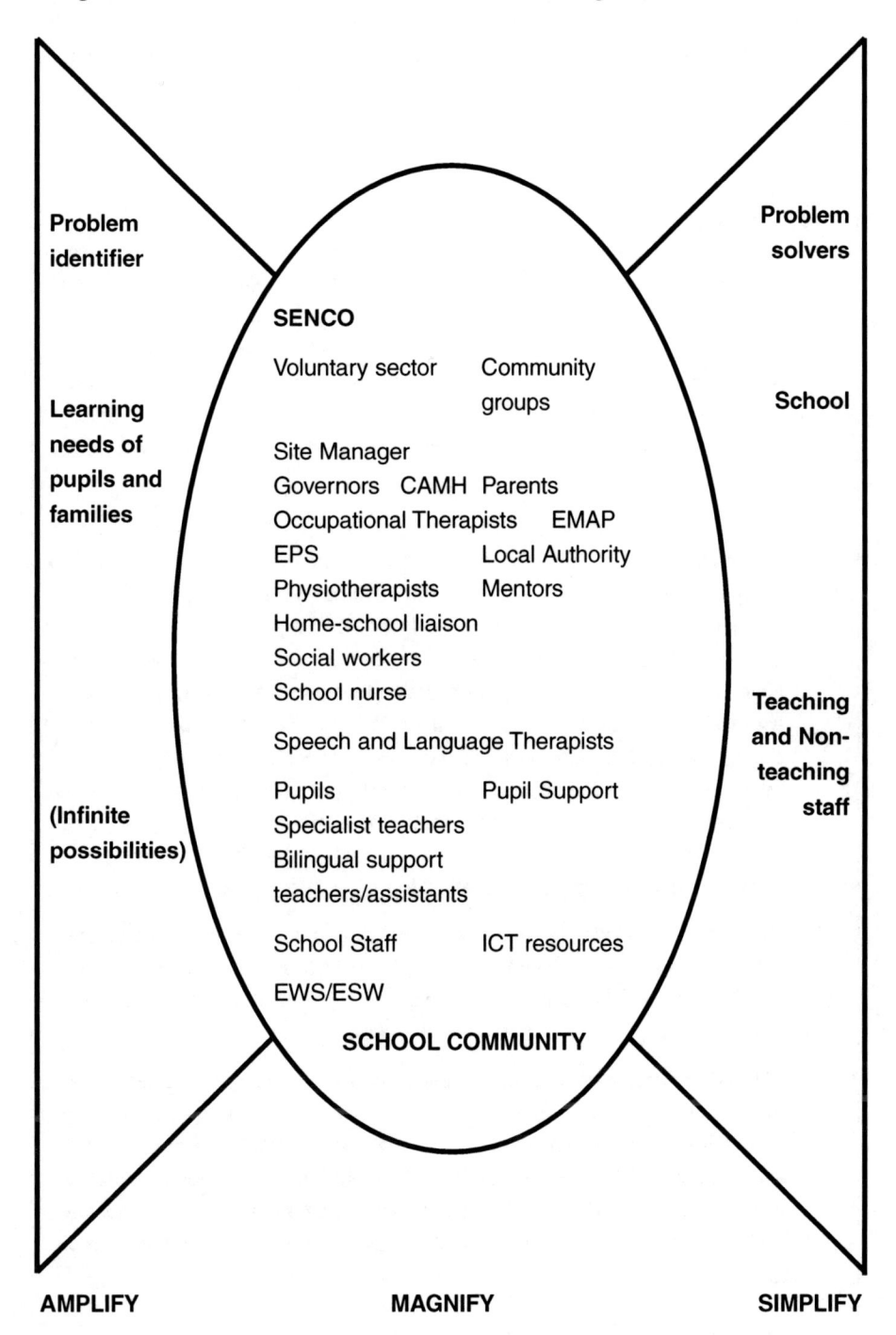

Problem identifier		Problem solvers
Learning needs of pupils and families		School
		Teaching and Non-teaching staff
(Infinite possibilities)		
AMPLIFY	MAGNIFY	SIMPLIFY

SENCO

- Voluntary sector
- Community groups
- Site Manager
- Governors CAMH Parents
- Occupational Therapists EMAP
- EPS Local Authority
- Physiotherapists Mentors
- Home-school liaison
- Social workers
- School nurse
- Speech and Language Therapists
- Pupils Pupil Support
- Specialist teachers
- Bilingual support teachers/assistants
- School Staff ICT resources
- EWS/ESW

SCHOOL COMMUNITY

implemented. This relieves pressure on the class teachers and parents to come up with answers that are based on their personal experience. The box below clarifies the key messages for teachers and SENCos that are considered central to effective co-ordination of support to pupils with LDD in general who also lack proficiency in English.

Key messages

1. The infrastructure: The SENCo must hold a senior position in school management and must have a solid knowledge base of LDD and also the skills and expertise to earn the respect of the teaching staff. As their position bridges the school management and teaching staff, the SENCo must be flexible and adopt a *can do* approach to support both management and teachers. The Headteacher must be a staunch supporter of inclusion and prioritise training to boost the quality of provision for children with LDD.

2. There must be a sincere commitment to develop excellent working relationships with parents. The SENCo must be aware of the stigma of LDD for families from certain cultures. The SENCo must be prepared to lead parents' groups to widen access to parents from cultures with a less developed conceptual base on SEN/LDD to increase their knowledge and understanding of SEN (see Chapters 7 and 9). They must position the parent as the expert in their child's needs. In practice, this may simply mean suspending judgements about families that are based on their ethnicity, culture or proficiency in English alone. Communication with parents who lack English proficiency will be more effective if the school provides hard signs of progress in the form of achievements that are quantifiable rather than soft signs such as qualitative feedback saying the child is 'improving'. The school should seek role models from among the community and reflect the ethnicity and class of the children.

3. There is no correlation between achievement and the availability of toys and reading material in the children's homes. Children from South and East Asian backgrounds are the highest school achievers, yet few have toys when they are very young (Gillborn, 1990; Ofsted, 2006).

4. Without communication pathways the system can collapse. The first communication pathway is between the subject leaders and the Inclusion Manager or staff who have key responsibility for pastoral care or behaviour. A confident and competent SENCo will be prepared to challenge teachers and non-teaching staff who stereotype pupils. Some may have stereotypical and even mythical views of pupils with LDD or those who are bilingual or black or who are from economically disadvantaged families.

> 5   Effective SENCos must have an enabling agenda so they help to break down barriers and defences by affirming everyone in the school community. This will feel unusual when the system is in transition from a system which is developing to one that is established, but over time it will become an automatic style of communicating feedback. As schools make the transition from a developing to an established system, the SENCo should facilitate team-teaching across all the year groups.
>
> 6   SENCos and Inclusion Managers need to be able to demonstrate how to meet the learning needs of pupils by modelling competence in their own teaching of whole classes, in addition to their specialisms and managerial skills. This will help them to:
>
>   - gain credibility with colleagues when advising them
>   - model good practice
>   - differentiate between a child with learning difficulties and one who is not being taught appropriately
>
> 7   SENCos must always differentiate between EAL and SEN. They should know the distribution of LDD across the ethnic groups in the school. The SENCo team has to be skilled in using appropriate and relevant objective-based assessments and must use them whenever possible. Such assessments should be used alongside more qualitative assessments to close the gap between the child's current level of skills and knowledge and their educational potential as assessed by parent, teacher and child in interviews and by qualitative assessments such as sampling their recorded work over time. Specific tools such as language assessment logs can throw light on how teachers of pupils learning through what is not their first language distinguish temporary issues of English proficiency from longer term learning difficulties (Hall, 1995).

The Primary National Strategy for EAL made available resources such as those found in *Excellence and Enjoyment: learning and teaching for bilingual children in the primary years* (2006). These materials continue to be evaluated.

The next section summarises action research conducted by Jeune Guishard-Pine that was built into a problem-solving process. It exemplifies the convergence of educational psychology and support for LDD and EAL. The research was provoked by a nursery teacher's request for a checklist that could predict which bilingual children might experience learning difficulties later in school. It was an interesting piece of research because language proficiency generally emerges between the ages of 30 months and 48 months. So the objective was to develop a form of assessment that could identify young emerging bilinguals who might have learning difficulties. A variety of cognitive and physical skills were assessed without recourse to spoken language.

Designing a non-verbal developmental checklist for bilingual under-5s

The Bullock report (DES, 1975) recommended that children with EAL be given '*as sharp a measure as possible of their SEN*'. There is much that teaching and non-teaching staff have to learn about formal and informal assessment of children whose LDD may be masked by limitations in English or general language skills (Cline, 1993). In the Ofsted report, *Raising the Achievement of Bilingual Learners* (Benton and White, 2007) the statistics on the visibility and invisibility of pupils with EAL came under scrutiny. Lindsay *et al* (2006) noted the under-representation of Asian and Chinese children with respect to MLD, SpLD and ASD and called for more in-depth research to investigate whether these children's needs were accurately identified or whether their EAL status skewed the recognition of their academic needs. They suggested that accurate identification and assessment was crucial for pupils being supported at School Action Plus and SEN statutory assessment stages (see also Chapter 7).

What follows is a description of action research conducted in two schools in inner London to bridge the technical gap in how well they differentiated between EAL and LDD. The 23 children in the research cohort were thirteen Sylheti speakers, three Cantonese speakers, two Ibo speakers and one each of Mende, Arabic, Italian, Turkish and Greek. The primary aim was to develop a checklist that would identify bilingual pre-school children whose lack of English might delay their cognitive development. The checklist would need to:

- reliably identify children who were currently experiencing learning difficulties
- be used in the classroom by nursery staff
- be proactive and identify areas for further learning support

The project also aimed to examine whether the children perceived by their teachers as having learning difficulties or delayed development of cognitive skills, would be identified by the checklist. Children aged 3 to 5 years from two nursery classes in different schools were given a battery of non-verbal tests including *The Hiskey-Nebraska Test of Learning Aptitude* (1966), *The Ravens Coloured Progressive Matrices Formboard* (1938), *The Harris-Goodenough 'Draw-a-person' Test* (1963), and the checklist. The class teachers were also asked to rank the children for general competence and social competence.

The checklist consisted of 45 items grouped in four areas: motor co-ordination, drawing, cognitive and communication skill (See pages 110-112). The areas selected were based on research indicating that fine motor, language and cognitive skills had a positive correlation with educational achievement. The investigators hypothesised that the cognitive items on the checklist would correlate with the pupils' scores on the *Hiskey-Nebraska* and the *Ravens Tests*; that the drawing items on the checklist would correlate with the pupils' scores on the *Draw-a-person Test* and that the scores obtained on the checklist would correlate with the teachers' ratings.

How the checklist was used

To assess whether or not the child could respond appropriately, the investigators mimed the instructions, using a range of non-verbal communication (NVC) including strong gestures such as pointing, holding out palm, beckoning, physical prompts such as taking the child's hand to touch the object after touching or holding it themselves and eye-pointing. To encourage or reinforce the child's responses, the investigators used NVC such as nodding, smiling, clapping and the thumbs-up signal.

Statistical analysis of the data confirmed that the scores on the cognitive items of the checklist predicted the scores on the *Hiskey-Nebraska* ($p < .01$) and the scores on the *Ravens* ($p < .05$). The scores on the drawing items of the checklist predicted the scores on the *Draw-a-Person Test* ($p < .01$). Analysis showed that the older the child, the higher their scores on the *Ravens* test. The correlation matrix showed a high correlation between the cognitive items and the drawing items on the checklist ($r = .75$). We concluded, therefore that these items demanded similar mental processes. The drawings item on the checklist correlated with the *Hiskey-Nebraska* ($r = .64$), and the *Ravens* Test ($r = .52$) whilst the cognitive items correlated with the *Draw-a-Person Test* ($r = .39$). All these proved more powerful measures of the child's cognitive skills than the teacher ratings.

Conclusion

We concluded that the checklist identifies those children with EAL who have a delay in the development of their cognitive skills. There may be occasions, or cases of specific pupils, that mitigate against the sole use of measuring or observing language use because expressive language can relate to the personality of the child and their existing opportunities to converse in their first and their additional language. This checklist gives a good indication of the viability of using a wider range of techniques to assess the cognitive skills of bilingual pupils in schools, and follows here.

PSYCHOLOGY, RACE EQUALITY AND WORKING WITH CHILDREN

NON-VERBAL PRE-SCHOOL CHECKLIST

Name of child: :..

D.O.B: ....

Age: ....

Class: ....

Date of completion of checklist:

PLEASE RING YES OR NO

CO-ORDINATION

1	Throws ball underarm	Yes	No
2	Throws ball over arm	Yes	No
3	Runs well	Yes	No
4	Can climb stairs in upright position	Yes	No
5	Jumps off one step	Yes	No
6	Catches large ball from 4ft Away	Yes	No
7	Users alternate feet when climbing stairs	Yes	No
8	Jumps down two stairs	Yes	No
9	Runs to kick a ball	Yes	No
10	Bounces a small ball	Yes	No
11	Bounces and catches a ball	Yes	No

DRAWING

12	Holds pencil – no scribbling	Yes	No
13	Scribbles when given pencil and paper	Yes	No
14	Scribbles in straight lines	Yes	No
15	Scribbles in circles	Yes	No
16	Copies straight line	Yes	No
17	Copies a circle	Yes	No

18	Draws a person	Yes	No
19	Copies a diamond shape	Yes	No
20	Completes a simple maze	Yes	No
21	Draws a square in imitation	Yes	No
22	Copies triangles in imitation	Yes	No

COGNITIVE

23	Matches three colours	Yes	No
24	Matches geometric form with pictures	Yes	No
25	Arranges objects in categories	Yes	No
26	Builds a bridge with blocks in imitation	Yes	No
27	Matches a sequence of blocks or beads	Yes	No
28	Copies a series of connected 'v' strokes	Yes	No
29	Completes 3 piece puzzle	Yes	No
30	Picks up a specified number of objects (0-5)	Yes	No
31	Picks out objects from memory	Yes	No
32	Shows what is missing when one object is removed from a group of three	Yes	No
33	Matches symbols (letters and numerals)	Yes	No
34	Builds pyramid of 10 blocks in imitation	Yes	No
35	Matches colours of objects	Yes	No
36	Matches equal sets to sample of 1-10 objects	Yes	No
37	Copies own first name	Yes	No
38	Prints own first name from memory	Yes	No

COMMUNICATION

39	Uses gestures to make wants known	Yes	No
40	Points to object outside classroom	Yes	No
41	Pulls person to show them toys or work	Yes	No
42	Uses gestures to relate to incidents	Yes	No
43	Points to a familiar person	Yes	No
44	Can fetch an object	Yes	No
45	Can fetch 2-3 objects	Yes	No

Section 3
Theories and suggestions for ways forward

12
Progressive African Caribbean masculinities – a challenge to domination

Taiwo Afuape

Introduction

In Britain the focus on trying to understand the assumed problem of African Caribbean males and education has tended to operate as though their experience in schools takes no account of the position of young African Caribbean men in British society and the institution of education as a form of domination. I am aware of the heightened scrutiny of young African Caribbean males and do not wish to position them as a homogenous group, in need of rescuing, controlling or excluding. On the contrary, I wish to:

- highlight the context of hegemonic masculinity and white superiority within which mainstream education systems are located
- examine how dominant discourses – the processes of talk and interaction between people and the products of that interaction, such as what we write, say and think – impact on the experiences of young African Caribbean men
- reflect on what can be learnt from community and voluntary sector organisations working with young people about education as community and community as education, that challenges systems of domination

As Channer (1995) points out 'Many recent government reports, other publications and media reports have documented *ad infinitum* the apparent academic failure of African-Caribbean British children. A plethora of articles, research papers and books have probed varying aspects of this apparent failure' (Channer, 1995:ix). A recent wave of authors have challenged this continued pre-occupation by turning their attention to educational success among young African-Caribbean people (for example Byfield, 2008; Channer, 1995; Rhamie, 2007; and Sewell, 2009).

Young African Caribbean males in education

Teachers and pupils come to education settings influenced by many social contexts, and not all racial minorities occupy the same political or social position in British society. Research suggests that many British teachers think about the experience of African Caribbean males in education in terms of 'causation' and 'blame', defining these in terms of problems with African Caribbean people, families and communities and not oppressive discourses in wider society (Sewell, 1997). Mac an Ghaill (1994) argued that teachers, no matter how liberal, are socialised by the act of institutional teaching to uncritically defend the dominant ethos of the school, how learning happens and what education is within the wider social context.

In addition to home experience, young people are influenced by discourses in mainstream society, subcultures and peer groups that interact to influence the development of complex identities. Here I focus on discourses of hegemonic masculinity and white superiority.

Hegemonic masculinity and white superiority

Hegemonic masculinity refers to mainstream Western society's *ideal masculine standard*. Compliance is enforced by privileging and rewarding those who come closest to it and penalising those who stray or are distant from it. Hegemonic masculinity is associated with domination and patriarchy, which privileges men over women but does not privilege all men equally. Ideal masculinity embodied by the elite, white, middle class, heterosexual male (Collins, 2006). For example, hegemonic masculinity dictates that to class oneself as a real man is to be in control and to use violence to achieve control. However, access to socially legitimate forms of aggression and tools of violence is dependent on race and class. African Caribbean and poor men only have access to street weapons and their own bodies as tools of hegemonic masculine violence, whereas elite White men run the police and the army and therefore have authority to manage the legitimate use of force while appearing not to be violent at all (Collins, 2006).

Though this ideal is dominant or hegemonic, it is not the only notion of masculinity. Through forms of resistance, lived experiences and interactions with communities, multiple ideas and practices emerge to constitute masculinity differently over time and place. Children may resist or take on dominant social norms but they are influenced also by the norms of their subgroups. Particularly at a time when young people are under attack from mainstream society and the forming of a coherent identity is hugely important, peer groups become a significant part of the socialisation of young people. Young men from varying subcultures view masculinity in different and complex ways. But African Caribbean boys are portrayed through and subjected to narrow images that do not mirror them, and that are controlled by a powerful white male elite, running the media: film, newspapers, magazines, television and the music industry.

We live in a world that degrades cultures that are not white whilst holding whiteness as a standard to live up to. The subtler forms of white superiority enable racism to thrive and adapt to changing climates such as the era of political correctness and its backlash.

Given a context of interacting hegemonic masculinity and white superiority, white men become an embodiment of a human ideal, whereas African Caribbean men are an embodiment of pathology and fear. This form of racism challenges the notion that African Caribbean men are privileged by gender and subordinated by race in all circumstances. At times African Caribbean men are oppressed by gender in addition to race. In other words they experience disadvantage by virtue of being African Caribbean and male.

African Caribbean men throughout history have been portrayed as both hypo masculine – lazy, weak, work shy, unable to be proper fathers – and hyper masculine: violent, sexually aggressive, homophobic, misogynistic. This positioning has generated policies that promote imprisonment, exclusion, detainment and marginalisation rather than policies promoting education. Stereotypes about African Caribbean men have always been, based on being racially inferior, but they are also sexualised and gendered as deviant in order to depict African Caribbean men as threatening.

It is the bodies of African Caribbean men that get focused on, not their hearts, minds and spirit. James Baldwin (1993) described how a dehumanising image of black men as 'walking phalluses' – sexual and nothing but sexual – is used to justify impeding their achievement of their full potential. Young African Caribbean men learn early that the standards applied to them are different to those applied to anyone else. They learn that despite their intention and actions, their presence is enough to provoke fear. They are often suspected of acts they have not perpetrated and are under permanent surveillance.

Coping with the pressure of constant surveillance, sexualisation and exclusion, emotional distress and mental health problems are an understandable response to life in the UK. Bhui and McKenzie's research (2008) suggests that although suicide rates vary between ethnic groups, it is young African Caribbean men aged 13 to 24 years, living in England and Wales who are at greatest risk.

Gendered racism in the school system

Many researchers and academics have highlighted that African Caribbean males undergo far more control and criticism in schools than members of other ethnic groups who commit the same offence (Gillborn, 1990; Gillborn and Gipps, 1996; Osler and Hill, 1999; Social Exclusion Unit, 1998). Research on students excluded from schools, mainly male, shows that white pupils are more likely to be of below average achievement, have a history of trauma and to be excluded for verbal abuse whereas those of African Caribbean origin are more often of above average achievement and more commonly excluded for challenging teachers' judgements (Ofsted, 1996; Osler *et al*, 2000).

Sewell (1997) rightly points out the creative ingenuity of young African Caribbean people: '*their talents as makers of positive identity for both black youth and white*' (pix) and observes that young African Caribbean males were '*either viewed as angels and/or devils in British schools*' (pix). They were the heroes of a street fashion culture that dominates most inner cities, yet experienced disproportionate amounts of punishment and exclusion. They were seen simultaneously as sexy and sexually threatening – and sexy only in relation to fashion, crime, sport and music (Sewell, 1997). How they were identified by others centred on their bodies and not their hearts and minds.

Sewell's qualitative study in London schools demonstrated the variety of ways in which African Caribbean boys resisted and responded to their circumstances, manifesting different masculinities at different times; changing their social identity depending on the context and their roles within it. In contrast to much of the literature that concentrates on African Caribbean pupils who are visibly resisting the schooling process, Sewell found that few were rebels. Most chose to adopt a pro-education, anti-schooling position, seeing school as a means to an end. They thus showed resistance within the realm of accommodation, but this strategy still produced negative consequences for them.

When young African Caribbean people are taught that the African Caribbean presence in the world began with slavery and not with ancient African civilisation, the message received is that they are subordinate to white people, thus '*relegating African Caribbean people to spectators and objects of history and current life*' (Mutua, 2006b:27). As hooks rightly points out: '*When already feeling a profound sense of disconnection, schooling that does not honour the needs of the spirit simply intensifies that sense of being lost, of being unable to connect*' (hooks, 2003:180). In contrast, she argues that students can learn that the purpose of education is not to conform, nor to be dominated, nor to prepare them to be dominators, but rather to create the conditions for freedom (hooks, 2003). Similarly, supporting the natural development of progressive African Caribbean masculinities in community settings is a viable response to gendered racism of this kind.

Progressive African Caribbean masculinities

Mutua (2006a) defines progressive black masculinities as *'unique and innovative practices of the masculine self actively engaged in struggles to transform social structures of domination'* (pxi) that constrain, restrict and suppress the full development of human potential.

Given the highly controlled and distorted images of African Caribbean masculinity we are subjected to, many of the experiences of African Caribbean maleness are not presented by mainstream media and society. Rarely do I come across mainstream media examples of the loving fathers, passionate community workers, nurturing uncles and elders, supportive brothers, gentle male friends that surrounded me as I grew up and surround me today. Even when these images are occasionally shown, they cannot counter the widespread stereotype of African Caribbean males as threatening.

Rather than African Caribbean fathers being unavailable or absent in the lives of their children through the ending of the parental relationship, Guishard-Pine (2002) has shown that, when granted contact, non-resident African Caribbean fathers continue to influence and play a significant role in the lives of their children. Her work has been built upon by the Babyfather Alliance.

Bambara's study of pre and post colonial Africa suggests that in many African societies before colonialism, women were not subordinate but shared policy-making and privileges (Bambara, 2005). Men of African descent today join the struggle for the emancipation of women alongside the antiracism struggle and challenge homophobia: examples of this are Michael Awkward, Michael Eric Dyson, Luke Harris, Devon Carbado, Greg Tate, Kevin Powell, Mark Anthony Neal and Benjamin Zephaniah.

Community education

Education can be defined in its broadest sense as all that is meant by contributing to the upbringing, care and development of young people, and relates crucially to the relationship of the individual to others. Despite the progressive potential of marginalised subjugated discourses, white-supremacist and hegemonic masculine thinking informs every aspect of our culture, including what is considered education, intelligence – how we learn, the content of what we learn and the way we are taught. White supremacist and hegemonic masculine ideologies underpin mainstream western schooling in the form of competitive individualism:

- those who put themselves first and do not complain about their social circumstances are rewarded
- childhood determinism: your adult potential is determined by the quality of your childhood experience
- innate ability: your ability is determined by your genetic inheritance
- environmental determinism eg African Caribbean children do not achieve academically because their social environments are inferior
- merit by competition: 'only the best students deserve the best opportunities' (Murrell, 2002:xxxi).

Mainstream schooling promotes competition among students rather than community.

The pressure to reach targets puts enormous pressure on teachers to teach for tests. This might mean abandoning their sense of creativity and autonomy in the classroom, ignoring the specificities of students' lives and being inattentive to the differences among students. Byfield (2008)'s qualitative study of 40 black students under the age of 25 years at universities in the USA and UK showed that black boys can and do succeed despite a system stacked against them. Byfield (2008) suggests that teachers – black and white – are often a major influence in the boys' success – particularly those whose approach to education goes beyond the focus of the school; seeing beyond challenges the boys presented to understand the oppression they face; displaying infectious passion for what they were teaching; taking into account individual needs values and experiences; being non-judgemental; spotting talent and developing a good relationship with their students.

Education does not necessarily have to reflect and promote dominant hegemonic values. My most empowering educational experiences inside and outside school were those that attempted to subvert domination. Such subversive education prepares young people to participate in challenging domination, creating their society and creating the context for freedom.

'Too much schooling, too little education' (Shujaa, 1994)

Many African Caribbean people have been exposed to various community-based learning settings such as Saturday schools, after school projects, community programmes, youth clubs – that aim to transmit cultural knowledge that is relevant and emancipatory. The distinction between education and schooling has been made by many in critical pedagogy such as Murrell (2002) and hooks (2003).

Critical pedagogy invites us to regard the aims of education as:

> *any curriculum developed ... to involve a confrontation with the meaning of the day-to-day reality of the students...a place that practices freedom and challenges oppression ... a constant engagement in laying bare the basis of our present society and the means by which power and privilege are maintained.* (Freire, 1975:29)

This makes the educator also a learner of the student's reality and knowledge.

Education according to these principles challenges mainstream views of knowledge as discrete bits of information and student achievement as measured by how much of this information they can reproduce (Murrell, 2002). Instead, it views education as a kind of dialogue or community. Rather than being viewed as passive, African Caribbean learners are seen as creative beings who both transform and are transformed by the social environment, and who, in transforming the world, become further transformed.

Community as education and education as community refers to education that is emancipatory, relevant to those whom it aims to reach and based on the principle that interpersonal learning is as important as intrapersonal learning; and that they essentially cannot be separated. Community education therefore goes beyond the individual and private world of achievement towards the communal, public and political arena of understanding and transformation. Being an educator then becomes a much deeper role than generally attributed to the classroom teacher. Based on Kiswahili – ie Swahili language – the term for this complete teacher is *mwalimu*. Murrel (2002) uses the term 'community teacher' to refer to what educators can do in their approach to education in any setting. Community education in this sense both builds a community of critical inquiry and builds the supports for learning and transformation; not just challenging what is but prefiguring what should be (Kilpatrick *et al*, 2003).

When we learn in this way we experience learning as a whole process rather than a restrictive practice that disconnects and alienates us from our experience and from others in the world (hook, 2003). Education of this kind means learning that despite structural oppression, individuals and groups can act to influence their circumstances, and that African Caribbean people '*are subjects and conscious actors in the creation of history and culture rather than the passive recipients of someone else's actions*' (Mutua, 2006b:29).

Implications for psychology and statutory services

The Labour administration's focus on 'closing the gap' serves to position young African Caribbean males as 'the other' and divert attention away from interrogating the deep-rooted gendered racist cultural values that are hostile to the positive identity development and community involvement of these pupils. On the other hand, a focus on African Caribbean male achievement should not be used as another stick to beat those who do not do well. For too long an 'if I can do it why can't you? There is *no* excuse' argument has put undue pressure on individuals. It is important therefore that a positive focus on black boys who do 'succeed' does not distract from the need to examine the social political context of oppression and the increasingly narrow ways in which we define 'intelligence' and 'success' and reinforce a focus on how to change the outcome of schooling rather than the nature of education itself.

Working with community based initiatives

As psychologists in the NHS we are often placed under great pressure to show concrete but often superficial results in unrealistic timeframes while working with client groups who are multiply oppressed, abused and disadvantaged. Yet our unique position means that we can use our understanding and political/ psychological analysis of the impact social conditions have on individuals and communities to guide interventions that are emancipatory. This might involve a community psychology approach to engaging in and working with young people and the community groups they access. For instance, community approaches like that of In-volve, formed in 1989, represent more than merely diversionary activities to 'keep young people out of trouble', and emphasise how young people can be active agents in exploring, highlighting and addressing the underlying causes of the difficulties they experience.

RAW is an In-volve programme that has a high success rate in getting young people to engage, and all those who do engage gain accreditation as social researchers who complete paid research in their communities. Most of the young people, many of them African Caribbean, successfully return to school, get training or employment, or go on to work as apprentices on subsequent RAW projects. The Communities Empowerment Network (CEN) seeks to ensure a just society in which every child is included in mainstream education and is enabled to fulfil their potential. They provide advice, counselling, support, representation and training for people experiencing mistreatment and discrimination in education and 95 per cent of their clients are from the African Caribbean communities.

Education as intervention

Many critical social theorists have highlighted the inter-relationship between knowledge and power – most notably French philosopher and social theorist Michel Foucault. These arguments, however, emphasised how domination works

(Foucault, 1977) rather than how knowledge can be used to decentre power and oppose domination. Strategies of education as intervention are forming debate teams and supporting African Caribbean boys to conduct social research as described above and in forming debating teams.

Debating teams are another way of learning how to influence and govern, based on an oral tradition. They foster rigorous and passionate discussions about social change and how it is to be achieved. Students learn the skills, knowledge and discipline of critical thinking, engaging in dialogue with others, respecting the positions different from their own and exploring how they become active advocates for progressive thinking (Giroux, 2006). All this promotes the idea that it is not just possible but often necessary to think against the grain. Education of this kind can create a relationship between the margins and the centre of culture and power. African Caribbean boys go from being invisible and disposable, to being central to the fabric of community life, thus linking the language of critique with the language of possibility (Giroux, 2006).

Giroux (2006) argued that '*critique and hope must inform each other*' (Giroux, 2006:5) with respect to what it means to imagine a future that does not merely imitate the present (Giroux, 2006). Hope, often masquerading as resistance, is the refusal to stand still in the face of prejudice and the commitment to keep moving forward for the good of oneself and others. Learning is linked not just to understanding but to social change and research becomes a form of 'moral witnessing' (Giroux, 2006) and social action, rather than an accumulation of data for self promotion.

Action points for educators and psychologists
Critical consumers
Educators and learners can become 'critical consumers' (Murrell, 2002:xxxv) of the overt and hidden curriculum, educational policy and institutional practice, and can interrogate them for gendered racism. Education can be seen as a form of social intervention which inverts the norm in which dominant groups influence policy and are in charge of the major ideas that circulate in society.

Developing critical thinking skills
Young African Caribbean males can be supported 'to conduct research, pursue knowledge on their own [and together], defend their ideas, be reflective about when to reject their own positions, be aware of the consequences of their ideas and actions, and always be willing to listen critically to others' (Giroux, 2006:19).

Research on achievement

The experience of African Caribbean boys who experience success in their education are obscured by the abundance of studies that concentrate on failure. The research that exists on successful education of young African Caribbean males needs to be foregrounded in government policy and research reports as well as augmented with an exploration that moves beyond static notions to more complex and enriching understandings of success. Rather than outdated notions of African-Caribbean male educational 'failure', research into empowering education should become the focus of government initiatives to challenge marginalisation.

Working across statutory and community settings

A focus on community might entail working across different professions and settings which aim to support the needs of young people. This would require harnessing a range of skills and knowledge about working with young people in the community.

Rather than a 'fix it' mentality based on a deficit model that circumvents research into successes and a deeper understanding of wider social issues, education that is emancipatory actively involves young African Caribbean males in debating, researching and promoting empowering solutions to the oppressive discourses that impact on their lives.

This chapter is dedicated to my beautiful nephew and friend Lanre, lovely brother Dele and very special father Mr Akanni Afuape. Many thanks also to Gerry German and Paulette Douglas from Communities Empowerment Network in Newham for their passion, their time, and for forging links.

13

The Virgin Father: psychological research with black fathers in Britain

Jeune Guishard-Pine

Introduction

Black extended families help to filter out the potentially harmful inputs from society. Although their social behaviour is consistently described harshly and their teachers describe them as emotionally deficient, black children are generally not negatively affected in the formation of their self-concept (see Benskin, 1994; Guishard-Pine, 1983; Stone, 1980 for reviews). Hayles (1991) wrote of the survival of the black family in any form as a 'miracle' indicating that the strengths of black families remain the kin networks.

There is a strong and pervasive psycho-history that actively promotes and supports the idea that the psychological and developmental needs of children are fulfilled exclusively through tasks carried out by the mother. Rutter (1974) commented on this in his examination of academic and school achievement:

> The father, the mother, brothers and sisters, friends and schoolteachers and others all have an impact on development. A less exclusive focus on the mother is required. Children also have fathers!' (Rutter, 1974:125)

Milligan and Dowie (1998) itemised the specific needs of the child that can be met by the father. These included safety and protection, comfort, the feeling of being loved, friendship, a role model, recognition of the child as an individual, and having a father who is adaptable and honest. Until I completed my series of studies, no known research had been conducted in Britain into the influence of the fathering behaviour of black and ethnic minority men specifically on the psychological development of their children.

My research aimed to address the issue of the invisibility of men, particularly in black families. I examined the style of fathering as defined by health, hygiene and grooming, intellectual, financial, disciplinary, emotional and leisure activities and the difference it made to the social, emotional, intellectual and academic development of the child. The paucity of research in these areas cannot be emphasised enough. Although there is some research on Caribbean fathers (Brown *et al*, 1997; Roopnarine, 2002), when my research was first presented in 2000, there were few published reports that had attempted to present a framework for developing the knowledge and understanding of black families and parenting in the British context (Guishard, 1992). My research revealed that self-esteem increased as a consequence of black 'generative' fathering in the British context. Generative fathering relates to the specific parenting activities carried out by fathers with the explicit intent of developing the next generation (Hawkins and Dollahite, 1997).

Background

The principal influence on my research was a module on my educational psychology training course entitled 'Paternal Deprivation'. Since the end of World War II psychologists have considered the psychological impact of 'father absence' by comparing the psychological profiles of children in 'intact' families and those in families without fathers. Research spanned three decades and fairly consistently reported adverse findings for fatherless children, including lower IQ scores, poorer academic achievement, lower self-esteem and motivation to achieve. But when these studies included black children the magnitude of such differences reduced significantly. The reason for this may well be the impact of the African Kin Network or extended family as a social support system (Martin and Martin, 1978). The African Kin Network includes both relatives and friends. Diagrams 13.1A and 13.1B illustrate how this arrangement is potentially protective of the child's psychological and physical development. The lines between kin are support pathways. In Diagram 1B, the removal of one node will have minimal effect in terms of support for the child, whereas with nuclear families, when the father node is removed, literally half of the child support has gone (see Diagrams 13.2A and 13.2B).

Nancy Boyd-Franklin is one of the leading authorities on work with families of African origin in the diaspora. She talks about 'familism,' which she defines as the value of black family life being played out with both kin and non-biological relationships. Given the relatively high number of children of African Caribbean descent who are born to lone mothers, I wondered whether there was a link between being reared in a lone mother household and poorer academic out-

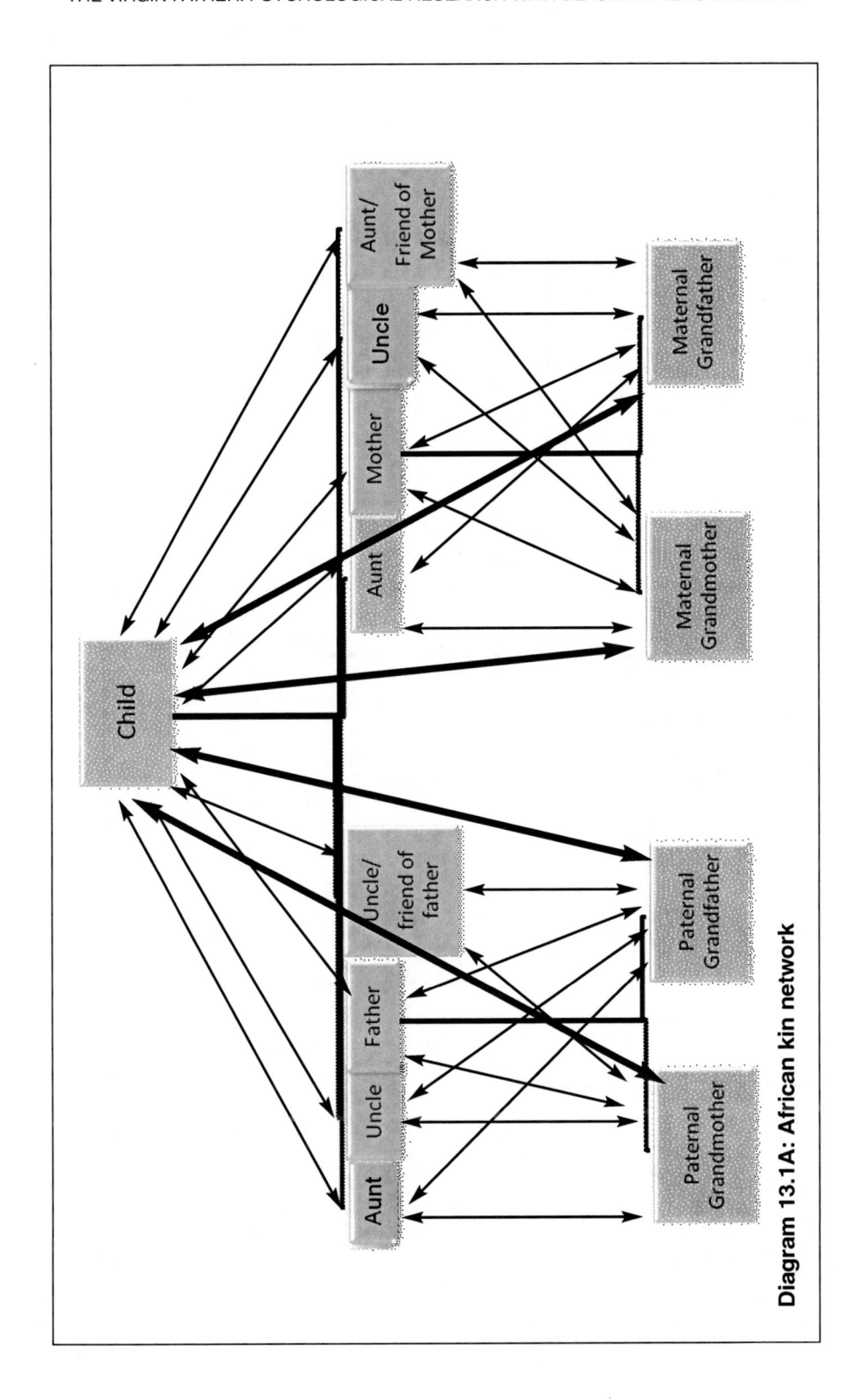

Diagram 13.1A: African kin network

Diagram 13.1B: 'Fatherless' African kin network

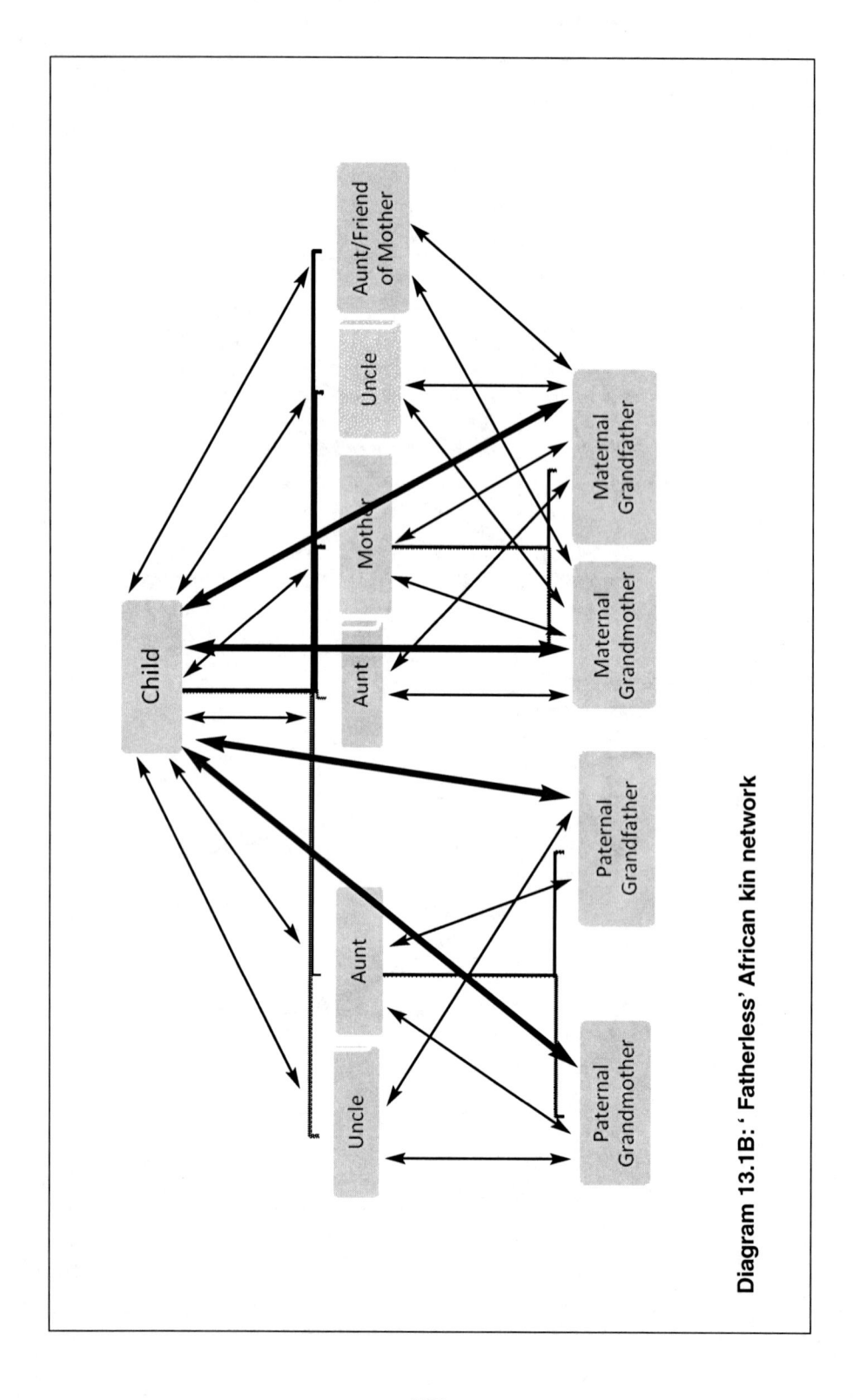

Diagram 13.2A: Nuclear family

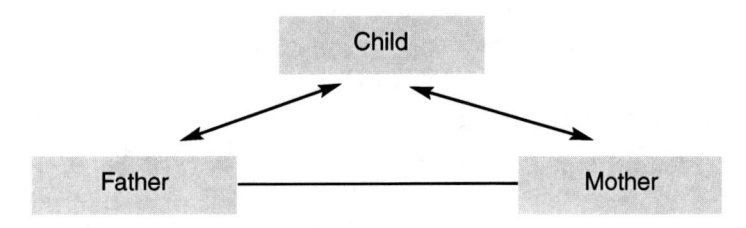

```
        Child
       ↙    ↘
   Father ——— Mother
```

Diagram 13.2B: 'Fatherless' Nuclear family

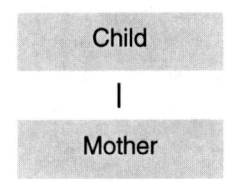

```
    Child
      |
    Mother
```

comes for black children? If there is, is the impact greater for boys than girls? I recognised intuitively that whatever I found, my research could be criticised for oversimplifying the issue of men in black families. Given the statistical facts of higher academic achievement levels and higher levels of married parenting practices amongst South Asian people, yet the negative caricatures and stereotypes of the male parent, I decided to constitute samples that included children of African Caribbean, South Asian and white British descent so as to compare and contrast these ethnic groups.

What I did

My research accessed fathers and children in order to examine four constructs: father availability, fathering 'style', father-child relationship and father involvement (the range or concentration of activities the father carried out with his children) and their influence on the child's reading and numeracy; their self-esteem and their cognitive skills.

What I found
Father availability and father involvement

Overall, compared to children in two parent households, children who lived in a lone mother household said that their fathers were scarcely involved in their lives. These children also reported having the lowest levels of positive feelings about their social status and their school experience. Perhaps most intriguing of all was the fact that the children who lived with both parents had more advanced mathematical skills – which indicates that increased access to the male parent has academic benefits for the child.

Evidence is emerging of the psychological significance of the child maintaining links with a non-resident father. The positive language of the Child Support Act (1991) helped to encourage the use of the more neutral terms of 'resident' and 'non-resident' father in place of 'present' and 'absent' fathers. This may be particularly useful in dispelling myths that absent fathers are necessarily less involved than present ones. In one of my studies, for example, children gave more favourable ratings for the involvement of non-resident fathers than of resident fathers. There are several possible explanations for this. It may be that the children were idealising the absent father, or it may be that the resident father is relatively inactive, believing that he is contributing well simply because he is living with the child. Studies have found that it is highly likely that resident fathers feel that their role is best summarised in terms mainly of just 'being there' (Snarey, 1993). A more radical explanation, which is also consistent with research done in the Caribbean (Brown *et al*, 1998), is that the non-resident father contributes a wider range of support across a narrower band of time, because his access to the child is restricted. Therefore on the occasions when he spends time with his child he is required to fulfill all the responsibilities of childcare, as the mother is not there to share them.

Fathering style

When I asked a group of fathers to rate their caregiving behaviour, the men of African Caribbean descent said that they were more likely to be involved in supporting the physical (health, hygiene and grooming) and intellectual development of their children. The children with fathers who provided the highest levels of intellectual and emotional support considered themselves well behaved, whilst those with the worst opinions about their own behaviour reported that their fathers gave them little emotional support.

The research also suggested that children whose fathers were actively involved in their overall care enjoyed feelings of emotional and social well-being. The best fathering behaviour fostered the child's appetite for learning, promoted the emotional development of the children and provided solid financial support. What the research gave was a clearer picture of the 'what?' that black fathers do to support the child's development.

Marital status

Given the increase in the number of couples who co-habit rather than marrying, and the break-up of many such relationships after the children are born, I examined whether the commitment of marriage made any difference to the way a black father behaved towards his children. I found that married fathers said they were likely to be involved with instilling discipline and with recreational and leisure activities. There was also a significant psychological impact: children whose parents were married to each other felt they had higher social self-esteem than the children whose parents were not married, whether or not they were cohabiting.

Father-child relationships

'...a father's function ...is turning boys into men.' (Park, 1996:4)

Fathers are generally less involved with their sons than their daughters (Morgan *et al*, 1988). Boys in my study felt that their fathers did not provide adequate emotional support. Fathers need to contribute to the emotional development and empathy of their sons, and to teach them the vocabulary to communicate their feelings (Downes, 1997). For their sons to find them affectionate, black fathers may need to develop their own personalised repertoire of physical and emotional, verbal and non-verbal signs, signals and actions to demonstrate the equal commitment to emotional development of their sons and daughters.

> "Stroking' may be used as a general term for intimate physical contact; in practice it may take various forms. Some people literally stroke an infant; others hug or pat it, while some people pinch it playfully or flip it with a fingertip....' Berne (1986:14)

Early research into paternal deprivation found evidence to suggest that boys who had no access to a father had a 'feminised' cognitive profile: they showed higher levels of verbal and reading skills than those who lived with their father. However, my research contradicted the idea that a boy who lived with a physically or emotionally unavailable father developed a feminised cognitive profile, as I found that boys who had closer relationships with their father had poorer reading skills.

Schools should involve men

A child's failure to acquire reading skills is worrying for both families and schools. My research pointed to an interesting paradox for my multi-ethnic sample: promoting the active involvement of fathers in childcare may reduce the language competence of children, as demonstrated by the proxy measure of reading attainments. No advanced society would promote the notion of lone-mother families or poor father-child relationships as a desirable alternative to a stable, nurturing two-parent family to increase reading skills. So what should an advanced society be doing?

Since the 1980s, studies on the influence of parental roles and attitudes on school achievement have found that parent and school partnerships support achievement. There is a fairly strong relationship between the level of attainment in absolute terms and participation in school activities. The overriding message therefore is that schools should involve men.

If male input does improve results in mathematics, schools might need to consider how to involve pupils' fathers. Teachers are not omnipotent – others can help children learn. Bloom (1980), for example, found a number of alterable and non-alterable variables that influenced achievement, such as the quality of teaching, the cognitive characteristics of learners, the affective characteristics of learning, the rate of learning and the home environment. Some variables have greater effect than others on learning, but Bloom's research showed that family factors and the cognitive status of the child were the least strong factors in promoting achievement following focused interventions. The findings of my research did not support Bloom's position: across all my studies, statistical analysis showed that an array of family-related variables such as the family structure, parent-child relationships and number of siblings in the household were significant predictors of the scores on the psychological and scholastic measures.

The question remains: how can the school be more open to fathers' involvement and specifically black fathers?

My research suggested that there is a huge issue around the visibility or invisibility of black fathers. The finding that his physical presence in the home is linked to the advancement of number skills is important as there was no specific fathering style linked with this. This suggested that 'just being there' is of crucial importance and that black men should be simply encouraged to come in to the school and just ... be there.

Generative fathering – the final word

The competing demands of father as nurturer and father as breadwinner have to be addressed before men can enact 'good-enough' fathering. The tension is that the material demands of both adults and children are so extraordinarily high today that it is potentially a disincentive for men to spend time on 'masculine domesticity'. The employment of women has already altered the role of fathers in family life, and has provided for many men a welcome opportunity to participate in generative fathering. But as my research shows, fathers cannot be conceptualised as mothers. However, research on generative fathering must not define childcare that resembles traditional 'mothering' tasks so it excludes such tasks from being required for motherless children too. All activities that contribute to the psychological, educational, emotional, physical, moral and spiritual development of the child are non-negotiable components of parenting and are therefore essentially the role of fathers as well as mothers.

It should also be noted that feminist ideologies within the disciplines of sociology and psychology have provided views that orientate at both ends of the spectrum. Feminism has proposed that men are of little value to families while at the same time emphasising the importance of fathers (Griswold, 1997). There has been a focus on the intellectual, moral, psychological, physical and spiritual development of their children and it will be these agents that will undoubtedly shape the future of fathering. If racism and discrimination seem particularly debilitating to the black male psyche, it is because such oppression relentlessly strips black men of their ability to do what men are supposed to do – work, earn money, take care of their partner and children, run their communities, rule their destinies – have power. The contribution of the growing body of literature on black masculinity is not being ignored (eg Lewis, 1986; Majors and Billson, 1992; Madhubiti, 1990; Sewell, 1997; see also Chapters 12 and 14), but there clearly needs to be more empirical research conducted on the perceptions and development of fathering models that are embedded within parallel models of masculinity.

Research has a role to play in exploring the mythology that exists around black fathering. One of the strongest ideas that I have taken away from my research is that positive involvement should be measured as opposed to more involvement, as there is no consistent evidence base to suggest that a father merely spending hours playing football or watching TV has significantly greater benefits for the child. This small-scale British research however goes some way to initiate closer looks at the issue of the influence of particular fathering styles on the psychological development of the children.

Perhaps this is an area where the role and support of educational psychologists can be enhanced within the school system. Given the very real phenomenon of the influence of parenting on academic achievement, strategies should be given to educational psychologists to disseminate to schools that have some utility for both parents in supporting their child's development. Clearly it is not the role of the educational psychologist nor the school to determine how the cultures of individual families should evolve. They should, however, promote the results from research of the benefits of the additional involvement of both resident and non-resident fathers.

This chapter is adapted from an article by Jeune published in *Race Equality Teaching*, 24(2), 2006.

14

Walking in Jung's shadow? Black Rage and domestic abuse

Luke Daniels

Introduction

> Jung discovered residues of racial history in the fantasies ... with the collective unconscious these are stored, inherited predispositions to respond with great emotions to specific events. These predispositions which Jung called archetypes include ... the shadow... (Monte, 1995:342)

Jung believed that when we minimise the shadow in ourselves we deny behaviours that do not fit with a positive view of ourselves. Like the personal shadow, the family shadow has its built-in taboos and forbidden areas that contain all that is rejected by a family's conscious awareness. In our society, wife battering and child abuse used to be hidden away in the family shadow. Today they have emerged into the light of day in epidemic proportions (Monte, 1995:xxi).

Some of the most traumatic experiences of violence a child can have can occur within the family. Whether it is direct physical assault or witnessing family violence it is bound to be psychologically damaging. Living with violence within the family may lead to mental health problems for children (Guishard-Pine *et al*, 2007), and in the worst scenario they can lose both their parents – one to a coffin and the other to a prison.

Men's violence towards women does not recognise race or class and is not always bound by gender. Family violence has been likened to a war that knows no boundaries: it destroys the psychological well-being of adults and children alike. In the final analysis, gender-based violence is predominantly about men's violence towards women and children but the term 'men' cannot describe a homogenous group that is solely to blame for violence. It is neither men's nature (biological factors) nor men's nurture (their socialisation) alone that offer sufficiently sophisticated explanations for family violence (Lang, 2001). So what are the possible reasons for it?

Coomaraswamy (2001) suggested that the primary cause of gender based violence is unequal gender relationships and assigned stereotypic notions of masculinity and femininity so constructed that superiority is ascribed to one gender and inferiority to the other. Greig (2001) suggests that men's violence towards women and children may be connected to other systems of violence and power. A leading expert in the area of research into family violence, Greig suggests that the work pivots around two main questions: 'Why men?' and 'Which men?'

As a black counsellor working with perpetrators of domestic violence, I am asked: 'Are black men more violent than white men?' The question raises certain key issues about race and violence, and I often wonder how my white colleagues would deal with this question. There is an interface between racism, class and men's violence towards women; moreover, cultural norms of many societies affect men's socialisation into violence. Race issues impact on the counsellor as well as the perpetrator. Research has shown that people have racist attitudes about black people even though they have had no direct contact with them, having formed their prejudices entirely from the messages put out by the media (see Chapter 17). It is not surprising that people hold the belief that black people are more violent, since any news received about them from the mainstream media is usually bad, and when a black man appears on television it is often because he is reported to have committed some criminal or violent act (Gutmann, 2001).

A historical context to black family violence

My parents hit me when I was a child and I complained to the woman living next door. She said that I was lucky. Her childhood punishment was being made to kneel on a grater in the hot sun after being beaten by her parents. Where did our parents learn such things? I'll tell you where: they learnt them from slavery.

Slavery was a humiliating and hurtful experience that was endured by a people collectively. I've been told many times to sweep it under the carpet. Often the people who say this have not looked at the legacy of the history and experience of slavery. To sweep it under the carpet and pretend it 'did not hurt' is exactly how children are expected to survive abuse. They may try hard not to give their abusers the satisfaction of showing they have hurt them, just as we may pretend that the barbarous things done to us in slavery did not damage us as a people. We have too much pride to admit it and are ashamed that our ancestors were the subjects of this heinous crime.

Richard Hart in his book *Slaves who Abolished Slavery* (1980) recounted the punishments for offending slaves in one parish of Jamaica:

> Adam, for running away, 'to be taken hence to the place from whence he came, there to have a halter put about his neck, and one of his ears nailed to a post, and that the executioner do then cause the said ear to be cut off close to his head...'

> 19th April 1783: Priscilla, for running away (simply), both her ears cut off close to the head immediately, to receive 39 lashes the first Monday of every month for one year and to be worked in irons during that time...

> Thunder, for running away ... to have his right leg cut off below the knee, by a surgeon, at the proprietor's expense, within ten days from the date hereof...

Jung's theory would suggest that such experiences are stored within the recesses of the collective unconscious as primordial images and are passed down from generation to generation as templates or models for current experience to follow (Jung, 1936:66ff). These primordial images of the collective unconscious are Jung's archetypes. The collective unconscious is inherited within the course of history, and is where day to day events experienced by all members of the group are stored (Jung, 1917:69). Archetypes are a product of the cumulative effect of continuous recurrent experiences on one's growth process. The repetitive subjective emotional reaction to the event is impressed on human unconscious mental processes. Their internal state gives them a predisposition to react in a similar way to repetitions of the physical event that is transmitted to future generations. Thus the collective unconscious's archetypes are a residue of ancestral emotional life (Jung, 1917:77).

The daily life of a black male in white societies

Although many of us would like to pretend that racism does not exist, it keeps raising its ugly head – sometimes when we least expect it. In times of economic depression it will be stronger. There is no escaping its ability to surface.

We live in a society where racism is deep-rooted and persistent – this is a fact. Black people are discriminated against in all fields. Black people live predominantly in poor boroughs, often in sub-standard housing. We do worse than most groups in education. Our health is the among the poorest (PSI, 5/8/97). In some parts of the UK we die younger from more heart attacks, stroke, diabetes, often because of poor diet. We are over represented in the penal system (see Chapter 4 in this book) yet have little representation at the top, where justice is dispensed. According to Justice Ministry statistics for 2009, black people are eight times more likely to be stopped and searched by the police, despite the landmark Macpherson report condemning the institutional racism of the police force and their subsequent promises to root it out. Ten years on, the situation has become still worse. In the mental health system we suffer the most, especially the generations born into this racist society.

Not only are our lives blighted by overt racism but we also have to worry about the effects of internalised racism. When we act out on each other the violent stereotypes created for us, we are in the grip of internalised racism; we are surely in its grip when we don't feel safe around other black people. Violence has become a way of affirming or defending our sense of masculinity. Majors and Bilson (1992) talk about black men who feel they are 'dissed' (disrespected) wanting to kill each other. By making much of our differences and continually highlighting the negative, the media helps perpetuate the difficulties we face in our communities.

Furthermore, Greig (2001) points out that approaching the discussion of black masculinity as a matter of nature or nurture can highlight but not explain the complexity of what it means to be a man: '... racism, economic disempowerment, political disenfranchisement, geo-political relations, colonial histories, ecological trends and movements of trans-national capital are also important, and cannot simply be subsumed in an explanatory framework of nature-nurture.'

Black Rage

Mental bondage is invisible violence. (Hilliard, 1985)

Understanding the role of historical trauma on family violence among Africans who are descendants of slaves requires more research. It may well connect to contemporary oppression and discrimination. There is also a historical context to the fact that black men and women have not been taught how to value one another, as poor relationship skills lie at the heart of intimate relationships that are violent. However research needs also to consider whether any of their conditioning – past or present – is sufficient to explain behaviour now.

The experiences black people have lived through and live through still are likely to have affected their psychological adjustment (Jenkins, 1990). Black people have certainly been victimised by this society and still are; so social violence possibly connects to other violence.

Mama (1995) reports on an ailment called 'dysesthesia Aethiopica', which was said to affect only slaves. 'Those smitten by it would cease to be loyal and content and begin to resent their work and their overseers.' (p10). Here are the beginnings of pathologising the behaviour of resistance (Thomas and Sillen, 1972). When doing research for this chapter, as well as finding the famous book by Grier and Cobbs (1968), I came across 'Black Rage'. This phenomenon is identified in the USA as one among the 'innovative defences' used. An innovative defence is a novel defence to reduce or remove one's criminal liability against committing (usually a violent) crime. Black Rage is a manifestation of the build-up of frustration from living in an oppressive, racist environment.

Hurt (1998) made a documentary entitled *I am a Man: black masculinity in America*. The film examines the multiple levels of abuse that occur in the outside world that exacerbate tension in the home and heighten the husband's desire to be a 'man'. If men believe their female partner perceives them as a sexual or financial failure, violence may be used to express their frustration. Bergman (1995) suggests that violence becomes a way to cope with such frustrations and feelings of helplessness, inadequacy, vulnerability or shame. He suggests that males in general have been socialised to externalise their distress.

Humanistic psychologist Jenkins (1982) agrees that mechanistic psychological views may describe the socialisation of violence in this way but he feels that this focus overlooks other important aspects of human psychology. His premise is that a reductionist or environmental contingency psychology tends to see African Americans only as passive victims.

The socialisation of violence

Men are socialised into a set of gender roles and stereotypes that produce violence from childhood. Theoretical explanations for men's relations with and violence toward women are drawn from the disciplines of psychodynamic, cognitive behavioural and social learning theories (Greig, 2001). Renvoize (1978) has come to see family violence as a gigantic web in which countless generations of people are caught. Both the victim and perpetrator are ensnared.

In response to the question about violent black men, I argue that black men are inherently no more violent than white men. It is not in their skin, or bones or genes, as some would have us believe. But the socialisation for violence affecting black men is arguably more intense because of the oppression and violence of racism, and it is therefore not surprising if black men are more prone to act out this violent stereotype. In short – violence breeds violence (Curtis, 1963).

Research with black families

Although there is no linear relationship, child rearing practices can be a major environmentally-sustaining factor of male violence. Experts met in 2001 to look at gender socialisation and domestic violence in the Caribbean (Commission on Status of Women, 2001). Bailey *et al* (1996) reviewed the research and found that:

- boys were allowed more freedom than girls; they were out more and therefore likely to be influenced by violence
- toughness was seen as masculine and therefore positively reinforced in boys
- this toughening up meant that boys more than girls were subjected to violence as punishment
- boys received less positive affirmation of their school self-esteem so it was unlikely to be high (Figueroa, 1996; Parry, 1996)
- by the age of 10, there was a sharp incline in boys' development of a construct of masculinity. Evans (1999) found that boys in the Caribbean had stereotyped notions of what it meant to be male and that violence was broadly manifest as gendered, unequal power relations and was also an expression of aggression
- physical punishment was seen as father's task. Chevannes (2001) found that it was important to understand the link between the expectations of fatherhood, gender socialisation and family violence
- girls tended to seek relationships with older men who could fulfil the role of 'breadwinner' as central to masculinity and these men made their male peers feel inferior. Boys would therefore leave school early in order to earn money to obtain a female partner

In the Caribbean, the socialisation of violence extended far beyond the models provided by parents. My research found also that the teachers' reliance on corporal punishment for discipline meant that children learned that violence was a legitimate means of resolving conflict. Many teachers also used a disciplinary style where they would silence or belittle the children (Parry, 1996).

Gender-based violence

Greig (2001) suggests that expecting males to be aggressive and violent is in itself a kind of gender-based violence. Churches add to the problem. Bent-Goodley and Williams (2003) found that rather than giving messages to reduce family violence, scripture was evoked to disempower women. In Indo-Caribbean cultures the Pundits (Hindus) and the Imams (Muslims) also sanction gender-based violence

(Wyatt, 2001). Overall, however gender roles for men are more rigid in the US than in the Caribbean (Chevannes, 2001).

Bailey *et al* (1996) showed that in the Caribbean tolerance of corporal punishment was linked to tolerance of family violence. They also showed links between family violence and substance misuse and poverty and noted that intervention programmes were based on dealing with the women and children as victims and averred that what was now needed was to look at the root causes of family violence.

A major piece of research in Detroit found twelve reasons for family violence: mental health, substance misuse, society's view of parenting, church, poor relationship skills, gender role socialisation, poor education about family violence, the silence of abuse, structural issues, the historical context and resources (Bent-Goodley and Williams, 2003). These authors found that for men mental health problems were taboo and they did not access the services they needed for fear of shame and stigma. Lack of treatment leaves women and children more vulnerable to the man's abuse as he is likely to consider abuse an option because he finds no other channel through which to discharge his frustration.

Walking in Jung's shadow

An alternative explanation of family violence can be taken from Jung's analytical psychology. Jung believed that we are capable of shifting an intra-psychic problem – which is a problem within an individual – to an interpersonal conflict, a difficulty that arises between two people. He defined this process as projective identification – mental acrobatics in which a person projects denied and disavowed aspects of their inner experience onto their partner. The next stage is that these dissociated feelings are experienced as a genuine aspect of their partner. One partner then deliberately provokes negative feelings in the other to make them behave as if they were real, as if the original negativity originated in them.

The shadow is thus an unattractive aspect of our personality. This archetype may be evoked in our relations with another when we feel uncomfortable with them, and often we cannot specify exactly what provokes the discomfort. The shadow is both a personal and a collective unconscious phenomenon (Jung, 1968:21-22). Jung's theories have been dismissed as irrefutable and therefore unscientific. However, his emphasis on the spiritual side of life and concern with goal oriented behaviour in a person's remote past is an active theory of human agency, observable and therefore available for interpretation.

Healing the hurts

> ...the person must form a psychological organisation that can reconcile all of the opposing and contradictory trends within the psyche. To this reconciliation of opposites, Jung gave the name 'self'. (Monte, 1995:342)

In the process of counselling black men, the explicit aims of their journey would be to:

- achieve genuine self-acceptance, based on more complete knowledge of who they are
- manage the negative emotions that disrupt their daily lives
- acknowledge the guilt and shame associated with negative feelings and actions
- recognise the projections that influence their opinions of others
- heal relationships through honest self-examination and direct communication

The stereotyping of black men is bound to affect their own behaviour and attitude towards themselves but it also cannot fail to affect the therapists/counsellors working with them. When training therapists and counsellors, argues McKenzie-Mavinga (2009), the main issues for black populations need to be reflected upon and understood but remain unresolved because of competing space in training programmes. We must not underestimate the impact racism can have on training programmes, although this does vary. Consideration must also be given to the problem of how receptive the trainee is to addressing the issues. (See Guishard 1992; M'gadzah and Gibbs 1999 and Chapter 3 here).

It is recognised that people who experience – or even only witness – a great deal of violence may suffer from post-traumatic stress disorder. All our ancestors could thus be deemed to have been suffering from post-traumatic stress disorder, since punishment was meted out in the most public of places to act as a deterrent to rebellious slaves. Our ancestors were in no position to parent well. To make sense of behaviour exhibited today we must understand the struggles they endured. This is not to excuse bad behaviour but to understand the reasons for it. The hurt must be acknowledged before we can move on. By hitting children we perpetuate the conditions for a violent society. If we do not begin the healing, we will pass on the hurt to our children. We have to break the cycle of mistreatment by resolving not to abuse our children.

Parenting for change

Most people who hit their children do so because they were beaten. Denying this will change nothing. We must accept that the hurt we endured as children has taken its toll and caused damage. For men to take time to talk about their own experiences is a starting point. Parents and children should ask their parents and grandparents about their experiences of being hit when they were children. This will show us clearly how mistreatment has been passed on.

Children look to significant adults as role models. Social learning theory would say that the way we behave and what we do and say will influence children. If children are not exposed to violence they are unlikely to expect violence as part of their adult relationships. Children whose parents take care to show that they respect their children's ideas and wishes will come to expect this in their relationships now and in the future. And this will ultimately contribute to breaking the cycle of violence.

Conclusion

> Love your enemy as yourself. (The Bible)

Jungian psychology shows us that light and shade are integral to being human. This suggests that the 'enemy' is constructed from denied aspects of our self. We create enemies not because we are intrinsically cruel but because focusing our anger on a target allows us to be part of an in-group. The discussion in this chapter suggests that the in-group to which violent men aspire is one that is carefully crafted by him as 'being a man'. Would we create evil because we need to belong?

Men still have to be men. But there is a first step in the process to reproduce a new masculinity for men, particularly fathers, that is non-violent, yet still authentically masculine. This can start with identifying and promoting new role models in the media and elsewhere. Meanwhile, family violence is reaching pandemic proportions (Hayward, 2001). As gender is part of the problem it needs to be part of the solution. We must actively seek roles for both males and females in ending violence; we need positive men to speak up against men who perpetrate family violence and we need the judicial system to take violence against women more seriously.

I leave you with the words of Keen (1990:202):

> If we desire peace we must begin to demythologise the enemy... and re-own our shadows; make an intricate study of the myriad ways in which we disown, deny and project our own selfishness, cruelty, greed and so on, onto others; be conscious of how we have unconsciously created a warrior psyche and have perpetuated warfare [on others].

15

User engagement and African Caribbean experience in child and family care service

Naomi Anna Watson

This chapter explores African Caribbean perspectives on user involvement in the processes of adoption and fostering. It looks at the terminology and the rationale behind its introduction into policy processes globally, nationally and locally. The chapter explores not only the theoretical frameworks and their importance but also the lived experiences of African Caribbean individuals and communities.

A case study helps illustrate the importance of people's lived experiences of user involvement, particularly in light of the historical marginalisation of vulnerable individuals and communities (Atkin and Rollins, 1993; Begum 2006). Although citing a single case limits the possibilities of generalisation, it gives readers an understanding of individual experiences and the factors that may be contributing to inappropriate outcomes of care delivery practices. Although Baxter and Jack (2008) assert that multiple case studies provide for more focused understanding, they accept that a single case study does much more than examine a single individual or situation and can facilitate complex understandings. Yin (2003) argues that a case study will include aspects of description and exploration rather than presuppositions, which will contribute to understanding the actual phenomena being questioned. Here we examine the phenomenon: *'How do African Caribbean service users experience involvement when dealing with child and family services?'*

User involvement – the international picture

The World Health Organisation (WHO) has an impact on health outcomes globally, as governments and countries across the world are encouraged to become more alert to innovative ways of improving the health of their subjects. The case for involving users in service development and delivery was strongly argued by the World Bank (2000), and formed a basis for action by all Governments. Consequently, European countries have made user involvement a major priority in their agendas for health, and the United Kingdom is no exception.

Public and service user involvement have become major foci of British health and social care policy and care delivery practice, forming the basis of much discussion in the literature and in most aspects of practice (Audit Commission, 2003; Department of Health (DH) 2004; Harrison et al, 2002; Health Care Commission, 2006; Marinetto, 2003; Stewart, 2008). The extent to which this is understood and applied to actual services at local level is a continual debate. Some feel that this concept has been allowed to become no more than rhetoric (Cowden and Singh, 2007) yet it remains an ongoing issue in the drive to improve service delivery to marginalised individuals and communities. Issues relating to both the politics and the actual practice of user involvement need to be explored, discussed and developed so as to clarify the meaning of the policy (Cowden and Singh, 2007; Crawford et al, 2002). The Government expects service providers – at all levels – to actively engage with the concept and develop and implement programmes of participation locally. This policy has focused the minds of everyone, even when the requirement at times appears confused (Milewa et al, 2002).

While the UK's health and social care systems are well regarded by most, its responsiveness to its users is not always thought adequate (Tritter, 2006) and has been critically challenged. The extent to which present policy contributes to real changes for individuals and communities is the major issue. Webb (2008) argues that the participation of citizens in service delivery practices has become a 'showpiece of good intentions' (p270). Arguably this is most obvious in services to vulnerable and marginalised communities. Begum (2006) and Stuart (2008) are both of this view and advocate an approach which ensures that vulnerable individuals and groups, in particular those in ethnic minority communities, are enabled to participate effectively in the services provided to them.

There have already been several political reforms aimed at increasing the profile of this important agenda across the health and social care interface. In the UK, these go back to 1974, when Community Health Councils were set up to provide a voice for individuals from the community, backed by the Government's 'Patient's Charter', and in 1997 these became part of new Labour's agenda to modernise public services. Further reinforcement by the Local Government and Public Involvement in Health Act of 2007 and the Health and Social Care Act of 2008 indicated the Government's commitment to improving the effectiveness of user involvement. Vincent-Jones and Hughes (2009), however, suggest that this overhaul of policy signifies a political shift from involvement of patients and the public, to choices of individuals as consumers within the context of economic regulation. Hence the role of available resources and the way they are allocated remains an important factor in determining how services are provided. However, this dependence on economic regulation is responsible for the patchy implementation of the Government agenda, with meaning and objectives lacking a client focus (Cowden and Singh, 2007).

What 'user involvement' means

The Royal College of Nursing (2007) defines user involvement as an engagement of people – members of the public, patients, carers or potential, present and past users – in the development of services or the evaluation of those services in health and social care settings. The vast range of abilities and skills that individuals and communities possess is recognised: users can provide knowledge about their communities and offer their personal experiences of their own situation and that of people in their family and community.

But what counts is how much this is taken on board by those providing services, and how it affects eventual user outcomes. This is particularly so for minority users of services, including African Caribbeans (Cowden and Singh, 2007; Mirza, 1996). Some commentators point out that an unequal partnership is typical of the regular experience of minority users (Barn *et al*, 1997; Barnes, 1999; Begum, 2006; Butt and Mirza, 1996; Dutt, 1998).

According to Rutter *et al* (2004), using and even abusing professional power is an added possibility when appropriate resources are lacking, and can influence purchasing issues and possibly lead to closure of local services. Evidence of meaningful impact of user involvement is thin, complicated by poor clarification and uncertainty of outcomes (Cowden and Singh, 2007; Crawford et al, 2002). So is real partnership actually possible? Rutter *et al* (2004) identify in their case studies that while staff and service users cooperated to improve services, providers and managers appeared to have a different agenda and tended to discount the contribution of users as being unrepresentative of the wider community.

Services for children and families

Psychological service providers understand the importance of involving users. The literature agreed that this should be the business of everyone delivering clinical psychological services. Soffe (2004) and Hayward (2005) argue that involvement in training professionals ought to be an important part of the agenda but there is scant evidence of any meaningful changes in the design and delivery of services in response to user participation. What evidence there is indicates that the influence has been slight (Harrison *et al*, 2002). Yet it is vital that both individuals and the institutions understand and apply approaches which are sensitive to social, cultural and discriminatory factors. Excluding the individual could negate the care delivery process and impede recognition of diversity (Macpherson, 1999; Thompson, 2001; Watson, 2001).

People who are involved with designing, organising and delivering services for children and families from ethnic minority communities should ensure that account is taken of the influence of factors such as racism and marginalisation (Dutt, 1998; Guishard-Pine 2005; O'Neale, 2000).

From rhetoric to reality

The following case study considers the rhetoric as opposed to the reality of user involvement in adoption and fostering services.

Adoption and fostering: a case study

Julie Brown is a single 39 year old professional woman of African Caribbean background. Her work as a specialist practitioner and family care worker frequently brought her in contact with other professionals who were directly involved in providing services to vulnerable children and families in the community. Before deciding to become an adoptive parent, Julie had two years experience as a respite foster carer. Julie was assessed and found suitable for the placement of a child with a view to adoption.

As part of the introductory process, she was invited to visit Gabriel (the adoptive child) every day for a week. He was living over one hundred miles from her home. His foster family comprised a white woman, her black partner and their teenage son.

On the preparation course, Julie was told that a social worker would be present at all introductory visits. She had not been included in drawing up this plan and when presented with it she noticed that the presence of a social worker was only included for the first visit. She requested the daily presence of a social worker but was told by her key worker that this was not necessary given her level of experience as a foster carer. Julie noted the dismissal of her request, but decided to cooperate.

Her visits were problematic from the start. The initial introductions were made in the presence of the social worker and Julie assumed she would remain for the rest of this first visit but after half an hour the social worker left Julie alone with the foster family. Immediately she left, the foster carer became uncooperative. Julie's efforts to interact were ignored and the foster carer actively discouraged Julie from developing a relationship with Gabriel. She refused to include Julie in any aspect of Gabriel's care and, despite being asked, would not discuss Gabriel's routine or how he was being cared for. Noticing the tension created by this evasive and uncooperative behaviour, her partner disappeared.

Julie expected a call or visit from the social worker to discuss the first session (again promised at the preparation course), but did not hear from her. She tried for eight hours to contact her key worker, and when she managed to speak with her she requested her attendance the following day. However, her key worker was unable to return because of the distance but said she would try to arrange for a local worker to attend the next day instead. Julie arrived at the placement the following day to find no social worker support and the tense situation unchanged.

The combination of the foster carer's attitude, what she saw as certain culturally insensitive childcare practices, and the lack of professional support, left Julie feeling upset and frustrated. The interrelated social and cultural issues surrounding her professional and foster carer roles, and her status as a single African Caribbean adopter were not addressed by the local authority or the voluntary organisation. She was disappointed at the lack of awareness of the cultural implications of Gabriel's race and dismayed by the ensuing discrimination in the interactive process – a situation that is well documented in the literature (Guishard-Pine, 2005; Thompson, 2003; Watson, 2001).

With the situation remaining unchanged on day three, Julie felt frustrated and totally unsupported. She was on the verge of abandoning the adoptive process.

Encouraged and supported by her family and friends to achieve the intended outcome, Julie agreed that Gabriel would go with her to his new home. His belongs were packed in a black bin bag, which further distressed Julie. She complained to local authority, but no one seemed to understand the appalling cultural implications. Rather, their attitudes suggested that Julie was creating a fuss about nothing. They completely missed the seriousness of such thoughtlessness.

> Following the investigation of her complaint, Julie was given feedback. She was told that the white foster carer had said she felt her competence and her relationship with the child were threatened by the presence of a black professional woman. Again, the rhetoric won out over the reality: Julie had taken care to request that the information that she is a professional should not be disclosed but this had been disregarded. Julie was made to feel frustrated but also vulnerable.

Analysis

Julie's exclusion from the planning process is characteristic of the gulf that exists between policy and practice. Even though the presence of a social worker as part of the entire introductions process was a declared matter of policy, the organisations failed to implement their own policies. They consequently ignored the voice of the service user. The explanation that this was simply due to a lack of resources was unacceptable and made more so when Julie discovered that white prospective adopters on her course had been accompanied by social workers during the introduction process. No explanation a was offered about why no local worker was available. Julie felt that once she had expressed her concerns about the lack of support on the first day, action should have been taken to ensure someone was observing the process. But this did not happen. Tritter *et al* (2005) point out that although Arnstein's typology of power in the decision making process is frequently quoted as the appropriate key framework, this is not always taken into account in practice: transferring any real power to service users may never get beyond being part of the rhetoric of policy. Begum (2006) and Cowden (2007) suggest that in the case of vulnerable and minority users, practice should make real the policy rhetoric to ensure that their voices are truly heard. However, Cowden himself questioned the extent to which this is possible.

Professional opinions instead of action dominate still, because there are no clear guidelines on how user involvement should be manifest in practice (Branfield and Beresford, 2008; Crawford *et al*, 2004). This prioritisation of opinion over policy essentially ignores the spirit of user involvement and makes a mockery of the concept.

Cowden and Singh (2007) argue that this prioritisation sustains the nature of service user involvement as being no more than rehetoric. These authors identified that the focus of services for children and families is more about managing risk than about genuinely engaging with the parents and children concerned. Julie surmised that there may well have been a genuine lack of resources, which simply illustrates the ineffectiveness of well meaning policies (Rutter *et al*, 2004). Policy statements about including service users at the service provision level must be implemented by ensuring that their voices are actually heard. Failure to implement the rhetoric is all too evident at service delivery level.

When the voice of the service user is ignored the reality becomes problematic (Cowden and Singh, 2007; Rutter 2004). Even where the service user is considered to be an expert (in this case an experienced foster carer and professional worker with families in the community), this made no difference to Julie's treatment as a black service user. The assumption that because Julie was a practitioner herself, she needed less professional support contradicts evidence from the literature that institutional racism strongly affects the lived experiences of ethnic minority individuals and communities. In short, the concept of ethnic minority user involvement is still not a fully functioning part of all service providers' agendas (Begum, 2006; Butt and Mirza, 1996; Dutt, 1998; Macpherson, 1999).

Julie felt oppressed by a disabling process which left her feeling she had been set up to fail. Without her community's support, the adoption process would have collapsed.

The response to Julie's formal complaint was equally disappointing. She received a letter which stated that the foster carer concerned had many years experience and would not have behaved in the ways Julie described. Although Julie's expertise had initially been welcomed as beneficial to the adoption process, the way she was treated actually undermined her professional skills. The conclusion to what should have been a happy affair was that Julie felt completely let down by the inadequacies of a system which ultimately refused to acknowledge her voice and denied that what she had seen and reported had really happened. Julie and her family had effectively been called liars, which further illustrated the relative weakness of the ethnic minority voice and the overall failure to recognise the impact of the rebuttal (Dutt, 1998; O'Neale, 2000; Sheldon *et al*, 2007; Singh 1999).

Enhancing the service user experience for vulnerable and minority groups

Services have to show an engagement with the needs of service users, carers and their families (DH, 2004; DH, 2006). The extent to which this engagement is meaningful is still debatable. The experiences of ethnic minority users remain problematic, despite various attempts to make services more inclusive (Begum, 2006). The pervasive impact of race and culture on ethnic minority users and their communities still influence how they experience the services (Stuart, 2003).

Local services need to ensure that effective frameworks are developed *with*, rather than just *for* service users (Begum, 2006). Services need to engage with the realities of people's lived experiences. The undeniable influence of institutional racism and its subtle but damaging impact must be recognised as being part of the daily experiences of marginalised service users (Begum, 2006, Guishard-Pine 2005, Watson, 2001).

Conclusion

Service user involvement was a central part of the Labour government's 'modernisation of health and social care' agenda, and as this book goes to press, it is still gathering momentum in service delivery across all sectors (Thompson *et al*, 1997; Vincent-Jones and Hughes, 2009). Some confusion exists, however, about the effectiveness and clarity of the approach in terms of user involvement at both policy and delivery level. Although there is much goodwill on the part of both users and staff who try to deliver this agenda, evaluation of effectiveness at both levels indicates little change (Bransfield and Beresford, 2008; Rutter *et al*, 2004).

Service delivery to vulnerable groups such as African Caribbeans has been identified in the literature as lacking focus and as tending to underplay, deny or ignore the impact of racism and discrimination on users' experience (Health Care Commission, 2006; Joseph Rowntree Foundation, 2001, 2003; Macpherson, 1999; Stuart, 2008). Service development in relation to children and families is vital, and more research is needed to explore how user involvement is interpreted in the delivery stages and how this compares to the lived experiences of vulnerable and marginalised individuals and communities.

16

Self-evaluation by primary school aged children: an existential intervention

Yvonne Mills and Jeune Guishard-Pine

It is impossible to have complete harmony in any situation – but we get as near to it as possible. (11 year old primary pupil quoted by Ofsted, 2002:8)

Introduction

Does this pupil know what many adults don't know; or is she saying what adults can't bring themselves to say? As trained primary teachers with over 50 years experience between us, we have seen interventions to enrich the pastoral curriculum come and go. However, much of the literature about black psychology suggests that the dominant approaches can be counterproductive for black pupils. This chapter introduces ideas from existential humanistic psychology as a vibrant approach to supporting the development of the *black self* and also behaviour management tools that can be used across the entire school.

Behaviour management techniques in the school context

Disobedience is the modal behaviour problem in childhood. In schools it mainly manifests as non-compliance with instructions, interrupting lessons and relentless chatter in class (Ofsted, 2002 cited in Steer, 2005). Thirty five years ago, tabloid headlines warned of degeneracy in urban schools, with headlines like this in the *Sunday Express* (9.6.74): *They turn our schools into a jungle of violence.* The Elton Report (1989) appeared confident that: ...'Our recommendations would secure a real improvement in all schools' (p11). The *Every Child Matters* (DfES, 2004) agenda has stimulated research into the ongoing roles in improving schooling of LEAs, the Department of Children, Schools and Families (DCSF), medical and social worker professionals.

Applied psychology offers group management techniques that will enhance teaching and classroom control. The dominant theoretical basis for many behaviour management interventions over the last four decades has been operant conditioning (learning) theory (Skinner, 1953, 1957). It remains a highly regarded approach that has made its constructs of *reinforcement,* manifested as rewards and sanctions, part of our mainstream language (see Steer, 2005). Generally described as *behaviourism,* the ideas were developed into strategies for shaping and modifying the behaviour of school children. Applied behaviour analysis is the process of systematically applying interventions based upon the principles of Skinner's learning theory to develop prosocial behaviours, and to demonstrate that the improvements are directly attributable to these methods (Baer, Wolf and Risley, 1968; Sulzer-Azaroff and Mayer, 1991). It assumes that the application of the techniques will produce identical outcomes and is therefore seen as an *objective* approach to managing behaviour.

Certain interventions permeated the education system: *Behavioural Approaches to Teaching Package* (BATPACK) (Wheldall and Merrett, 1985); *Preventive Approaches to Disruption* (PAD) (Chisholm *et al,* 1986); *Building a Better Behaved School* (BABBS) (Galvin *et al,* 1990); *Assertive Discipline* (Canter and Canter, 1992); *Circle Time and Golden Time* (Mosley, 1996) and the *Problem-Solving Approach* (PSA) which is now revived as a specific behaviour management technique (Zellmer, 2003).

Later in his career Skinner wrote *Beyond Freedom and Dignity* (Skinner, 1972) in the attempt to promote his philosophy of science, the technology of human behaviour, his conception of determinism, and what he called 'cultural engineering'. Skinner's theories have been criticised as dehumanising, mechanistic and generally ignoring the autonomy of humans (Chomsky, 1971). A further criticism is that they promote totalitarianism. This criticism applies particularly to the socialisation of black children. In his seminal work, Wilson (1978) wrote that the development of a negative black self-concept was the consequence of oppressive behaviour modification techniques across generations. Jenkins (1982) suggests that black psychologists look towards humanistic psychology to describe and develop black self-theories.

The development of the black self
When other cultures are judged against European norms, European cultures are assumed to be superior and as such the desired norm for all people. The school curriculum presents historical events from a European standpoint, as if non-European cultures had no history, development or civilisation until discovered by

Europeans (Leicester, 2008). The discipline of black psychology seeks to counteract such omissions (Guthrie, 1976; White, 1971).

Most of the work on the development of self for diasporean Africans has been done by American psychologists. The seminal work of Kardiner and Ovesey (1951) stated as fact: 'The Negro has no possible basis for a healthy self-esteem' (p197). This view changed somewhat with the Civil Rights Movement (see Guishard, 1983 for a review). In Britain, Stone (1981) recast her PhD thesis to create the influential book *The Education of the Black Child in Britain: the Myth of Multiracial Education*, using overlapping discourses within sociology and psychology.

Stone researched black self-concept. She argued that the learning aptitude of black pupils in Britain were, despite the lack of evidence, declared to be rooted in 'personality factors' such as low self-esteem and that this mistaken thinking

> ... manages to ignore the vast body of evidence showing that working class and black families have much less access to power ... Self-concept becomes a way of evading the real and uncomfortable issue of class and privilege in our society. (pxx)

Stone cited research that indicated the contrary – that: '...the grammar school may be failing to promote self-confidence amongst youngsters' (Musgrove, 1971: 10). Upper and middle class children were possibly more anxious and had lower self-esteem, as their competitive environment compelled them to join the race to occupational success and consequent high SES, whereas the lower classes nurtured both the potential elite children and those who would remain in lower classes. Musgrove concluded that negative self-concept may be a necessary price of high academic attainment under fiercely competitive conditions.

Radical for its time, Musgrove suggested that school should be a place for affective as well as cognitive development. He challenged the insensitive, behaviourist child-rearing practices of the elite classes such as putting a baby on its own in a room and ignoring its cries so they learn to self-soothe. Musgrove stresses individual meaning and subjective experience as defining social reality – ideas consistent with existential humanistic psychology. The next section discusses the potential of such ideas to enhance discipline and behaviour management in schools.

The advent of the subjectivity in the management of self

> Rather they have argued that human beings should be understood in terms of the actuality of their lived existence: as non-object-like flows of experiencing that act towards their work in freely chosen ways. Existential philosophers, however, have not argued that human beings are completely free. Rather, they have pointed out

that human freedom faces unavoidable limitation, challenges and paradoxes...(we) cannot choose not to make choices! (Cooper, 2001:34)

Skinner (1972) maintains that when we consider scientific enquiry, people are not free to choose their behaviour:

In the traditional view a person is free. He is autonomous in the sense that his behaviour is uncaused. He can therefore be held responsible for what he does and justly punished if he offends. That view, together with its associated practices, must be re-examined when a scientific analysis reveals unsuspected controlling relations between behaviour and environment. (p17)

An existentialist might criticise the dominance of behaviourist ideas because it ignores the potential of intrinsic motivation. Individuals may well determine their behaviour according to their own self-driven goals and wish to determine their behaviour rather than be subject to external manipulation by, for example, money, praise or grades. According to Van Deurzen (2001), Sartre believed that people do not like to face up to their fundamental nothingness and their essential freedom and that in their denial, they pretend to be no different from a solid object. Thus we continue to deceive ourselves because, she maintains, we are always free to choose to be something other than we are.

When practiced as a therapeutic intervention, existential psychology has no tool-box of techniques. Instead it stresses the creation of understanding about who you are and who you would like to be (Guishard-Pine, 2006b), thus connecting with other humanistic models of 'self-as-tool'. The existential perspective on the promotion of self is that the primary drive in one's life is towards a search for meaning and that each person has unique and specific meanings that can be fulfilled by that person alone; one's striving toward existence (accepting what it means to be you) takes willpower and motivation.

These ideas are also linked to *self-determination theory* (Deci, 1975; Deci and Ryan, 1991, 1995) which emphasises that humans have the free will to make choices. This theory is explained by the Johari Window (Luft and Ingham, 1955). Although affiliated to cognitive psychology in its origins, this model is much used to explain social phenomena such as communication and relationships. Luft and Ingham observed that we are more open about some aspects of our self than others. They suggest that there are qualities or behaviours that others see in us but to which we pay little or no attention. There is a final group of personal characteristics that are unknown to anyone. They used a *four-pane* window to illustrate their model.

Diagram 17.1a and 17.1b: The Johari Window

	1 Known to me and others	4 Known to me but not other
	2 Known to others but not me	3 Not known to me or to others

OTHERS (− top, + bottom)

ME (+ I know, − I don't know)

	I know (+)	I don't know (−)
You Know (+)	The Public Self	The Blindspot
You Don't know (−)	The Hidden/Private Self	The Unknown Self

The public persona is openly known and described to others and consequently the characteristics can be evaluated as strengths or weaknesses. The private self contains information about us that we choose not to share with others. Both of these are within our direct control. The blindspot contains aspects of ourselves that others observe that they may not choose to feed back to us. Again, as they could be positive or negative behaviours, they affect the way that others act towards us. The *unknown* self contains things that nobody – including ourselves – knows about us. This may be because of a lack of experience; some believe it is because these characteristics are buried deep in the subconscious.

The model suggests that either of these panes can expand or contract according to the social setting that we are in. So if we are amongst people who are familiar and liked by us, most of our public self will be on display; conversely if we are amongst a group of people who are unfamiliar or whom we like or distrust less of our public self will be observable, leaving the observer with an opportunity to evaluate us using a more limited amount of information (see diagram 17.2).

Diagrams 17.2 and 17.3: The Johari window model when we are in different social settings

	I know(+)	I don't know(-)
You Know (+)	The Public Self (bigger when around familiar people)	The Blindspot
You Don't know (-)	The Hidden/Private Self	The Unknown Self

	I know(+)	I don't know(-)
You Know (+)	The Public Self	The Blindspot
You Don't know (-)	The Hidden/Private Self (bigger when surrounded by unfamiliar people)	The Unknown Self

Existential humanistic thinking and child mental and emotional health

Humanistic thinking recognises existence as a positive force that contributes to humility, greater sensitivity in personal relationships and creative utilisation of one's potential. It emphasises that the individual's world is unique.

The tenets of humanistic thinking are characterised by the following:

- our reactions depend on how we experience and perceive phenomena within our environment
- our behaviour is rooted in a drive to satisfy our needs and therefore the best way to understand an individual's behaviour is through their internal frame of reference
- we adapt most of our behaviour to be consistent with our self concept
- we all exist at the centre of a continually changing world of experiences
- and incongruence between our intentions and our behaviour is the consequence of a poor fit between our self-concept and our experiences
- we become anxious when there is a major discrepancy between our self-image and our experiences

Contemporary psychologists believe that trying to separate behaviour management in school from individual mental health issues is a false distinction, particularly when drugs and psychotherapy are increasingly being requested and used to control behaviour in school. Thus the manipulation of the self concept becomes an interpersonal rather than a mental health goal. Breggin (2001) argued that the gradual but consistent rise in treating young people in England with drugs is because school-based professionals fail to understand the total effect of drugs on children and largely ignore the additional benefits of psychosocial interventions. He concludes that such professionals are willing to subdue children rather than meeting their needs for a satisfying family and school life.

Yet the goals of applied psychology and humanistic therapies are ostensibly the same: that the individual is freed from anxiety and enabled to take responsibility for their behaviour and make choices that are consistent with behaviour change and personality development: The goal is 'to establish the proper therapeutic conditions to allow the normal developmental patterns of the individual to be brought back into play' (George and Cristiani, 1990:64).

Self-management in the school setting

The explicit role of existential humanistic therapy is to promote decision-making so that the individual improves their relationships, moves away from defensive behaviour and develops their social skills. The outcome to be desired is that the individual is more confident and more self-directing, that their values are determined by their own unique process and that they experience acceptance from significant others. But in reality, the individual is always at the centre of their continually changing world no matter what others want (Rogers, 1951). Fell (2004) writes about self-evaluation and self-control – a welcome aspect to introduce into the panoply of ideas.

When we are dealing with problems of poor conduct, anxiety and depression in children and adolescents, the existential approach is specifically useful in presenting a view that we can survive the challenge of living with ambiguity, whilst acknowledging that uncertainty is stressful for a youngster. Accordingly, the task for adults is to model the pursuit of self-development and self-acceptance and to tolerate the tension of misjudgements, impulse and risk. This is where the idea of 'normalcy' is maintained – this reality is something all humans face.

Youngsters learn with increasing clarity throughout their lives that 'Who can I be?' and 'Who can I not be?' are essentially the same question, and that the answers have infinite possibilities. Self-acceptance means understanding that we are living as we are because we can be no different and that it is the individual and not other people who make the change. The changes a youngster makes in their self are rooted first in the drive towards harmony and second in their opposing tendencies towards independence (self-assertion) and their relatedness to adults (eg parents and teachers) and other children (eg siblings, peers and classmates). According to an existential viewpoint, paradoxes are precisely the meat of life and that the incompatibilities are those we all must manage.

Four activities to enhance self-management

The following activities were carried out in a large school in an area with high levels of social disadvantage. When they arrive at Forward School, the skills of many of the children are measurably lower than those typical of the age group. A third of the pupils are asylum seekers, and three-quarters are from a visible minority. Half the school population has English as an additional language and a large proportion of these are only starting to acquire English. There is a high level of pupil mobility as many families move to the area on a temporary basis. The number of pupils with learning difficulties or disabilities is above the national average and most of them have severe learning difficulties and/or behavioural, social and emotional needs. Community care is provided for children on weekdays and Saturday mornings and the school has won a National Award for Community Cohesion.

The methods described developed from groupwork with an all-age group of children identified by their teachers in Term 2 as having issues regarding their self-esteem.

GROUPWORK ACTIVITIES

1. **What makes you unique?**
   Children are asked to characterise themselves according to cards bearing given and self-generated adjectives – thus affording each child their own permutation of adjectives. This emphasises the uniqueness of each child and consequently increases the prospect of self-acceptance. Children are also less anxious about difference because they can clearly see the individuality of everyone in the group. This stresses existentialism as 'you' being a unique construct.

2. **What's in a name?**
   Children are asked: *What do you want to hear when you hear your name spoken?* A secondary question would be: *What do you want others to hear when your name is spoken?* This exercise uses the concept of self-respect, examining what behaviours and attitudes lead to people being either respected or disrespected. It emphasises African and Asian cultures where children are named according to specific meanings – meanings that the family hope will be reflected in the child's character or that they will aspire to.

3. **Stuck on you**
   Children are asked to write adjectives on post-its. They are encouraged to write both positive and negative attributes (*things you like about you/are great about you/what people say is good about you* and *things you don't like much about yourself/that is not so great about your people say they don't like about you*). They then stick them on to a life-sized outline of themselves. Seeing the labels that are stuck onto the child has a powerful impact. Children then discuss the descriptions they feel are undeserved or that they want to change. The children are then invited to monitor the behaviour that has earned them these labels and that they would like to peel off. At the next session they are permitted to indulge in the empowering exercise of peeling off the post-its they have been stuck with but which are truly undeserved, and to explain their reasons. The process gives immediate feedback on their achievements and progress. Children report that it makes them feel that a burden has been lifted. At the third session they discuss the fact that some positive and some negative labels will remain but that these labels can be peeled off, added to or replaced across a whole school year if appropriate. This has a psychological impact on the child's self esteem and self acceptance. The activity is also powerful when training probationary teachers and for continuing

professional development. An empathy with the children can be created when these teachers apply the exercise to themselves.

The Deficit Zone and the Asset Zone
This is a choice-centred activity. It uses the analogy of a bank balance sheet to examine how self perceptions can drive or influence changes in the behaviour of primary aged children. The Deficit Zone is explained in terms of a child thinking they are not worthy and with this belief they will not gain money. The Asset Zone relates to any gains/worthiness/value the children can see in themselves that others can also see. The group discusses the behaviour and attitudes that may get them in to the Asset Zone. The activity can be used with preschool children, but is ideal for children from years 2-6 (ages 6-11 years). This activity encompasses discussions of skills, qualities and behaviours. It can be used as a device for curriculum development for years 1-3 and also with each class as a whole-school approach.

Conclusion

Schools that manage to raise the achievement of their black pupils note that a genuine attempt to respect and celebrate diversity through the relationships and interactions, structures and routines, and through the daily work on pupils' learning and personal development is central to their ethos. The activities discussed fit this view. Society is value-based and children can be taught to understand this by being helped to value themselves. By making choices, they use self management as a tool to negate or neutralise the projections and perceptions of themselves. This is potentially more ego strengthening than putting children's names on the good side or the bad side of the board. Children can physically see how labels change as they mature and this is empowering and reduces anxiety. The activities can be extended to whole classes and children can generate examples of both group and individual behaviour. These activities can also teach skills such as co-operation, active listening and debating skills.

Psychology subscribes to the theory that self-concept develops from experience. Since black experience is viewed as emasculating and dehumanising, one can assume that it leads to self hatred. This in turn assumes that black people are incapable of rejecting negative images of themselves as perpetuated by the dominant white society. We now know that this is not the case (Guishard-Pine, 2005). The activity *Stuck on You* is particularly powerful evidence of this.

Section 4
Contexualisation and experiences of racism

17
'Blank darkness': the invisibility of black women in the history curriculum

*Isis Guishard-Pine and
Jeune Guishard-Pine*

Introduction

> When young African Caribbean people are taught that the African Caribbean presence in the world began with slavery and not with ancient African civilisation, the message we receive is that African Caribbean people are always and only subordinate to white people... (Afuape: 2010: Chapter 12 of this book, p118)

*B*lank Darkness, the title of this chapter, comes from a book by C Miller (1986) alluding to the blank canvas that symbolised westerners' knowledge of Africa and Africans (Mama, 1995). It bears an uncanny resemblance to the contemporary picture of the black female living in Britain. Research for this chapter led to only a handful of texts written over the last two decades (Amos and Parmar, 1981; Bryan *et al*, 1985; Mama, 1995; Mirza, 1992; Mirza, 2002). What is a marvel is just how relevant that title remains despite the longstanding inclusion agenda. The two generations of black British women writing this chapter could not cite anything our British schooling taught us about black females.

Rather than accept our representation as blank darkness, we sought information on scientific or social scientific research, specifically on black females. We quickly discovered the stereotypes and caricatures of the black female portrayed through European sciences, justified as Social Darwinism. We end by investigating worthy black women in British history. Jeune wrote the first section of this chapter and Isis the second.

Section 1
Sociology and social psychology in education

Allport (1958) wrote that 'no person knows his own culture that only knows his culture' (cited in Verma and Ashworth, 1986). Although the sociology of education is concerned with the transmission of culture, a closer look at the history curriculum soon destroys any illusion that Allport's assertion is honoured.

Education in developed societies has two main functions. The first is to equip the individual with knowledge and skills valued by society and the second is to equip them with the skills the society requires to continue its evolutionary path. Bernstein's (1971) sociological theory of the role of education in British society postulates a tripartite system:

- a curriculum that promotes the information that is considered to be valid knowledge
- an accepted pedagogy through which to transmit that information
- an accepted system for evaluating the successful retention of that information

The idea has long had currency that knowledge is socially constructed and that the curriculum is merely socially organised knowledge (Banks, 1976). Leicester (2008) suggests that one way of assessing whether the school curriculum is inclusive is to see whether the history curriculum goes well beyond the study of great men. But the history curriculum in Britain is the study of powerful white able-bodied men – and we question the establishment's determination to maintain this focus because it so openly excludes that there have been calls to overhaul it (Hopkin, 2005; Hunt, 2006; Lyndon, 2003).

The disciplines of sociology and social psychology have an interest in how curricula influence personal and lifelong education. Both examine the way that society impacts on the individual and vice versa. Here we use ideas from social psychology to look at what obstinate loyalty to the current history curriculum can precipitate.

From a symbolic interactionist perspective (Mead, 1934) the exclusive approach to teaching history that persists in British schools has a potentially detrimental impact on those in society who are not powerful, white, able-bodied and male. We argue that the impact is immense and we focus on black females to put forward a radical range of images and ideas that can be taken into the classroom.

The development of self-concept and self-esteem

In his theory of the 'looking-glass self' Cooley (1902) suggested that we develop an idea of who we are from the way others see and/or respond to us. Our self concept is therefore based on a reflection not just of our direct experience but also of the experiences of people around us whom we consider to belong to the same groups as we do. The way we feel about it – our self esteem – is a measure of whether or not the images are considered to be positive or negative; worthy or unworthy. Thus the development of self is inextricably linked to the values that society holds of what is good or bad. Since Cooley (1902) much has been written on how the self develops.

George Mead (1934) proposed that a child develops a sense of 'I' and 'me' from the way she is viewed by the people who are important to her. He states that:

> The behaviour of the individual can be understood only in terms of the behaviour of the whole social group of which he is a member, since his individual acts are involved in larger, social acts which go beyond himself and which implicate the other members of the group'. (Mead 1934:6-7)

The logical conclusion is that the black girl will develop a sense of her self from the images of black females available to her in her personal life, in school and in the media.

What are black females taught to make them feel good about themselves?

A 13 year-old friend of the family once exclaimed: 'I hate TV! You would never think that black women ever washed their hair!' It was a bizarre accusation yet entirely justified. So is the view that positive images of black sexuality have been banned from British TV. Just look at a few images of black females that are featured in European and American literature. Some were presented under the guise of 'scientific discovery', such as Saartjie Baartmaan, the *Venus Hottentot*.

The African female in Europe

The story of Saraatjie Baartman, the Venus Hottentot (1789-1815)
Ethnological expositions or 'Human Zoos' were popular in the 19th and 20th century for parading mainly nude Africans. Marketed as a version of Social Darwinism, they were later criticised as being highly degrading and racist.

One of the most famed black females that came to British shores as an exhibit was Saartjie 'Sara' Baartman. She was brought to England as a slave with Dutch owners and became known throughout Europe as the 'Hottentot Venus'. Fascinated by her fleshy body she was seen as both erotic and mystical. She was hypersexualised and forced to entertain people by gyrating her

PSYCHOLOGY, RACE EQUALITY AND WORKING WITH CHILDREN

LOVE and BEAUTY -- SARTJEE the HOTTENTOT VENUS.

© Courtesy of Westminster Library Archives

nude buttocks immodestly, showing to Europeans what were thought of as highly unusual genitals. Following her death in France, an autopsy was carried out and her skeleton, genitals and brain were preserved and exhibited in Paris' *Musée de l'Homme* until 1974. Thus she was abused by European society well beyond her death. Her story symbolises historical European ideas on race and sexuality. (Crais and Scully, 2008)

The African female in America
Black females in America fared no better. African American literature features three main kinds of mythological image of the African woman in America: the 'Mammy' or 'Aunt Jemima' (a maid or housekeeper), the 'Jezebel' (the promiscuous, lustful temptress), and the 'Sapphire' (the asexual, aggressive, single woman). Ammons (1995), notes that these images were based on misogynistic mythology. She added two stereotypes that developed much later: the 'Matriarch' (the dominating maternal woman) and the 'Welfare Queen' (the feckless 'baby-mother')(Yarborough and Bennett, 2002).

Section 2
Increasing the visibility of black females in the school curriculum
It was good timing that my mother asked me to write this chapter with her as I have just begun a sociology course at A level. I was also motivated to get involved because neither my siblings nor I chose to do history GCSE because it does not allow us to study the history of how we came to be black British and so the course was of no interest to us.

My mum and I were both born in Westminster, London. My mum is now a citizen of her parents' birthplace – a nation known as the Federation of St Kitts and Nevis, famous for being the smallest sovereign state in the western hemisphere. Another thing my mum and I have in common is that, along with my two sisters, Janae and Ifetaiyo, we are part of a community group called the Yaa Asantewaa Carnival Arts Group (YAA). YAA is a touring carnival group and has performed regularly in Denmark, Germany, France and Trinidad as well as at Notting Hill Carnival and elsewhere in the UK.

So what is the significance of this information? Well, there are more important questions that could be asked, such as: *Where is St Kitts and Nevis? Who is Yaa Asantewaa? What is the Notting Hill Carnival?* Or even, *What is the importance of any of this to British history?*

We congratulate any readers who could answer even two of those four questions – especially if they are not of Ghanaian or Kittitian heritage. Let me tell you what I found out on *Wikipedia* about Yaa Asantewaa.

Yaa Asantewaa was a royal of the Asante tribe in Ghana in the latter part of the 19th century. She is well known and well regarded in Ghana for her bravery and determination. When the king was exiled, she tried to encourage the remaining warriors to fight for his return with the words:

> Is it true that the bravery of Asante is no more? I cannot believe it. It cannot be! I must say this: if you, the men of Asante, will not go forward, then we will. We, the women, will. I shall call upon my fellow women. We will fight the white men. We will fight till the last of us falls in the battlefields. (Addy, 2001 cited on *Wikipedia*)

The tale continues that Yaa Asantewaa and her army fought the British but lost. Consequently 'on January 1, 1902, the British were finally able to accomplish what the Asante army had denied them for almost a century, and the Asante empire was made a protectorate of the British crown' (Berry, 1995; cited in *Wikipedia*). Such stories are of historical significance but they are ignored in British schools because they are marginalised as black history. However, these accounts involve Britain, so are equally part of British history and should be taught as such.

Black women who could be integrated in to the national curriculum

The women I name are of British historical value and happen to have African heritage. My research was all done via the internet, which proves how easily available the information is.

Curriculum Area

English;History; sociology

Name

Mary Prince (circa 1788-1833)

There are no surviving images of Mary Prince, but her book The History of Mary Prince (1831) (edited by Sara Salih) is still in print

Biography

b Bermuda
Married Daniel James

© Penguin Books

Information

First book ever published in 1831 in England by a black female author. Was autobiographical and the torture described was so horrendous that it was initially not believed that she had endured such a catalogue of abuse

Elizabeth Barrett Browning
by Michele Gordigiani,
oil on canvas, 1858
© National Portrait Gallery

Curriculum Area
English

Name
Elizabeth Barrett Browning (1806-1861)

Biography
b England
Family were from Jamaica and were part Creole. Married distinguished poet, Robert Browning in 1846

Information
Wrote her first ;epic' poem aged 12 years and first publication The Battle of Marathon was published when she was 14 years old. First collection of her poems An essay on mind and other poems was published in 1826. Also published her translation of the Greek drama Prometheus Bound in 1833 and Poems in 1844

PSYCHOLOGY, RACE EQUALITY AND WORKING WITH CHILDREN

Charlotte Sophia of Mecklenburg-Strelitz
by Johann Philipp Haid, published by Johann Daniel Herz the Younger, after Unknown artist, mezzotint, after 1761
© National Portrait Gallery, London

Curriculum Area
History

Name
Queen Charlotte Sophia (1744-1818)

Biography
b Germany
Married 'Mad' King George III. Had 15 children

Information
Her African ancestry is seen as a "riddle". Her family are a black branch of the Portuguese monarchy. Is the great-great-grandmother of Queen Elizabeth II. Famous Queen Charlotte Maternity Hospital in West London named after her

Mary Jane Seacole
(née Grant)
by Albert Charles
Challen, oil on
panel, 1869
© National Portrait
Gallery

Curriculum Area
History; Science

Name
Mary Seacole (1805-1881)

Biography
b Jamaica
Married to Edwin Seacole

Information
Refused official status with the British army, determined to use her nursing skills in the Crimean war effort, she raised the finance to travel and to open a British hotel near Balaclava for convalescing soldiers. She received much praise from the British Commanders. In 1857 she published her autobiography

© Claudia Jones Foundation

Curriculum Area
Media; Visual and Performing Arts

Name
Claudia Jones (1915-1964)

Biography
b Trinidad
Married to Abraham Scholnick in 1940

Information
Described as the 'mother' of Notting Hill Carnival which started in 1959 in London. Started the first black weekly newspaper in Britain The West Indian Gazette.

Philippa of Hainault
by John Faber Jr, after Thomas Murray,
mezzotint, possibly mid 18th Century
© National Portrait Gallery, London

Curriculum Area
History

Name
Queen Phillipa of Hainault ((1314 -1369)

Biography
b France
Married to King Edward II. Had 14 children the most well-known of who is 'The Black Prince' Edward III

Information
The Queen's College at Oxford University was named after her

Curriculum Area
PE

Name
Tessa Sanderson CBE (1956-)

Biography
b Jamaica

Information
In 1984 became the first British black woman ever to win Olympic gold. She set a new Olympic record with her winning throw. She now holds both an OBE and CBE for her contribution to British sport

Valerie, Baroness Amos of Brondesbury; Rosalind, Baroness Howells of St Davids; Patricia, Baroness Scotland of Asthal
© Robert Taylor, cibachrome print

Curriculum Area
Sociology; Law; History

Name
Baroness Patricia Scotland of Asthal (right) (1955-)

with Baroness Valerie Amos of Brondesbury (left) and Baroness Rosalind Howells of St Davids (centre)

Biography
b Dominica
Married to Peter Mahwhinney. Has two sons

Information
In 1991 was the first black woman to be made a QC and later in 2007, she became the first ever woman and black person to hold the office of the Attorney General for England, Wales and Northern Ireland since its foundation in 1315. She was made a life peer in 1997

Joan Armatrading
by Andrew Catlin, toned bromide print, 27 April 1988
© National Portrait Gallery, London

Curriculum Area
Music

Name
Joan Armatrading MBE (1950 -)

Biography
b St Kitts & Nevis

Information
First black British female musician and composer to achieve prominence acknowledged by 3 Grammy nominations, 25 gold and 10 platinum records for her self-penned songs. First British female artist to achieve Number 1 in the US Billboard Blues charts

Curriculum Area
Business

Name
Yvonne Thompson CBE (1955-)

Biography
b Guyana

Information
Founder and President of the European Federation of Black Women Business Owners (EFBWBO). has been described as Britain's first black self-made woman millionaire. She is managing director of the marketing and PR company ASAP Communications, a former director of Choice FM radio

Curriculum Area
Science

Name
Professor Elizabeth Anionwu CBE (1946-

Biography
b London

Information
Considered one of Britain's leading authorities on blood disorders with a specialism in sickle cell and thalassemia. Director of the Mary Seacole Centre for Nursing Practice at the Thames Valley University

Curriculum Area
Business; Food Technology

Name
Dounne Alexander MBE FRSA (1949 -)

Biography
b Trinidad
Married to Rudolph Walker OBE. Has two children

Information
With no formal business training, experience or finance, she established 'GRAMMAS' (herbal foods) single-handedly supplying prestigious stores including Harrods, Selfridges, Harvey Nichols, Fortnum & Masons, plus top 7 supermarket chains. A true pioneer and winner of 8 National Awards; included in the first official list of 100 greatest/most influential black people in British history; gained Public Health Minister approval to use her products in hospitals and hospices. Her contributions were recorded (by the BBC) and stored in the British National Library, as part of the 2000 Millennium history archives.

Conclusion

> The teaching of black history is often confined to topics about slavery and post-war immigration or to Black History Month. The effect, if inadvertent, is to undervalue the overall contribution of black and minority ethnic people to Britain's past and to ignore their cultural, scientific and many other achievements. [History: 2004/5 annual report on curriculum and assessment (QCA)]

When Jeune attended school, the standard image of an African was of someone wearing a loincloth with a bone through the nose, living in a mud hut and boiling white missionaries in cauldrons. This image has been replaced with images of starving, diseased and still barely-clothed Africans – although these are counter balanced with politicians of global significance. But where are the positive images of the jewels of African heritage? Although some thought has gone into including white women and black men in the history curriculum, attention has yet to focus on black women. Perhaps, as Cline *et al* (2002) suggest, within the school context the lead needs to come through national education policies (p12). The QCA acknowledges that the history curriculum needs to 'make history more relevant to pupils' (QCA website).

Isis takes the view that there needs to be a completely new GCSE humanities course called Ethnic Studies. There are now over 4 million people from visible ethnic minority groups in Britain (ONS website), so this course would walk the talk of an inclusive curriculum and therefore be not just welcome and popular, but relevant to all.

18

Looking back at being black and gay in school

Lloyd Hamilton

The past

When discussing prejudice and social injustice, issues inevitably arises of power, its construction and sustenance. One could ask what those who have the power to influence change have to lose? Being black and being gay, I can readily question the subject as though I am from the outside, or from the margins looking in. The pain of the lived reality of marginalisation entrenches the dichotomy of being 'inside or out', 'visible or invisible'. The valourisation of fairness in this society therefore is a curiosity to me.

I can still connect to my feelings of pain when I recall the events of a decade ago when a gay pub in Soho, the Admiral Duncan, was bombed. Through both my blackness and my gayness, I felt personally attacked. The bombing was associated with a series of attacks, first on the black community with a bomb in Brixton, and then on the Asian community with a bomb in Brick Lane. Tragically, three people died in the Soho bombing. Many more were injured in the attacks and countless more were affected.

But marginalisation is an everyday occurrence, mostly subtle and seldom making the headlines. Marginalisation occurs within the to-ing and fro-ing of everyday interactions; tensions that arise because of assumptions, expectations, fears and prejudices of two people in interaction, the primary act of society making.

Since 2005 same sex couples can celebrate their relationships with civil partnerships and be granted the same legal rights as married heterosexual couples. The

Adoption and Children Act 2002 allows both married and unmarried adults to adopt, regardless of their sexuality. We also have the same employment rights and an equal age of consent. I think it has become widely understood that life, certainly in Britain's major cities, appears to have evolved dramatically for lesbians and gay men.

With the increasing numbers of openly gay and lesbian personalities and depictions of gay and lesbian characters in film and television, our lifestyles are no longer just targets for crude mockery or, as in the Hollywood film tradition, symbolic portrayals of malevolence (Russo, 1987). It seems that the qualitative change in the day-to-day lives of lesbians and gay men has been real, systemic and far-reaching.

Recent research suggests that life for young gay and lesbian people in schools contrasts with the hard won progress made and reported in wider society. Homophobic bullying and an absence of Lesbian, Gay, Bisexual and Transexual (LGBT) themes in the curriculum reflects persistent and wilful disregard of the responsibility of schools to address the psychological needs of young LGBT people for their healthy development and the acquisition of the skills and knowledge they needed for achievement in adult life. This neglect contradicts the atmosphere of diversity and tolerance proposed by then Prime Minister Tony Blair in 2006.

Studies of the experience of black boys in school and the social contexts of black gay men in Britain point to more complex and harder to challenge processes of homophobia for black gay boys than white. Research into the lives of black lesbians and gay youths and adults reflect the continuing relative invisibility of lesbians and black lesbians in particular. As a male author I acknowledge that in reflecting my experience in this chapter under-represents black lesbianism.

However, today communication technology has transformed the capacity for all young people in Britain to create independently their own information and social networks of resources. This communications revolution has taken shape against a background of endemic homophobic bullying in many secondary schools:

> Young people who are homophobically bullied are less likely to do well at school ... They are more likely to truant, to leave school at 16, to harm themselves or to attempt suicide. Ask your class how often they hear words like 'gay' used as an insult or put down. (Jennett, 2004:2)

Is it only protest that will enable progress? I was born in London in 1968. My parents' generation brought feminism to Britain. They lived through the Vietnam war – some even learnt to protest then. Like many black children in Britain, I learnt through my parents' stories and through images on television of their struggles –

the struggles of true pioneers to find a life despite the pervasive nature of racism they found here in Britain: inequality in the work place, in housing and subsequently in the schools they could access for their children. Flats for rent and boarding houses announced 'no blacks, no Irish, no dogs'. It is astounding that my decent church-going mum and dad, aunts and uncles who left the green hills of rural Jamaica, found a way to survive life in 1950s and 60s London.

The need to act for social justice found expression first for me in the protests against fascism and the British National Party (BNP) in Lewisham, South-East London in 1977. The numbers and influence of the BNP at that time had grown in many parts of the country. Their decision to march through Lewisham, an area with a large African Caribbean community, was a direct and aggressive challenge. To me, aged 9, it appeared to be an attack and confirmation of white hatred of black people. Four years later, thirteen black people, mainly children, were killed in a house fire in New Cross. I joined the crowds marching through central London days after the fire, without my parents' knowing. I was 13. I can remember being struck by the angry words of people around me that 'the Queen doesn't care!' She hadn't visited the site of the fire but was said to be visiting the relatives of a family lost in an arson attack in Northern Ireland. It was a frightening march for me but now I can reflect on those events which began to construct an idea of social justice in my young mind. My past experience indicated that visibility was the only means to achieve social justice.

Before I was 13 I stopped attending church. As with many life changing rites of passage, this decision to go against my parents' wishes was made easier as my elder brothers had taken my parents through similar grief and confusion before me. However, unlike my brothers, I didn't stop going to church because 'it was boring'; it was because I was different. I was gay and I had learnt that there was no place for homosexuals in church society.

School had no place for me either. Up to the age of 11, I was a funny and popular boy in school. My primary school was predominantly white and I remember only the occasional racist comment or joke – until Alex Haley's *Roots* was shown on TV when I was 9. I found it compelling, a true landmark in black visibility. But what followed was a devastating increase in racist comments, jokes and general abuse from neighbours, school and TV comedians. I recall my confused feelings of exposure, growing self-hatred and the accumulation of internalised racism.

In secondary school I was withdrawn and became increasingly characterised as 'quiet'. Many of my opinions were formed during the early years of Margaret Thatcher's government – opinions about the 3,000,000 unemployed, the miners' strike in the 80s and the ugly turning of the state against working class communities. I became absolutely determined to counter any stereotypical images held of black boys so, although I loved sport, I never wore trainers or owned a tracksuit. I carried my school equipment proudly in a smart bag – never a plastic carrier bag – my own quiet form of resistance. But as I came to relate more readily to my sexuality, I learnt that, like church and primary school, secondary school was not a place for me. Secondary school was fundamentally homophobic. Going away to university would finally give me the freedom to learn and to express how my life could be. Until then I continued to be quiet.

Like many multiracial schools today, my secondary school was self-segregated by colour. Children inevitably gravitate toward others who are like them, thus inclusive policies and strategies organising how teachers structure the learning environment will to some degree fail. At break-times, a significant minority of working class African Caribbean students hung out in one particular area, whilst the white working class pupils occupied the rest of the site. Within this environment I learnt to fear rejection from anyone in my peer group, as I perceived that it might lead to rejection from my black community. Given the microcosmic school context of segregation and homophobia, perhaps it was a tragically understandable fear for an adolescent boy. There was nobody in the school, no role model on any TV or cinema screen, who could mitigate my fears.

So I left for Exeter, where I was able to express myself as a design student, amongst a small circle of gay friends who are still my second family. By 1987, my fresher year, gay life in Britain had changed because of acquired immune deficiency syndrome (AIDS). The now iconic tombstone and iceberg public information films of 1986, with John Hurt's chilling narration, seemed to capture and galvanise the nation's sense of fear of this killer 'gay plague', as it was labelled in both *The Daily Mirror* and *The Daily Telegraph* (02/05/1983). Section 28 of the Local Government Act 1988, forbidding the promotion of homosexuality and 'the teaching in any maintained school of the acceptability of homosexuality as a pretended family relationship' was an attack on our place in society. Whilst homophobia in school oppressed isolated gay pupils, the government and press attacks of the 80s galvanised the gay community across Britain to protest and lobby for equal rights, adequate health care, and social justice. The founding of Stonewall, the LGB lobbying group, was one of the enduring responses to this legislation.

My teaching career between 1992 and 2000 was marked by the repeal of section 28, an equalising of the age of consent (involving a night of protest, raging at the Lords' defeat of the second motion with a siege of parliament's gates) and other landmark social and legislative victories. Sadly, it was also marked by the murder of Stephen Lawrence, a black teenager, in southeast London in 1993 and

Macpherson's recognition (1999) of *The Stephen Lawrence Inquiry report* identified as 'institutionalised racism'.

The present

So what about being gay and black in school today? After Section 28 was repealed in 2003, what difference should be made to the school curriculum? The Qualifications and Curriculum Authority (QCA, now QCDA) website (2009) set out the aims and objectives for the curriculum at key stages 3 and 4:

> The curriculum should enable all young people to become:
> - Successful learners who enjoy learning, make progress and achieve
> - Confident individuals who are able to live safe, healthy and fulfilling lives
> - Responsible citizens who make a positive contribution to society

The National Curriculum claims to have brought teaching in schools into public ownership. Developments are through open consultation and the duty to implement the curriculum across all state schools in England, Wales and Northern Island is legislated through parliament. The developments of the new or revised curriculum (2000) address the dichotomy of a curriculum that meets the needs of society and economic growth or of personal development. Ian Colwill, Director of QCDA's Curriculum Division, says the first purpose of the new Curriculum is 'to secure for all pupils, irrespective of social background, culture, race, gender, differences in ability and disability, an entitlement to a number of areas of learning and to develop knowledge, understanding skills and attitudes necessary for their self fulfilment and development as active responsible citizens.'

Creative resources to support teachers to discuss sexuality and homophobia are available from the QCA (Bennet, 2004). They bring together research, advice and support, including a homophobic bullying audit and a checklist for challenging and responding to homophobia and homophobic bullying. The publication is poignantly prefaced with a quote from Archbishop Desmond Tutu, 25 February 2004:

> Everyone is an insider, there are no outsiders – whatever their beliefs, whatever their colour, gender or sexuality.

The Ofsted inspection framework required that schools be asked

- Whether learners feel safe from bullying, whether on religious, racial, (including Gypsy/Roma and Travellers of Irish heritage) sexual and homophobic grounds.
- The extent to which learners have confidence to talk to staff and others when they feel at risk

- How well learners make a positive contribution to the community? For example:
  - Learners' growing understanding of their rights and responsibilities, and respect for others who are different from themselves
  - The extent to which the curriculum helps pupils understand how we can live in a cohesive community, and the opportunities there are for pupils from different backgrounds to interact and work together.

The political and legislative context for British schools (Race Relations (Amendment) Act, 2000) explicitly calls for an attitude of inclusivity that actively challenges prejudice. It is a context in which Stonewall has supported schools and has tested the limits of the inclusivity agenda with provocative curriculum events. A spokesman for Stonewall, actor Ian McKellan, attended a Leytonstone comprehensive secondary school's staging of an adaption of Romeo and Juliet: *Romeo and Julian*, in 2009 during LGBT history month. *FIT*, a hip-hop musical commissioned by Stonewall, was written for Key Stage 3 by Rikki Beadle Blair, an openly gay black British writer, actor and director. Staged in 2008 in an East London Community school, the play tells the story of children coming to terms with their sexuality. In Lewisham, the Metro Centre, an LGBT community resource, has developed an advice and consultation service to schools as well as presenting curriculum events to actively engage students in discussing issues of sexuality and homophobia.

The ESRC funded *No Outsiders Project* which ran from 2006-2008 and involved 15 schools across Britain, was the first to tackle homophobia at primary level (No Outsiders Project Team, 2010).

None of this is achieved without resistance. Philip Davies, Conservative MP for Shipley expressed his concern at the staging of *Romeo and Julian*, proposing a parliamentary debate on political correctness! The BBC news programme Inside London broadcast a ten minute report *Gay education in schools – the cases for and against*, which looked at resourcing libraries with fiction and fairy tales that include gay and lesbian characters, and noted the curriculum events and resources available. The BBC website hosts a selection of viewers' comments: the emailed responses were 55 in favour and 56 against.

Challenges and resistance to progress in the curriculum persist. What is the experience of being black and gay in school today? Should students be faced with the double oppression of racism and homophobia? *Ethnic minority gay men, redefining community, restoring identity* (Keogh *et al*, 2004) is a London based research report that compares British born Black Caribbean with White Irish gay men. The research sought to 'investigate the relationship between ethnicity and gay sexuality [and to] isolate the range of factors that influence the identity and social interactions of gay men' (p2), and also to comment on the social environment in which gay men are situated.

Black respondents and white identified with the notion of a 'gay scene' – a conflation of a commercial environment of pubs and nightclubs, organised community groups, and familial and friendship groups. The commercial environment is the most visible and accessible sector of the scene and is often the first place young lesbians and gay men meet others like them. Across all ethnic groups, gay men experience the commercial sector as highly sexualised, with an associated culture of the indulgence of the body. The research showed a fetishisation of Black gay men by white men. Despite the acknowledgement of their objectification as a cross-ethnic product of the scene, black men found this fixation problematic. The commercial sector was also experienced as an 'impoverished form of social contact' (Keogh *et al*, p41).

This research found that the motivation behind coming out as gay and remaining openly gay, was perceived as being a particularly white discourse. For gay black men, the emphasis was on moving in and out of relationships with family, their church community and the gay scene as crucial to maintaining a sense of their identity. Being openly gay was described as a set of behaviours that might apply in one context but not another:

> The way in which the men managed this dilemma was to negotiate their space within both [black and gay] environments. This was done within a series of slow and subtle acceptances and rejections, disclosures and withholdings. (Keogh *et al*, p23)

Research by Wright *et al* (1989) discusses the continued over representation of black boys excluded from school, describing a culture of hyper-masculinisation within the group. If this is how black boys in school are seen by others, and if the common discourse of male homosexuality as the antithesis of masculinity pertains, black gay boys and young men at school face difficulties. The research suggests that for the healthy development of their identity, black gay men must find a way to navigate between black social groups and the gay scene. Homophobic peer pressure is, however, a justification for the invisibility of black gay students as a subpopulation of barely visible gay school age males. This intricate set of issues reflects the barriers to an inclusive curriculum that will enable black lesbian and gay young people.

The future

The story of the hypermasculine black male continues to be challenged (see Chapter 12). But I would question what the stories black gay boys and young men are told about who they are, and how these affect their sense of self. What are their true stories – the stories they have of themselves, which they tell each other, the stories that constitute their own emerging identities? And how do the stories they are told of hypermasculinity affect their own stories of self? What stories do they anticipate from others? More to the point, what is the effect on their own identity of the stories black heterosexual boys tell about black homosexuality?

I would ask members of the BNP past and present: what are the stories they hold about immigrants? What do those stories mean in relation to who they are? What is the effect of the stories we hold of the 'other' on who we think we are and how we see ourselves? If we construct our worth in relation to others, our history in relation to an anticipation of change, and our values in relation to social difference, what value do equity and social justice have? If power is the capacity to act on the impact of 'difference' and of 'the other' and to deny change, then power and its misuse function to fuel 'identity preserving systems' – systems in this case determined by exploitative egoism rather than justice and egalitarianism (Maturana and Varela, 1992).

Choosing egalitarianism from a position of power is perhaps how Britain navigates its way between diversity and (*in*)tolerance. This may explain the lag in schools' awareness of LGBT groups and all their diversity, compared to wider society. Paradoxically, once our children have all the advantages of being like 'us' (straight, white, powerful), with corresponding beliefs and ways of life, they too will be able to choose brotherhood and equality.

I remain convinced that without visibility black gay pupils cannot affect fundamental curriculum change and social justice. In an environment where gay men and lesbians can take for granted the legislative gains of the last ten years, I applaud the efforts of Stonewall and youth LGBT organisations across Britain. And I am fascinated by the opportunities offered by the evolving world of technology that give our technologically gifted young people unprecedented access to information and new genres of social networks, so creating allies in the striving for an inclusive curriculum. I am a product of my history and my hopes for the future, yet I cannot believe that real change for black gay pupils will come undemanded and without protest.

19
Conclusion

There are always more questions than answers. This book could have been double the length: much vibrant research and practice on ethnic minority populations in the UK still remains unpublished. However, it has been a hugely important step in the right direction to have these messages presented at all.

The book reminds us that not all traditional white psychological theory is useless when applied to ethnic minority groups. Many of the chapters make explicit references to the usefulness of theories and thinking from mainstream psychology. For example, existential psychology, with its recognition of pain and struggle as an unavoidable condition, applies equally to the lives of black people and white. References to behavioural, cognitive, psychoanalytic understandings and various theories from social psychology are all relevant across society.

Not only does the book present exciting work that is being done with a diverse range of ethnic groups currently channelled through the statutory services, it offers models for practitioners of how culturally-competent interagency work can be achieved through increasing the knowledge base and understanding of the people who are actively engaged in child-focused practice. It is heartening to see the wide application of psychology to this endeavour.

However, psychologists in the UK lag behind their American counterparts in that we have yet to develop coherent models of black psychology based on consistent empirical research. What black psychology in the UK can learn from black psychology in America is the overall message that research has to continue to focus on the strengths of black children and their families. It is also vital that black heroes and 'sheroes' are made more visible; not only the financially successful. There are also other people whose activities are erecting signposts towards race equality. These are people who serve as role models for all children.

List of contributors

Olatayo Afuape is a child and adolescent psychoanalytic psychotherapist and chartered education and child psychologist. She has been a senior specialist psychologist on domestic violence projects; a clinical child psychologist; senior psychologist and lead psychotherapist. Her specialist knowledge and skills are in the areas of race and culture, looked after children, adolescents, domestic violence, and pervasive developmental disorders.

Taiwo Afuape is a principal clinical psychologist and systemic psychotherapist for the Medical Foundation for the Care of Victims of Torture and at the Tavistock in a Community CAMHS. She has managed a Systemic Consultation Service for people experiencing complex psycho-social difficulties and has helped to set up community therapeutic services for transitional people.

Jan Carter is an education consultant. Formerly she worked as a teacher and she has 40 years experience in primary education, including being the teacher in charge of a language unit. For many years she worked as both a SENCo and inclusion manager in a multilingual school.

Christine Cork was born in Trinidad. She is a qualified nurse, midwife, neonatal nurse and health visitor and has 30 years experience of working with parents and young children. She has a masters degree in psychoanalytical observational studies and works in a community outreach mental health service in Bedfordshire.

Luke Daniels is a social activist, counsellor and consultant on domestic violence, working with men and couples and also with adolescent boys in schools. The television documentary 'Pulling the Punches' was based on his work. He currently combines his work as a primary care development worker with writing. His chapter on domestic violence appeared in *Working with Men for Change* (Wild, 2008) and his book, *Pulling the Punches: Defeating Domestic Violence*, was published in 2009.

Isis Guishard-Pine is attending Further Education College with the hope of becoming a writer. She has interests in events management, black history and media.

Jeune Guishard-Pine is an activist psychologist. Throughout her career in the health, education, social services, voluntary and private sectors, she has devoted herself to working with marginalised or disenfranchised groups of people. She is a trained teacher, educational psychologist, humanistic psychotherapist and systemic practitioner. She and her husband have six children.

Lloyd Hamilton is a systemic psychotherapist and team manager of the Lewisham Child and Adolescent Mental Health Service looked after children team, part of the South London and Maudsley NHS Foundation Trust. A former teacher who began working with diverse communities of young people in London schools in 1992, he is studying for his doctorate.

Alex Harborne is a qualified nurse, clinical psychologist and systemic practitioner, and principal lecturer in clinical psychology at the University of Hertfordshire. She has a special interest in early infant development having worked with neglected children in Romania and with children who have learning disabilities. She is deputy lead clinician for Luton early intervention service, where she has a remit to develop services for 0-4 year olds and their families.

Sarah Hawes began her nurse training in 1967, and worked as a nurse-midwife and health visitor in the UK, West Africa and the Middle East. Diplomas in counselling and infant mental health augment this experience to inform her present work as a primary mental health worker.

Valerie Jackson is currently a senior practitioner educational psychologist based within CAMHS in Newham. Since 1993 she has worked in a range of London boroughs as a local authority educational psychologist. She has taught in Inner London state schools and voluntary West Indian complementary schools.

Yvonne Mills was schooled in Wiltshire before she trained in both primary and secondary teaching. She made a conscious decision to work in an area with an ethnically diverse population and consequently chose to work in Brent, where she has remained for her entire career.

Karina Ng was born in Hong Kong and came to England in 1990. She is a senior educational psychologist with Croydon Education Authority. She has special interest in transcultural issues which impact on children and family life and has published articles in the Chinese press in the UK on various educational issues.

Clare Nichols began her nursing career as an undergraduate in 1974. After practicing health visiting for some years, in 2000 she joined the child and adolescent mental health team in Luton, which has developed an award winning community service with local schools. She recently completed a systemic practice diploma.

LIST OF CONTRIBUTORS

Randa Price has worked for many years as a chartered educational psychologist, community worker and teacher. Randa has held a senior specialist position related to refugees and asylum seekers. Apart from clinical work with children, their families and schools, Randa has conducted research in the area of responsiveness of local service providers to the needs of newly settled communities in Britain.

Hazel Sawyers is a trainer and facilitator with 20 years' experience of working in race relations, equality and diversity in the UK. She currently provides learning and development solutions to individuals and organisations.

Sarah Took is a specialist senior educational psychologist with Durham local authority. The experience of living and going to school in different countries has heightened her interest in culture, the things people give value to and listening to the stories people tell.

Naomi Anna Watson is a lecturer with the Open University and specialist practitioner in primary care. Her research interests include: primary care, diversity and ethnicity in nursing, health and social care practice and education and public health, distance learning in pre-and post-registration nursing education and its implications for practice. She is past chair of a fostering and adoption panel and member of a voluntary sector organisation supporting children in public care and their families.

References

Adams K and Christenson S (2000) Trust and the Family-School Relationship. *Journal of School Psychology* 38(5) p477-497

Addy E A (1960) Yaa Asantewaa – the Queen mother of Ejisu. p54-58. In E Addy (ed) *Ghana: A History for Primary Schools: Book Two.* London: Longmans

Ahmed S, Cheetham J and Small J (eds) (1986) *Social work, black children and their families.* London: Batsford

Allport G (1958) *The Nature of Prejudice.* New York: Doubleday Anchor Books

Alvarez A and Reed S (1999) *Autism and Personality: Findings from the Tavistock Autism Workshop.* London: Routledge

American Psychiatric Association (1994) *Diagnostic and statistical manual of mental disorders* (4th ed) Washington,DC: American Psychiatric Association

Ammons L (1995) Males, Madonna, babies, bathwater, racial imagery and stereotypes: and African American women and the battered woman syndrome. *Wisconsin Law Review*, 5, p1003-1080

Amos V and Parmar P (1981) Resistances and responses: the experiences of black girls in Britain: An adventure story, in A McRobbie and T McCabe (eds) *Feminism for Girls.* London: Routledge and Kegan Paul

Andersen T (1987) The reflecting team: dialogue and meta-dialogue in clinical work. *Family Process.* 26(4) p415-428

Antonopoulos G (2003) Ethnic and Racial Minorities and the Police: A review of the literature. *The Police Journal.* 76, p222-245

Archer L (2003) *Race, Masculinity and Schooling: Muslim Boys and Education.* Buckingham: Open University Press

Archer L and Francis B (2005a) Constructions of racism by British Chinese pupils and parents. *Race, Ethnicity and Education* 8(4) p387-407

Archer L and Francis B (2005b) They never go off the rails like other ethnic minority groups: teachers' constructions of British Chinese pupils' gender identities and approaches to learning. *British Journal of the Sociology of Education* 26(2) p165-182

Archer L and Francis B (2005c) British Chinese pupils' constructions of gender and learning. *Oxford Review of Education* 31(4) p497-515

Archer M (2002) *Being Human: The problem of agency.* Cambridge: Cambridge University Press

Armstrong D, Hine J, Hacking S, Armaos R, Jones R, Kissinger N, and France A (2005) *Children, Risk and Crime: the On Track Youth Lifestyle Surveys (Home Office Study 278).* London: Home Office

Association of Educational Psychologists (1988) *Working Party Report on Racism.* Durham: AEP Publications

Atkin K and Rollins J (1993) *Community care in a multiracial Britain: A critical review of the literature.* London: HMSO

Audit Commission (2003) *Connecting with users and citizens.* London: Audit Commission

Baer D, Wolf M, and Risley R (1968) Some current dimensions of applied behavior analysis. *Journal of Applied Behavior Analysis,* 1 p91-97

Bailey W, Branche G and Stewart S (1996) *Family and Gender Relationships in the Caribbean.* Mona: Kingston Institute of Social and Economic Research, University of West Indies

Baldwin J (1970) *African (Black) Psychology: Issues and Synthesis.* US: University of Michigan

Baldwin J (1989) The role of black psychologists in black liberation. *The Journal of Black Psychology.* 16(1) p67-76

Baldwin J (1993) *Nobody Knows my Name.* New York: Vintage

Bambara T C (2005) *The Black Woman: an anthology.* New York: Washington Square Press

Banks N (1992) Techniques for direct identity work with black children. *Adoption and Fostering,* 16(3), p19-25

Banks O (1976) *The Sociology of Education.* London: Batsford

Barclay G and Mhalanga B (2000) *Ethnic Differences in decisions on young defendants dealt with by the Crown Prosecution Service.* London: Home Office

Barn R (1993) *Black children in the public system.* London: Batsford in association with British Agencies for Adoption and Fostering (BAAF)

Barn R, Sinclair R, and Ferdinand D (1997) *Acting on principle: An examination of race and ethnicity in Social Service provision for children and families.* London: BAAF

Barnes E (1991) The black community as a source of positive self-concept for black children: a theoretical perspective. In R Jones (ed) *Black Psychology.* 3rd edition. CA: Cobb and Henry

Barnes M, Harrison S, Mort M and Shardlow P (1999) *Unequal Partners – User Groups and Community Care.* Bristol: Policy Press

Barrat S, Burch C, Dwivedi K, Stedman M, and Raval H (1999) Theoretical Bases in Relation to Race, Ethnicity and Culture in Family Therapy Training. *Context.* 44, p4-12

Basit T (1997) 'I want more freedom, but not too much': British Muslim girls and the dynamism of family values. *Gender and Education* 9 p425-439

Baxter P and Jack S (2008) Qualitative Case Study Methodology: Study Design and implementation for Novice Researchers. *The Qualitative Report.* 13(4) Dec. p544-559

Begeer S, Bouk S, Boussaid W, Terwogt M, and Koot H, (2009) Underdiagnosis and referral bias of autism in ethnic minorities. *Journal of Autism & Developmental Disorders.* 39(1) p142-8

Begum N (2006) *Doing it for themselves: participation and black and minority ethnic service users.* London: Race Equality Unit, SCIE

Bennett M (2004) *Stand Up for Us, Challenging homophobia in schools.* London:HMSO

Benskin F (1994) *Black Children and Underachievement.* London: Minerva Press

Bent-Goodley T and Williams O (2003) *Community insights on domestic violence among African Americans: conversations about domestic violence and other issues affecting the community.* Detroit, Michigan:Institute on domestic violence in the African American community. http://www.dvinstitute.org/media/publications/Detroit-CommInsights.pdf

Benton T, and White K (2007) *Raising the Achievement of Bilingual Learners in Primary Schools: statistical analysis.* Available online. http://www.dfes.gov.uk/research/data/uploadfiles/DCSF-RR006.pdf Research Report DCSF-RR006. DCSF: Nottingham

Bergman S (1995) *A new psychology of men.* NY:Basic Books

REFERENCES

Berne E (1986) *Games People Play.* Harmondsworth: Penguin

Bernstein B (1971) *Class Codes and Control, vol 1. Theoretical studies towards a sociology of language.* London:Routledge and Kegan Paul

Berry L (ed) (1994) *Ghana: A Country Study.* Washington: Federal Research Division, Library of Congress

Bhui K and McKenzie K (2008) Rates and risk factors by ethnic group for suicides within a year of contact with mental health services in England and Wales. *Psychiatric Services* 59(4), p414-420

Bion W (1959) Attacks on linking. *International Journal of Psychoanalysis.* 40, p308- 315

Bion W (1991) *Learning from Experience.* London: Heinemann

Bloom B (1980) *The State of Research on Selected Alterable Variables in Education.* Chicago: Department of Education, University of Chicago

Bolton P (1984) Management of compulsorily admitted patients to a high security unit. *International Journal of Social psychiatry* 30(1-2) p77-84

Bonnie R, Coughlin A, Jefferies J and Low P (1997) *Criminal Law.* Westbury, NY: The Foundation Press

Boyd-Franklin N (1989) *Black Family Therapy: A Multi-Systems Approach.* New York: Guildford Press

Branden N (2001) *The Psychology of Self-Esteem: A Revolutionary Approach to Self.* London: Wiley

Branfield, G and Beresford, P (2008) *Making user Involvement work: supporting service user networking and knowledge: The findings.* York: JRF

Brazelton T and Cramer B (1991) *The Earliest Relationship.* London: Karnac

Breggin P (2001) What people need to know about the drug treatment of children. In C Newnes, G Holmes and C Dunn (eds) *This is Madness Too.* Ross-on-Wye: PCCS Books

Briggs P and Guishard J (1988) Developing a Non-Verbal Pre-School checklist for Bilingual Pupils. Unpublished MSc Dissertation: University of London

British Psychological Society (1988a) *The Future of the Psychological Sciences: Horizons and Opportunities for British Psychology.* Leicester: The BPS

British Psychological Society (1988b) Key equal opportunities issues that should be covered in the BPS criteria for evaluating training courses in applied psychology. Report by the working party on the training of psychologists for the SCPEO. *Educational Psychology in Practice*, 5(3)

British Psychological Society (2001) *Promoting Racial Equality Within Educational Psychology Services: A Report From The DECP Working Party On Anti-Racism.* Leicester: BPS

British Psychological Society (2005) *Code of Ethics and Conduct: Draft Consultation Document.* Leicester: BPS

Brown J, Newland A, Anderson P and Chevannes B (1998) Caribbean fatherhood: Under researched, misunderstood. In J Roopnarine and J Brown (eds) *Caribbean Families: Diversity Among Ethnic Groups.* Advances in Applied Developmental Psychology series

Brown R (1995) *Prejudice: Its Social Psychology.* 2nd Edition. Oxford: Blackwell

Bryan B, Dadzie S and Scafe S (1985) *The Heart of the Race.* London: Virago

Bryans T (1988) Educational psychologists working in multicultural communities: An analysis. *Educational and Child Psychology* 5(2), p8-18

Bulhan H (1985) *Frantz Fanon and the Psychology of Oppression.* Boston: Boston University Press

Burnham J Alvis Palma D and Whitehouse L (2008) Learning as a context for differences and differences as a context for learning. *Journal of Family Therapy,* 30 p529-542

Butcher J and Pope K (1993) Seven issues in conditioning forensic assessment: Ethical responsibility in light of new standards and new tests. *Ethics and Behaviour*, 3 p267-288

Butt J and Mirza K (1996) *Social Care and Black Communities: A review of recent research studies*. London: HMSO

Byfield C (2008) *Black boys can make it – how they overcome the obstacles to university in the UK and USA*. Stoke on Trent: Trentham

Bygott D (1992) *Black and British*. Oxford:Oxford University Press

Canter L and Canter M (1992) *Assertive discipline*. USA: Lee Canter Associates

Carroll H and Leyden G (1988) Training EPs for working in Multicultural Communities: What are the training courses in England and Wales doing? *Educational and Child Psychology*. 5(2)

Carpenter B (1997) *Families in context. Emerging trends in family suport and early intervention*. London: David Fulton

Carter R (1995) *The Process of Racial Identity Development*. London: Wiley

Carter B and McGoldrick M (1999) *The Expanded Family Life Cycle: Individual, Family, and Social Perspectives*. Minneapolis: National Council on Family Relations

Cassara B (1991) *Adult Education in a Multicultural Society*. London: Routledge

Channer Y (1995) *I am a promise: the school achievement of British African-Caribbeans*. Stoke on Trent: Trentham

Charmaz K (1995) Grounded theory. In J Smith, R Harre, L van Langenhove (eds) *Rethinking methods in psychology*. London: Sage

Chau R and Yu S (2001) Social exclusion of Chinese people in Britain. *Critical Social Policy*, 21 p103-125

Chen Y (2007) Equality and inequality of oportunity in education: Chinese emergent bilingual children in the English mainstream classroom. *Language, Culture and Curriculum* 20(1) p36-51

Cheung Y H (1986) *Chinese Community in Lambeth*. London: CCRL

Cheetham J (1972) *Social Work with Immigrants*. London: Routledge

Chevannes B (2001) *Learning to be a Man: Culture, socialisation and gender identity in five Caribbean communities*. Mona: The University of West Indies Press

Child Support Act (1991) London: HMSO

Chisholm B, Kearney D, Knight H, Little H, Morris S and Tweddle D (1986) *Preventive Aproaches to Disruption (PAD)*. London: Macmillan Education

Chomsky N (1967) A Review of B. F. Skinner's Verbal Behavior. In Leon A. Jakobovits and Murray S. Miron (eds) *Readings in the Psychology of Language*. Prentice-Hall, p142-143

Chomsky N (1971) The Case Against B.F.Skinner http://www.chomsky.info/articles/19711230.htm (accessed 01.06.09)

Cline T (1987) The practice of educational psychology in a multi-racial society. *Input, Journal of the Hampshire Educational Psychology Service*, 1-3. Winchester: Hampshire Education Department

Cline T (1993) Educational assessments of bilingual pupils: Getting the context right. *Educational and Child Psychology*, 10(4), p59-69

Cline T, Abreu G, Fihosy C, Gray H, Lambert H and Neale J (2002) *Minority Ethnic children in mainly white schools*. London: HMSO

Cline T and Lunt I (1990) Meeting equal opportunities criteria: a review of progress in educational psychology training. In 'Training for Professional Practice', *Educational and Child Psychology*, 7, p3

Cline T and Shamsi T (1999) *The Assessment of Learning Difficulties in Literacy among children learning English as an Additional Language*. London: HMSO

REFERENCES

Coard B (1971) *How the West Indian Child is made Educationally Subnormal in the British School System*. London: New Beacon Books

Collins P (2006) A telling difference: dominance, strength and black masculinities. In A D Mutua (ed) *Progressive Black Masculinities*. London: Routledge

Colt G (2006) *November of the Soul: the enigma of suicide*. London: Simon and Schuster

Commission for Equality and Human Rights Be Inspired. Online publication http://83.137.212.42/sitearchive/eoc/PDF/pns_be_inspired.pdf (accessed 3.6.09)

Commission on Status of Women (CSW) (2001) *Racism, class and masculinity: the global dimensions of gender-based violence*. INSTRAW and UNICEF http://www.eurowrc.org/13.institutions/5.un/un-en/16.un_en.htm (accessed 13.7.09)

Conference of Congolese Community Organizations Report (2006)

Conference of Congolese Churches Report (2006)

Connelly N (1989) *Race and Change in Social Services Departments*. London: Policy Studies Institute

Connolly P (1995) Boys will be boys? Racism, sexuality and the construction of masculine identities among infant children. In M Blair and J Holland (eds) *Equality and difference: debates and issues in feminist research and pedagogy*. Clevedon: Multilingual Matters

Cooley C (1902) *Human Nature and the Social Order*. New York: Scribner's

Coomaraswamy R (2001) [http://www.unhchr.ch/html/menu2/7/b/mwom.htm] http://www.un-instraw.org/en/special-collections/violence-against-women/racism-class-and-masculinity/view.html

Cooper M (2001) Existential Therapy. *Counselling Psychology Journal*. Dec. p34-36

Cooper S (1973) A look at racism in clinical work. *Social Casework*, 54, p76-84

Corbett C and Perepa P (2007) *Missing Out? Autism, Education and Ethnicity: The reality for parents today*. London: National Autistic Society

Council of National Psychological Associations for the Advancement of Ethnic Minority Interests (2003) *Psychological Treatment of Ethnic minority populations* p13-23. Washington: Association of Black Psychologists http://www.apa.org/pi/oema/programs/empa_ptemp.pdf

Cowden S and Singh, G (2007) The User: Friend, Foe or Fetish? A critical exploration of user involvement in Health and Social Care. *Critical Social policy.* 27(5) p5-22

Crais C and Scully P (2008) *Sara Baartman and The Hottentot Venus: A Ghost Story and a Biography*. New Jersey: Princeton University Press

Crawford M, Rutter D, Manley C, Weaver T, Bhui K., Tyrer P (2001) Systematic Review of involving patients in the planning and development of Health Care. *British Medical Journal. (BMJ)* 325 p1263-1265

Crozier G and Davies J (2007) Hard to reach parents or hard to reach schools? A discussion of home-school relations, with particular reference to Pakistani and Bangladeshi parents. *British Educational Research Journal* 33(3) p295-313

Curtis G (1963) Violence breeds violence – perhaps? *American Journal of Psychiatry*, 120, 386

Dadzie S (1993) *Older and Wiser. Participation in education by older black adults*. Leicester: National Institute of Adult Continuing Education

Dagitcibasi C (2007) *Family, Self, Human Development across Cultures: theory and applications*. London: Lawrence Erlbaum

Dale N (1996) *Working with families of children with special needs: Partnership and Practice*. London: Routledge

Davenhill R, Hunt H, Pillary H and Harris A (1989) Training and selection issues in clinical psychology for black and minority ethnic groups. *Clinical Psychology Forum*. Leicester: BPS

Dawson G and Osterling J (1997) Early Intervention in Autism. Chapter 14. In M Guralnick (ed) *The Effectiveness of Early Intervention*. Baltimore: Brookes

Deaton A. and Lukotsky D (2004) *Mortality, Inequality and Race in American Cities*. Michigan: University of Michigan

Deci E (1975) *Intrinsic motivation*. New York: Plenum

Deci E and Ryan R (1991) A motivational approach to self: Integration in personality. In R Dienstbier (ed), *Nebraska symposium on motivation: Vol. 38. Perspectives on motivation* (p.237-288). Lincoln: University of Nebraska Press

Deci E and Ryan R (1995) Human autonomy: The basis for true self-esteem. In M. Kernis (ed) *Efficacy, agency, and self-esteem* (p31-49). New York: Plenum

Denscombe M (2007) Critical incidents and learning about risk: the case of young people and their health. In M Hammersley (ed) *Educational research and evidence-based practice*. London: Sage

DCSF (Department of Children, Schools and Families) (2005) *Every Child Matters: Change for Children*. London: Stationery Office

DCSF (Department for Children, Schools and Families) (2007a) *Learning and teaching for bilingual children in the primary years*. London: Stationery Office

DCSF (Department for Children, Schools and Families) (2007b) *Safe to Learn: embedding anti-bullying work in schools*. London: Stationery Office

DES (Department for Education and Science) (1975) *A language for life*. Report of the Committee of Enquiry apointed by the Secretary of State for Education and Science under the Chairmanship of Sir Alan Bullock FBA. London: HMSO

DfES (Department for Education and Skills) (2004) *National Curriculum Assessment, GCSE and Equivalent Attainment and Post-16 Attainment by Pupil Characteristics in England 2004*. London: HMSO

DfES (Department of Children, Schools and Families) (2005) *Raising the Achievement of Bilingual Learners in Primary Schools. Interim Report, April 2005*. London: National Foundation for Educational Research

DfES (Department for Education and Skills) (2006) *Excellence and Enjoyment: Learning and teaching for bilingual teachers in the early years*. London: Stationery Office

Department of Health (2004) *National Standards, Local Action. Health and Social Care Standards and Planning Framework*. London: Stationery Office

Department of Health (2009) *Health Inequalities in Britain*. London: Stationery Office

Dobson D and Dobson K (2009) *Evidence based practice of cognitive behaviour therapy*. London: Guilford Press

Docker-Drysdale B (1968) *Therapy in Child care*. London: Longman

Downes P (1997) Crisis Time for Boys? *The Parenting Forum Newsletter*. No. 8 p3 London: National Children's Bureau Enterprises

Du Bois W E B (1903) *The Souls of Black People*. US: Courier Dover

Dutt R (1998) The best for black users. *Community Care* 30/4/98-6/5/98

Elder J, Valcante G, Won D, Zylis R (2003) Effects of in-home training for culturally diverse fathers of children with autism. *Issues in Mental Health Nursing*. 24(3) p273-95

Elias P, Jones P and McWhinnie S (2006) *Representation of Ethnic Groups in Chemistry and Physics: a Report Prepared for the Royal Society of Chemistry and the Institute of Physics*. London: Royal Society of Chemistry/Institute of Physics

Else D, Newton A, Williams J, Fitzpatrick M and Roddis M (1999) *West Africa*. Singapore: Lonely Planet

REFERENCES

Elton B (1989) *Enquiry into Discipline in Schools*. London: HMSO

Erikson E (1950) *Childhood and Society*. US:Triad

Evans H (1998) *Gender and Achievement in Secondary Education in Jamaica*. Kingston: Planning Institute of Jamaica

Eysenck, H (1971) *Race, Intelligence and Education*. London: Temple-Smith

Fanon F (1967) *A dying colonialism*. NY: Grove

Fell P (2004) Overcoming barriers to successful suport: an examination of issues for teachers and suport workers. In Gray P (ed) *Working with emotions: Responding to the challenge of pupil difficult behaviour in school*. NetLibrary, Inc. Routledge

Feltzer M and Hood R (2004) *Differences or Discrimination. Report for the Youth Justice Board*. London: Youth Justice Board

Festinger L (1956) *A theory of cognitive dissonance*. Peterson: Evanston III Row

Figueroa M (1996) Male Privileging and Male Academic Performance in Jamaica. Paper presented at symposium on the Construction of Caribbean masculinity. St Augustine: Centre for Gender and Development Studies, University of West Indies

Finch J and Mason J, (1993) *Negotiating Family Responsibilities*. London: Routledge

Finn S, and Camphuis J (1995) What a clinician should know about base rates in J Butcher (ed) *Clinical Personality assessment* p229-235 NY: Oxford University Press

Franklin A (1984) Contemporary psychological in a multicultural society. *Educational and Child Psychology*. 1(1), p2-8

Freire P (1972) *Pedagogy of the Oppressed*. Harmondsworth: Penguin

Freud S (1915) *Instincts and Their Vicissitudes – Collected Papers IV*. London: Hogarth Press

Freud S (1916) *Introductory Lectures on Psycho-Analysis*. Standard Edition 15 & 16 London: Hogarth Press

Freud S (1920) *Beyond the pleasure principle*. Standard Edition. London: Hogarth Press

Frisby K (1998) Culture and cultural differences. In J Sanderwell, K Frisby, I Ramos and J Schwuneman (eds) *Test Interpretation and Diversity: Achieving Equity in Assessment*. Washington: American Psychological Society

Fryer P (1993) *Aspects of British black history*. London: Index

Fryer P (1984) *Staying power: The history of black people in Britain*. London: Pluto Press

Galvin P, Mercer S and Costa P (1990) *Building a Better Behaved School: A Development Manual for Primary Schools*. Harlow: Longman

Garcia-Moreno C, Jansen H, Ellsberg Heise L and Watts C (2006) Prevalence of intimate partner violence: findings from the WHO multi-country study on women's health and domestic violence. *The Lancet*, 368(9543), p1260-1269

Garner, R (2007) Chinese pupils eclipse all other ethnic groups in English tests. *The Independent on Sunday* 16.2.07

George R and Cristiani T (1990) *Counselling, Theory and Practice*. Englewood Cliffs: Prentice-Hall

German M (2008) Educational Psychology promoting the emotional well-being and resilience of refugee parents. *Educational and Child Psychology*. 25(2), p91-103

Gillborn D (1990) *'Race', Ethnicity & Education: Teaching and Learning in Multi-Ethnic schools*. London: Unwin

Gillborn D and Gipps C (1996) *Recent Research on the Achievement of Ethnic Minority Pupils*. London: Ofsted

Giroux H (2006) *America on the Edge: Henry Giroux on politics, culture and education*. New York: Palgrave Macmillan

Gilovich T, Keltner D and Nesbitt R (2006) *Social Psychology*. London:WW Norton.

Goldson B and Muncie J (2006a) Rethinking Youth Justice: comparative analysis, international human rights and research evidence. *Youth Justice* 6(2) p91-106

Goldson B and Muncie J (2006b) *Youth Crime and Justice: critical issues.* London: Sage

Gondola D (2002) *The history of the Congo.* UK: Greenwood Publications

Gordon P (1983) *White Law: Racism in the police courts and prisons.* London: Pluto Press

Gordon P (1996) Black People and the criminal law: rhetoric and reality. In P Braham, A Rattansi, and R Skellington. *Racism and antiracism.* London: Sage

Gordon R (1980) Research on IQ, Race, and Delinquency: Taboo or not Taboo? In R Edward and G Sagin (eds) *Taboos in Criminology.* NY: NCJRS Publications

Göktürk D Turkish delight-German fright: migrant identities in transnational cinema: http://www.transcomm.ox.ac.uk/working%20papers/mediated.pdf (20.04.09)

Gray D (1993) Negotiating Autism: Relations between Parents and Treatment Staff. *Social Science and Medicine.* 36, p1037-1046

Gray-Little B (1995) The assessment of psychopathology in racial and ethnic minorities in J Butcher *Clinical Personality assessment.* NY:OUP

Gray-Little B and Kaplan D. (1998). Interpretation of psychological tests in clinical and forensic evaluations. In J Sanderwell, K Frisby, I Ramos and J Schwuneman (eds). *Test Interpretation and Diversity: Achieving Equity in Assessment.* Washington: American Psychological Society

Greig A (2001) Racism, class and masculinity: the global dimensions of gender-based violence: towards a politics of masculinity. http://www.eurowrc.org/13.institutions/5.un/un-en/16.un_en.htm

Grier W and Cobbs P (1968) *Black Rage.* New York: Basic Books

Griffin C (2002) Discourses of Crisis and Loss: Analyzing the boys' underachievement. Debate in the *Journal of Youth Studies,* 3(2), p167-188

Griffiths E (1994) *Racial and Ethnic Identity: Psychological Development and Creative Expression.* London: Karnac

Griswold R (1997) Generative fathering: A historical perspective. In A Hawkins and D Dollahite, *Generative Fathering: Beyond Deficit Perspectives.* California: Sage

Guishard J (1983) Black self concept is a negative self concept: A re-examination of the black child in Britain. Unpublished Dissertation. University of Hull

Guishard J (1992) People who live in Posh houses....*Educational and Child Psychology Special Issue: Educational Psychologists working with Social Services.* 9(3) p42-47

Guishard J (1998) The Parent Suport Service: Brief Family work with parents and adolescents in school. *Educational Psychology in Practice.* 14(2) p135-139

Guishard-Pine J (2000) Promoting Inclusion in Further Education Colleges: Staff Consultation Groups. *Educational Psychology in Practice,* 16 p205-212

Guishard-Pine J (2002) Beyond Father Absence: An investigation into black fathering in Britain. Unpublished PhD thesis. University of London

Guishard-Pine J (2005) How to prevent racism from destroying the minds of Black Children. *Nex Generation, Family and Community* p14-15

Guishard-Pine J (2006a) MEN IN BLACK families: The impact of fathering on children's development. *Race Equality Teaching* 24(2) Spring 2006

Guishard-Pine J (2006b) Can Humanistic and Existential therapy help the psychological problems of adolescents in the National Health Service? *Journal of Critical and Counselling Psychology.* 6(1), p48-55

REFERENCES

Guishard-Pine J (2006c). Daddy Can You Spare Me Some Time? Fathering; Family Breakdown And Delinquency In Black Youth: Are They Linked?. Home Office Briefing Paper. www.publications.parliament.uk/pa/cm200607/cmselect/cmhaff/181/18106.htm (accessed 2.6.09)

Guishard-Pine J, Hamilton L and McCall S (2007) *Understanding Looked After Children: An Introduction to Psychology for Foster Care*. London: Jessica Kingsley

Guthrie R (1976) *Even the rat was white: A historical view of psychology*. New York: Harper and Row

Gutmann M (2001) *Racism, Class and Masculinity: Gender-based violence in Latin America*. http://www.eurowrc.org/13.institutions/5.un/un-en/16.un_en.htm (last accessed 13.7.09)

Haas J, Lee L, Kaplan C, Sonneborn D, Phillips K, and Liang S (2003) The Association of Race, Socioeconomic Status and the Health Insurance Status with the Prevalence of Overweight Among Children and Adolescents. In *American Medical Journal of Public Health*, 12(2) p105-109

Hagan T and Smail D (1997) Power mapping: I. background and basic methodology. *Journal of Community and Aplied Social Psychology*. 7 p257-268

Hall D (1995) *Assessing the Needs of Bilingual Pupils (Living in Two Languages)*. London: David Fulton

Hanko G (1987) Group consultation with mainstream teachers' *Educational and Child Psychology*, 1987 4(3&4), p123-130

Hanko G (1990) *Special needs in ordinary classrooms: suporting teachers*. Oxford: Basil Blackwell

Hannah C and Guishard J (2001) *The Community Psychotherapy Project*. Dunstable: Bedfordshire and Luton Child and Adolescent Mental Health Service Academic Unit

Harris D (1963) *Children's Drawings as Measures of Intellectual Maturity*. New York: Harcourt, Brace & World, Inc

Harris M (2001) Racial and Ethnic Differences in Healthcare Access and Health Outcomes in Adults with Type 2 Diabetes. *Mar24*(3), p456-9

Harrison M (1987) Social construction of Mary Beth Whitehead. *Gender and Society* 1 p300-311

Harrison S, Dowsell G and Milewa T (2002) Public and User involvement in the NHS. *Health and Social Care In the Community*. 10(2) p63-66

Hart R (1980) *Slaves Who Abolished Slavery, Volume 1: Blacks in Bondage*. Mona: University of West Indies Press

Hatchschild J L and Scovronick N (2004) *The American Dream and the Public Schools*. US: Oxford University Press

Hawkins D (1987) Devalued lives and racial stereotypes: Ideological barriers to the prevention of family violence among blacks. p189-205 In R Hampton (ed) *Violence in the black family*. Lexington, Mass: Lexington

Hawkins A and Dollahite D (1997) Beyond the role-inadequacy perspective of fathering. In A Hawkins and D Dollahite. *Generative Fathering: Beyond Deficit Perspectives*. California: Sage

Hayles Jr. V (1991) African-American Strengths: A Survey of Empirical Findings. In R Jones (ed) *Black Psychology*. California: Cobb and Henry

Hayward R, Kaufman M, Lang J and Prewitt G. *ICD-9-CM: International Classification of Diseases, 9th revision; Clinical Modification, 6th edition, 2006 / Practice Management Information Corporation (PMIC)*. Published Los Angeles, CA : PMIC, C2005. Online Edition. <http://icd9cm.chrisendres.com/>

Hayward M (2005) Clinical Psychology and service user involvement: Our business? *Clinical Psychology*, 37, p15-18

Hayward R (2001) Working with men to end gender based violence http://www.europrofem.org/contri/2_04_en/en-viol/87en_vio.htm (accessed 20.7.09)

Health Care Commission (2006) *Race Equality Scheme*. London: Commission for Health Care Audit and inspection

Heider F (1958) *The Social Psychology of Interpersonal Relationships*. Kansas: University of Kansas

Heilbrun K, Goldstein N and Redding R (2005) *Juvenile Delinquency: prevention, assessment and intervention*.US: Oxford University Press

Henwood K L (1994) Resisting racism and sexism in academic psychology: A personal/political view. *Feminism and Psychology*. 4 p41-62

Hickman L and Alexander T (eds) (1998) *The Essential Dewey: Volumes 1 and 2*. Indiana:Indiana University Press

Hiliard A (1985) Introduction. In *The Stolen Legacy*. San Francisco: Julian Richardson

Hiliard A (1994) What good is this thing called intelligence and why bother to measure it? *Journal of Black Psychology*. 20(4), p430-444

Hiskey M (1966) *The Hiskey-Nebraska Test of Learning Aptitude in Hearing-Impaired Samples*. (H-NTLA)

Home Office (2004) *Race and the Criminal Justice System: An overview to the complete statistics 2002-2003*. London: HMSO

Home Office (2007) *Young Black People and the Criminal Justice System: 2nd Report*. London: HMSO

hooks b (2003) *Teaching Community. A pedagogy of hope*. New York: Routledge

Hopkin D (2005) Why I....think the history national curriculum would benefit from a little more colour. *The Times Higher Education*: 24.06.05. http://www.timeshighereducation.co.uk/story.asp?storyCode=196926&sectioncode=26 (accessed 04.06.09)

Horsford B (1986) Psychology, Education and Race: a black perspective. *Psychology News*. 9(3)

Howitt D and Owusu-Bempah J (1994) *The Racism of Psychology: Time for a change*. Hemel Hempstead: Harvester and Wheatfield

Hunt T (2006) Slavery: The long road to our historic 'sorrow'. *The Observer*: 26.11.06. http://www.guardian.co.uk/politics/2006/nov/26/race.immigrationpolicy2 (accessed 3/6/09)

Inner London Education Authority (1985) *Education for all?* (The Fish Report). London: ILEA

Institute of Race Relations (IRR), (2005). *Creating Criminals*. IRR website. http://www.irr.org.uk/2002/november/ak000004.html (accessed 2.6.09)

Jackson E (2008) The development of work discussion groups in educational settings. *Journal of Child Psychotherapy*, 34(1) p62-82

Jackson G (1982) Black Psychology: an avenue to the study of Afro-Americans. *Journal of Black Studies*. 12(3) p241-260

Jenkins A (1982) *The psychology of the Afro-American: A humanistic approach*. Oxford: Pergamon Press

Jenkins R (2008) *Social Identity*. London: Routledge

Jennett M (2004a) *Stand up for us: challenging homophobia in schools*. London: Health Development Agency

Jennett M (2004b) (ed) *Out in School*. London: Terrence Higgins Trust

Jensen A (1969) How much can we boost IQ and scholastic achievement? *Harvard Educational Review*, 39 p1-123

Johnson T, Robinson K, Sharon E, Rayale A, Nedondo P, Tovar-Gamero Zoila G (2005) *Measurement and Evaluation in Counselling and Development*. Vol 38,No 2, 92-104

Jordan R (1999) Evaluating practise. *Autism* 3, p411-434

REFERENCES

Jordan R (1999) *Autistic Spectrum Disorders. An introductory Handbook for Practitioners.* London: David Fulton

Joseph Rowntree Foundation (JRF) (2001) *Involving black disabled people in shaping services.* York: JRF

JRF (2003) *Issues raised by users on the future of welfare, rights and suport.* York: JRF

Jung C (1917) Two essays on analytical psychology. In *Vol 7 of The collected works of C G Jung.* NJ: Princeton University Press, 1953 and 1966

Jung C (1936) The archetypes and the collective unconscious. In Vol 9 of *The collected works of C G Jung.* NJ: Princeton University Press, 1959 and 1969

Jung C (1968) *Analytical psychology: its theory and practice.* (The Tavistock Lectures). NY: Pantheon

Kaechele H, Schachter J and Thomae H (2008) *From Psychoanalytic N=1 to Empirical Single Case Narrative Research: Implications for Psychoanalytic Practice.* London: Taylor and Francis

Kamya H (1994) *A study of African immigrants in the USA: Interrelationships of stress and self-esteem.* Boston: Boston University

Kardiner A and Ovesey L (1951) *The Mark of Oppression: A Psychological Study of the American Negro.* New York: W. W. Norton and Co, Inc

Keen S (1990) The Enemy Maker. In C Zweig and J Abrams (eds) *Meeting the shadow: the hidden power of the dark side of human nature.* NY: Madison

Keiser S (1948) *The Psychoanalytic Study of the Child.* London: Hogarth Press

Kelly J (1966) Ecological constraints on mental health services. *American Psychologist*, 21 p535-539

Kilpatrick S, Barratt M and Jones T (2003) *Defining Learning Communities.* CRLRA Discussion Paper d1/2003. Australia: University of Tasmania

Klein M (1957) *Envy and Gratitude.* London: Tavistock

Kolb D (1984) *Experiential learning: Experience as the source of learning and development.* Englewood Cliffs, NJ: Prentice-Hall

Kraenzle C (2009) At Home in New Germany? Local Stories and Global Concerns in Yüksel Yavuv's *Aprilkinder and Kleine Freiheit'The German Quarterly*, 82(1) p90-105

Kumar S (1988) A survey of assessment of ethnic minority pupils. In S Wolfendale, I Lunt and T Carroll (Eds), Educational psychologists working in multicultural communities: Training and Practice. *Educational and Child Psychology,* 5(2) p51-56

Lane C (1998) *The Psychoanalysis of Race.* NY: Columbia University Press

Lang J (2001) Racism, Class and Masculinity: The global dimensions of gender-based violence – An Introductory Statement. http://www.eurowrc.org/13.institutions/5.un/un-en/16.un_en.htm (accessed 13.7.09)

Laubschov L (2005) Towards a (De) constructive Psychology of African American Men. *Journal of Black Psychology.* 31(2) p111-129

Lee C, Oh M, and Mountcastle A (1992) Indigenous models of helping in non-western countries: Implications for multicultural counselling. *Journal of Multicultural Counselling Development.* 20. p3-10

Leicester M (1993) *Race for a Change in Continuing and Higher Education.* Milton Keynes: Open University Press

Leicester M (2008) *Creating an Inclusive School.* London: Continuum

Lesbian, Gay, BiSexual, and Transexual Youth Scotland (2006) *Toolkit for Teachers, Dealing with Homophobia and Homophobic Bullying in Scottish Schools.* http://www.lgbtyouth.org.uk/schools-and-education/toolkit.htm

Lewis C (1986) *Becoming a Father*. Milton Keynes: Open University Press

Lewis D, Balla D, Shanok S (1979) Some evidence of race bias in the diagnosis and treatment of the juvenile offender. *American Journal of Orthopsychiatry.* 49(1) p53-61

Lindsay G, Pather S and Strand S (2006) *Special Educational Needs and Ethnicity: Issues of Over-Representation and Under-Representation.* University of Warwick

Lisak D Hoper J and Song P (1996) Factors in the cycle of violence: gender rigidity and emotional constriction. *Journal of Traumatic stress*, 9, p721-743

Lopez S (1989) Patient variable biases in clinical judgement: conc'l overview and methodological considerations. *Psychological Bulletin* 106 p184-203

Lopez S and Hernandez P (1986) How culture is considered in evaluation s of psychopathology. *Journal of Nervous and Mental Disesase* 176 p598-606

Loring M and Powell B (1988) Gender, race and DSM-III: A study of the objectivity of psychiatric diagnostic behaviour. *Journal of Health and Social Behaviour* 29 p1-22

Louvinger J (1976) *Ego Development: conceptions and theories.* San Francisco: Jossay-Bass

Lowe F (2007) Colonial Object Relations; Going underground black-white relationships: A Discussion paper. *British Journal of Psychotherapy*, 24(1), p20-33

Luft J and Ingham H (1955) The Johari window, a graphic model of interpersonal awareness. *Proceedings of the western training laboratory in group development.* Los Angeles: UCLA

Lunt, I (1993) EPs in multicultural communities: report from study day. *Educational and Child Psychology.* 5(2), p43-50

Lyndon D (2003) Teaching Black and Asian History in Schools. *History Teachers' Discussion Forum.* http://www.schoolhistory.co.uk/forum/index.php?showtopic=1518 (accessed 04.06.09)

Lyndon, D (2006) Integrating black British history into the national curriculum. *Teaching history*, 122, p3-19

Mabey C (1981) Black British Literacy. *Educational Research.* 23 p83-95

Machin S and Vignoles A (2005) *What's the good of Education: The Economics of Education in the UK.* New Jersey: Princeton University Press

Mac an Ghaill M (1994) *The Making of Men, Masculinities, Sexualities and Schooling.* Buckingham: Open University Press

Mac Innes J (2004) The Sociology of Identity: Social Science or Social Comment? *The British Journal of Sociology.* 55, p541-543

Macpherson W (1999) *The Stephen Lawrence Inquiry (Macpherson Report).* London: Stationery Office

Madhubuti, H (1990) *Black Men: Obsolete, Single and Dangerous? The Afrikan American Family in Transition. Essays in Discovery, Solution and Hope.* Chicago: Thirdworld Press

Magana S, and Smith M (2006) Psychological distress and well-being of Latina and non-Latina White mothers of youth and adults with an autism spectrum disorder: cultural attitudes towards coresidence status. *American Journal of Orthopsychiatry.* 76(3) p346-57

Majors R and Billson J (1992) *Cool Pose: The Dilemmas of Black Manhood in America.* New York: Lexington Books

Malik R and Krause I (2005) Before and beyond words:embodiment and intercultural therapeutic relationships in family therapy. In: C Flaskas, B Mason, and A Perlesz, (eds)*The Space Between: experience, context and process in the therapeutic relationship.* London: Karnac

Mama A (1995) *Beyond the Masks: Race Gender and Subjectivity.* London: Routledge

Mandell D, Wiggins L, Carpenter L, Daniels J, DiGuisepi C, Durkin M, Giarelli E, Morrier M, Nicholas J, Pinto-Martin J, Shattuck P, Thomas K, Yeargin-Allsop M and Kirby R (2009) Racial/

REFERENCES

ethnic disparities in the identification of children with autism spectrum disorders. *American Journal of Public Health*. 99(3) p493-498

Marcia J (1966) Development and Validation of Ego- Identity status. *Journal of Personality and Social Psychology*. 3(5), p551-553

Markus H R and Kittayama S (1991) Culture and Self: Implications for cognition, emotion and motivation. *Psychological Review* 98 p224-253

Martin E and Martin J (1978) *The Black Extended Family*. Chicago: Chicago University Press

Maturana H R and Varela F J (1992) An aspect of 'Autopoeisis' p47 In H Maturana and F Varela *The Tree of Knowledge. The Biological Roots of Human Understanding*. London: Shambhala Publications Inc.

Maximé J (1993) The Therapeutic Importance of Racial Identity Work with Black Children who Hate. In V Varma (ed) *How and why Children Hate*. London: Jessica Kingsley

May L (1998) *Masculinity and Morality*. New York: Cornell University Press

McClain L C (2005) Bend it Like Beckham and Real Women Have Curves: Constructing Identity in Multicultural Coming-of-Age Stories. *DePaul Law Review*, vol. 54, p701-753

McDermott J (ed) *The Philosophy of John Dewey*. Chicago: University of Chicago Press

McGoldrick M, Giordana J and Pearce J (eds) (1996) *Ethnicity and Family therapy* 2nd Edition. New York: Guilford Press

McGonigal J (2007) Learning to Read a New Culture: how immigrant and Asylum seeking children experience Scottish Identity through Classroom Tasks. The Scottish Executive

McIntyre K (1993) Pastoral care, The Educational Reform Act and vulnerability of black pupils. *Educational and Child Psychology*. 10(3), p39-42

Mckenzie-Mavinga I (2009) *Black Issues in the Therapeutic Process*. London: Palgrave Macmillan

McManus D (2001) The Two Paradigms of Education and the Peer Review of Teaching. *The NAGT Journal of Geoscience Education*. 49(6) p423-434

Mead G (1934) *Mind, Self, and Society*. Chicago: The University of Chicago Press

Menzies-Lyth I (ed) (1959) The functioning of social systems as a defence against anxiety, In I Menzies-Lyth I (1988) *Containing anxiety in institutions*. London: Free Association Press

M'gadzah S and Gibbs S (1999) Challenging Racism and Inequality in Education and Child Psychology. *Educational and Child Psychology*. 16(3)

Milewa T, Dowsell G and Harrison S (2003) *Partnerships, Power and the new politics of Community Participation in British Health care*. London: Blackwell

Miller C (1986) *Blank Darkness: Africanist discourses in French*. Chicago: University of Chicago Press

Milligan C and Dowie A (1998) What do Children Need from their Fathers? Centre for Theology and Public Issues, University of Edinburgh. *Occasional Paper*. No. 42

Minsky R (1998) *Psychoanalysis and Culture*. New Jersey: Rutgers University Press

Mirza H (1992) *Young, Female and Black*. London: Routledge

Mirza H (1997) *Black British Feminism: a reader*. London: Routledge

Monte C (1995) *Beneath the Masks: An Introduction to theories of personality*. 5th edition. Texas: Harcourt Brace

Morgan S, Lye D and Condran G (1988) Sons, daughters and the risk of marital disruption. *American Journal of Sociology*. 94 p110-129

Morrier M J, Hess K L and Heflin L J (2008) Ethnic disproportionality in students with autism spectrum disorders. *Multicultural Education*, Sept, p31-38

Mosley J (1996) *Quality Circle Time in the primary classroom*. Cambridgeshire: LDA

Moynihan D (1965) *The Negro Family: the case for national action.* Washington DC: Department of Labor, Office of Policy, Planning and Research

Murphy R (2001) *British Cinema of the 90s,* London: British Film Industry

Murrell P C (2002) *African Centered Pedagogy: developing schools of achievement for African-American children.* Albany: State University of New York Press

Musgrove F (1971) *Patterns of Power and Authority in English Education.* London: Methuen

Mutua A D (2006a) Introduction: mapping the contours of progressive masculinities. In A D Mutua (ed) *Progressive Black Masculinities.* London: Routledge

Mutua A D (2006b) Theorising progressive black masculinities. In A D Mutua (ed) *Progressive Black Masculinities.* London: Routledge

Myers L (1991) Expanding the psychology of knowledge optimally: the importance of world view revisited. In R Jones (ed) *Black Psychology.* 3rd edition. CA: Cobb and Henry

Myers L, Young A, Obasi E and Speight S (2003) Recommendations for the psychological treatment of persons of African descent. In Council of National Psychological Associations for the Advancement of Ethnic Minority Interests. Washington DC: Association of Black Psychologists

Neenan M and Dryden W (2002) *Life Coaching: A cognitive behavioural aproach.* London: Brunner-Routledge

Ng K (1992) Chinese Parents' Perception of Special Educational Needs. Unpublished MSc thesis, University of Sheffield

Nobles W (1973) Psychological research and the black self-concept: A critical review. *Journal of Social Issues,* 29, p111-131

No Outsiders Project team (2010) *Undoing Homophobia in Primary Schools.* Stoke on Trent: Trentham Books

Nsamenang A B (1987) A West African Perspective. In M E Lamb (ed) In *The Father's Role: Cross-Cultural Perspectives.* New Jersey: Lawrence Erlbaum Associates

Nursing and Midwifery Council Circular (07/2007 Annexe 2) *Introduction of Essential Skills Clusters for Pre-registration Nursing Programmes.* London, www.nmc-uk.org

Nwadiora E (1996) Nigerian Families. In M McGoldrick, J Pearce and M Giordano (eds) *Ethnicity and family therapy.* New York: Guilford Press

Nzegwu F (1993) Outpatient care and consumer's response. In Nzegwu, F *Black People and Health Care in Contemporary Britain.* Reading, Berks: The International Institute for Black Research

Obama B (2006) *The Audacity of Hope: Thoughts on Reclaiming the American Dream.* Crown Publishing Group/Three Rivers Press

Office of National Statistics. http://www.statistics.gov.uk/cci/nugget.asp?id=455 (accessed 3.6.09)

Office for Standards in Education (Ofsted) (1996) *Exclusions from Secondary Schools 1995/6.* London: HMSO

Ofsted (2002) *Achievement of Black Caribbean Pupils: Three Successful Primary Schools.* London: Stationery Office

Ofsted (2004) *Achievement of Bangladeshi Heritage Pupils.* HMI 513. London: Stationery Office

Ofsted (2006) *Inclusion: Does it matter where children are taught?* London: Stationery Office

O'Hagan K (1999) Culture, Cultural Identity, and Cultural Sensitivity in Child and Family Social Work. *Child and Family Social Work.* 4, p269-281

O'Neale V (2000) *Excellence not excuses: Inspection of Services for Ethnic Minority children and families.* (DH) London: HMSO

Ohri A, Manning B and Curno P (eds) (1982) Community Work and Racism. *Community Work,* 7, London: Routledge and Kegan Paul

REFERENCES

Olivier P and Yocom J (2002) Race and disparities in Criminal Justice: Maddison and Dane county in Context. *The Institute for Research on Poverty discussion* Paper No 125, p7-20

Orford J (1992) *Community psychology: theory and practice*. Chichester, UK: John Wiley and Sons, Ltd

Orford J (2008) *Community psychology: challenges, controversies and emerging consensus*. Chichester, UK: John Wiley and Sons, Ltd

Osler A and Hill J (1999) Exclusions from school and racial equality: an examination of government proposals in the light of recent research. *Cambridge Journal of Education* 29(1) p33-62

Osler A, Watling R and Busher H (2000) *Reasons for Exclusion from School. Research Report 244*. London: Department for Education And Employment (DfEE)

Pace J and Hemmings A (2006) *Classroom Authority: theory, research and practice*. London: Routledge

Pantzer K, Rajmil L, Tebec Codina F, Serra-Sutton V, Ferre M, Reeves-Sieberer, U, Simaoni M and Alfonso J (2000) Health Related quality of Life in Immigrants and Native Children. *Journal of Epidemiology and Community Health*. 60, p694-698

Papadopoulos R (1999) Working with Bosnian Medical Evacuees and their Families. *Journal of Clinical Child Psychology and Psychiatry*, 4(1), p107-120

Park J (1996) Fathers and sons. *The Parenting Forum Newsletter*. No.4, p4, London: National Children's Bureau Enterprises

Parker D (1998) Emerging British Chinese identities: issues and problems. In E Sinn (ed) *The Last Half Century of Chinese Overseas*. Hong Kong University Press

Parker D (2000) The Chinese takeaway and the diasporic habitus: space, time and power geometrics. In B Hesse (ed) *Unsettled Multiculturalisms*. London: Zed Books

Parry O (1996) In One Ear and Out the Other: Unmasking Masculinities in the Caribbean Classroom. *Sociological Research Online*. 1(2) www.socresonline.org.uk/1/2/2.html

Pavkov T, Lewis D and Lyons J (1989) Psychiatric diagnoses and racial bias: An empirical investigation. *Professional Psychologist: Research and Practice* 20 p364-368

Phoenix A (1987) Theories of gender and black families. In G Weiner and M Arnot (eds) *Gender under Scrutiny: new enquiries in education*. London: Unwin

Piaget J (1923) *The Language and Thought of the child*. Paris: Delachaux et Niestlé.

Price R (1990) The Somali Community in Tower Hamlets. Report to the Race Equality Council

Price R (2006) Needs Analysis of the Congolese Pupils in School. Report to the educational Psychology Service in Camden

Price R (2008) Somali Mothers' Group Report to the Somali Conference in Sheffield

Prince M and Salih, S (1831) *The history of Mary Prince: A West Indian Slave*. London: Penguin

Qureshi T, Berridge D, and Wenman H (2000) *Where to turn? Family support for South Asian communities: a case study*. National Children's Bureau and Joseph Rowntree Foundation

QCA (online) *National Curriculum*. http://curriculum.qca.org.uk/key-stages-3-and-4/aims/index.aspx (accessed 13.07.09)

QCA website http://www.qca.org.uk/history/innovating/history_matters/worked_for_me/ks3/cameo9.htm (accessed 04.06.09)

QCA website http://curriculum.qca.org.uk/key-stages-3-and-4/curriculum-in-action/casestudies library/case-studies/History_matters.aspx?return=/key-stages-3-and-4/subjects/history/index.aspx (04.06.09)

Race Relations (Amendment) Act 2000. London: HMSO

Rampton A (1981) *West Indian children in our schools. Interim report of the Committee of Inquiry into the education of children from ethnic minority groups.* London: HMSO

Raven J (1936) Mental tests used in genetic studies: The performance of related individuals on tests mainly educative and mainly reproductive. Unpublished MSc Thesis. University of London

Reed T (1999) The millenium objective: give our minority communities a good deal by eliminating white yardsticks and institutional racism. *Educational and Child Psychology.* 16(3) p89-100

Reicher S (1999) Differences, self-image and the individual. *The Psychologist.* 12(3), p131-133

Renvoize J (1978) *Web of violence.* London: Routledge

Reynolds T (2006) *Caribbean mothers in the UK: Identity and experience in the UK.* London: Tufnell Press

Rhamie J (2007) *Eagles who soar: how Black learners find the path to success.* Stoke on Trent: Trentham

Richardson, B (ed) (2005) *Tell it like it is: How our schools fail Black children.* London: Bookmarks

Roffe M, Wenban-Smith, J and Guishard J (1990) *Psychology in Residential Care.* City of Birmingham Psychological Service

Rogers C (1951) *Client-centered Therapy: Its current practice, implications and theory.* Boston: Houghton Mifflin

Roopnarine J (2002) Father involvement in English-speaking Caribbean Families. In C Tamis-Lemonda and N Cabrera (eds) *Handbook of father involvement: Multidisciplinary perspectives.* New Jersey: Lawrence Erlbaum Associates

Roper S (1987) Foreword. in Commission for Racial Equality (1988) *The Needs of the Chinese Community in Scotland and the North East of England.* London: CRE piii

Rosenfeld H (1971) A Clinical Approach to the Psychoanalytic Theory of the Life and Death Instincts: An Investigation Into the Aggressive Aspects of Narcissism. *International Journal of Psycho-Analysis.* 52 p169-179

Rosenfeld S (1984) Race difference in involuntary hospitalization: psychiatric vs labeling perspectives. *Journal of Health and Social Behaviour* 25 p14-23

Roth D L and Coles E M (1995). Battered woman syndrome: a conceptual analysis of its status vis a vis DSM-IV mental disorders. *Medicine and Law.* Vol. 14(7-8): p641-658

Royal College Of Nurses (RCN) (2007) *User Involvement in research by nurses.* London: RCN

Rubin, L B (1992) *Worlds of pain: life in the working class family.* New York: Basic Books

Russo V (1987) *The Celluloid Closet, Homosexuality in the movies.* New York: Harper & Row

Rutter D, Manley C, Weaver T, Crawford M, and Fulop N (2004) Patients or Partners? Case Studies of User Involvement in the planing and delivery of adult mental health services in London. *Social Science and Medicine.* 58 p1973-84

Rutter M (1974) *Maternal Deprivation Reassessed.* Harmondsworth: Penguin

Rutter M (1999) Autism; two way interplay between research and clinical work. *Journal of Child Psychology and Psychiatry.* 40 p169-188

Said E (1975) *Orientalism.* NY: Random House

Sandler A, Davies R, Green A, Stern D and Steiner R (2000) *Research, Roots of a controversy.* London: Karnac

Sargant N (1993) *Learning for a purpose: Participation in education and training by adults from ethnic minorities.* Leicester: National Institute of Adult Continuing Education

Sawyers P (2007) *MePLC Your Life is Your Business.* London: My Life is My Business Limited

REFERENCES

Scottham K, Sellers R, Nguyen H (2008) A measure of racial Identity in African American Adolescents: the Development of the Multidimensional Inventory of Black Identity-Teen. *Cultural Diversity and Ethnic Minority Psychology.* 14(4), p297-306

Seacole M (1857) *The wonderful adventures of Mrs Seacole in many lands.* London: James Blackwood

Sender H, Littlechild B, and Smith N (2006) Black and minority ethnic groups and youth offending. *Youth and Policy.* 93 p61-76

Sewell T (1997) *Black Masculinities and Schooling.* Stoke on Trent: Trentham

Sewell T (2009) *Generating Genius.* Stoke on Trent: Trentham

Seymour D (1997) An Annotated Bibliography of the Construct 'Lazy' in Psychological Literature of the 20th Century. Carleton University Website

Sheldon H, Graham C, Pothecary N, and Rasul F (2007) *Increasing response rates amongst BME and seldom heard groups.* Picker Institute Europe. Available online at www.nhssurveys,org/docs/Inpatient_Survey_2007_Increasing_response_rates8.pdf (accessed 30.6.07)

Sherwood M and Spafford M, (1999) Whose freedom were Africans, Caribbeans and Indians defending in the Second World War? *Teaching history, Historical Association,* Volumes 112, 2003, 120, 2005, 122, 2006 Savannah Press

Shohat E and Stam E (2003) *Multiculturalism, postcoloniality and transnational media,* New Jersey: Rutgers University Press

Shujaa M (1994) *Too Much Schooling, Too Little Education: a paradox of black life in white societies.* Trenton: Africa World Press Inc

Singh S (1999) Developing same race placements. *Community Care: Inside Supplement*

Skinner BF (1953) *Science and Human Behavior.* New York: Macmillan

Skinner BF (1957) *Verbal Learning.* New York: Appleton-Century-Crofts

Skinner BF (1971) *Beyond Freedom and Dignity.* New York: Knopf

Smith K (1996) Race and Difference-developing practice in Lifelong Learning Published online. http://www.memset.com/casestudies.php?study=privateeye

Smith R (2003) *Youth Justice – ideas, policy practice.* Dorset: Willan Publishing

Snarey J (1993) *How Fathers Care for the Next Generation: A Four Decade Study.* Cambridge, MA: Harvard University Press

Social Care Institute for Excellence (SCIE) (2006) *Black and minority ethnic service users.* London:SCIE

Social Exclusion Unit (1998) *Truancy and School Exclusion.* London: Cabinet Office

Soffe J (2004) Service Innovations: Service user involvement in training. *Journal of mental Health* 9 p575-587

Sokoloff N, Pratt C and Richie B (eds)(2005) *Domestic violence at the margins: readings on race, class, gender and culture.* London: Blackwell

Solity J (1995) A psychological perspective on teacher professional development. *Journal of Teacher Development,* 4(3) p5-14

Solity J (1996). Reframing psychological assessment, *Educational and Child Psychology.* 13(3) p94-102

Stafford-Clark D (1965) *What Freud Really Said.* Louisiana:Penguin

Staples R and Mirande A (1980) Racial and cultural variations among American families: A decennial review of the literature on minority families. *Journal of Marriage and the Family.* 42(4), p887-903

Steer A (2005) *Learning Behaviour: The Report of the Practitioners' Group on School Behaviour and Discipline.* http://publications.teachernet.gov.uk/default.aspx? PageFunction=productdetails andPageMode=publicationsandProductId=DFES-1950-2005 (accessed1.6.09)

Stein S, Christie D, Shah R, Dabney J, and Wolpert M (2003) Attitudes to and knowledge of CAMHs: differences between Pakistani and white British mothers. *Child and Adolescent Mental Health* 8(1) p29-33

Stewart O (2008) *User Participation in health care services.* London Race Equality Foundation (7) p1-7

Stone M (1980) *The Education of the Black child in Britain: The Myth of Multicultural Education.* London: Fontana

Strachey, J, Freud, A, and Richards, A (1962) *The Standard Edition of the complete Psychological works of Sigmund Freud.* London: Hogarth Press

Strauss, A and Corbin J (1998) *Basics of qualitative research: Techniques and procedures for developing grounded theory.* London: Sage

Strickland T, Jenkins J, Myers H and Adams H (1988) Diagnostic judgements as a function of client and therapist race. *Journal of psychopathology and behavioural assessment* 10 p141-151

Stuart M and Thomson,A (eds) (1998) *Engaging with Difference. The 'Other' in adult education.* Leicester: NIACE

Sue S (1983) Ethnic minority issues in psychology: a re-examination. *American Psychologist.* 38 May p583-92

Sue S (1999) Science, Ethnicity and Bias-Where Have We Gone Wrong? *American Psychologist.* p1070-1077

Sue S (2003) Cultural Competence in the treatment of ethnic minority populations. In Council of National Psychological Associations for the Advancement of Ethnic Minority Interests. *Psychological Treatment of Ethnic minority populations.* Washington: Association of Black Psychology

Sulzer-Azaroff B.and Mayer R (1991) *Behavior analysis for lasting change.* Fort Worth, TX: Holt, Reinhart and Winston, Inc

Swann M (1985) *Education for all. Report of the Committee of Enquiry into the Education of Children from Ethnic Minority Groups.* Scotland: HMSO

Taylor M (1987) *Chinese Pupils in Britain.* Berkshire: NFER-Nelson

Thomas A and Sillen S (1972) *Racism and Psychiatry.* New York: Brunner

Thompson L, Lobb C, Elling R, Herman S, Jurkiewicz S, and Hulleza C (1997) Pathways to Family Empowerment: effects of family-centred delivery of early intervention services. *Exceptional Children.* 64, p99-113

Times Educational Supplement (1974) They're not black so they can't be in our gang. And they're certainly not white now, are they?

Timisui S (2005) *Naughty Boys: Anti Social Behavior, ADHD and the Role of Culture.* London: Macmillan

Tizard B and Phoenix A (1992) *Black, White or Mixed-Race? Race and Racism in the Lives of Young People of Mixed Parentage.* London: Routledge

Tomlinson S (1982) A case of non-achievement: West Indians and ESN-M schooling. In S Tomlinson *Ethnic Minorities in British Schools.* London: Heinneman

Torrey E (1986) *Witch Doctors and Psychiatrists.* San Francisco: Harper and Row

Trevarthen C, Aitken K, Papoudi D and Robarts J (1998) *Children with Autism: Diagnosis and Interventions to meet their needs.* London: Jessica Kingsley

REFERENCES

Tritter J and McCallum A (2006) The Snakes and Ladders of user involvement. *Health Policy* 76 p156-168

Tuakki-Williams, J (1997) West African children. In G. Johnson-Powell and J Yamamoto (eds) *Transcultural child development. Psychological assessment and treatment.* New York: John Willey and Sons

Universal Declaration of Human Rights (1948) United Nations

Unknown. (2008), 'Fatih Akin, Crossing Borders and Boundaries on Film' http://www.npr.org/templates/story/story.php?storyId=90643082 (accessed 23.04.09)

Usmani K (1999) The influence of racism and cultural bias in the assessment of bilingual children. *Educational and Child Psychology.* 16(3), p44-54

Van Deurzen E (2001) The Meaning of Life. *Counselling Psychology Journal.* Dec. p32-33

Verma G and Ashworth N (1986) *Ethnicity and educational achievement in British schools.* Basingstoke: Macmillan

Vincent-Jones P and Hughes D (2009) New Labour's PI Reforms: Patient and Public Involvement in Healthcare Governance? *Modern Law Review* 72(2) p247-271

Wadlow R (2000) States of conflict: gender violence and resistance. In R Jacobsen, J Marchbank (eds) London: Zed

Wajid S (2007) They bought me as a butcher would a calf or lamb. *The Guardian:* 19.10.07 http://www.guardian.co.uk/uk/2007/oct/19/race.historybooks (accessed 04.04.09)

Walker Lenore E (1979) *The Battered Woman.* New York: Harper and Row.

Warnock M (1978) *Special educational needs.* Report of the Committee of Enquiry into the education of handicaped children and young people. London: HMSO

Watson N (2001) Equal Value, Equal Care: Dealing with differences and diversity in Primary Care: In N Watson, and C Wilkinson (eds) *Nursing in Primary Care: a handbook for students.* Basingstoke: Palgrave

Webster-Stratton C (2000) *The incredible years training series.* Office of Juvenile Justice and Delinquency Prevention, Juvenile Justice Bulletin. Washington DC: USA.

Wellard SJ, Bethume E and Heggen K (2007) Assessment of learning in contemporary nurse education: do we need standardised examination for nurse registration? *Nurse Education Today* 27 p68 – 72

Wheldall K and Merrett F (1985) *Manual for the Behavioural Approach to Teaching Package (BATPACK): for use in primary and middle schools.* Positive Products

White D and Woollett A (1992) *Families: A context for development.* London: Falmer Press

White J (1970) *Towards a black psychology.* Ebony

Wikpedia http://en.wikipedia.org/wiki/Yaa_Asantewaa (accessed 3.6.09)

Willey R (1984) *Race, Equality and Schools.* London: Methuen

Williams J (2010) Black UK families and the labour market: the difficulties of establishing a firm economic base. In Ochieng, B and Hylton, C. *Black families in the UK as a site of struggle.* Manchester: Manchester University Press

Williams O (1993) Group work with African American men who batter; toward more ethnically-sensitive practice. *Journal of comparative family studies.* 25, p91-103

Williams P, Turpin G and Hardy G (2006) Clinical psychology service provision and ethnic diversity within the UK: a review of the literature. *Clinical Psychology and Psychotherapy.* 13(5) p324-338

Williams R (1983) *Keywords: A Vocabulary of Culture and society.* London: Fontana

Wilson A (1978) *Developmental Psychology of the Black Child.* New York: Africana Research Publications

Wilson A and Beresford P (2000) Anti-opressive Practice: Emancipation or Appropriation? *British Journal of Social Work.* 30 p553-573

Wilson D and Moore S (2003) *Playing the Game – The Experiences of young Black Men in Custody.* London: Children's Society

Wing L (1996) *The autistic spectrum,* London: Constable

Wing L and Gould J (1979) Severe impairments of social interaction and associated abnormalities in children: Epidemiology and classification. *Journal of Autism and Developmental Disorders.* 9(1), p11-29

Winnicott D (1958) *Primary Maternal Pre-occupation. (Collected papers in through paediatrics to psychoanalysis.* London: Tavistock

Woodrow D and Sham S (2001) Chinese pupils and their learning preferences. *Race, Equity and Education* 4 p377-394

World Bank (2000) *Listening to the voices of the poor.* Washington DC: World Bank

World Health Organisation (1992) *International Classification of Diseases, 10th Edition. Classification of Mental and Behavioural Disorders: Clinical descriptions diagnostic guidelines.* Geneva: Author

Wright C (1992) Early education, multiracial primary school classrooms in D Gill, B Mayor and M Blair (eds). *Racism in education, structures and strategies.* London: Sage

Wyatt D (2001) Racism, Class and Masculinity: Race, class, culture and gender-based violence. http://www.eurowrc.org/13.institutions/5.un/un-en/16.un_en.htm (accessed 13.7.09)

Yarborough M and Bennett C (2002) *Mammy Sapphire Jezebel and Their Sisters.* http://www.artesana.com/articles/mammy_saphire.htm (accessed 3.6.09)

Yeargin-Allsop M., Rice C, Karapurkar T, Doernberg N, Boyle C, and Murphy C (2003) Prevalence of autism in a US metropolitan area. *Journal of the American Medical Association,* 289, 49-55

Ye_ilada K. E. (2008) Turkish-German Screen Power – The Impact of Young Turkish Immigrant on German TV and Film, *gfl-journal,* n°1, p73-96

Yin R (2003) *Case study Research: Design and methods.* CA: Sage

Young E (1998) *Psychoanalysis and Racism: A Loud silence.* London: Macmillan

Youth Justice Board (2004) *Race audit and action planning toolkit for Youth Offending Teams.* www.youth-justice-board.gov.uk (accessed 19.7.09)

Zellmer K (2003) *Problem-Solving Skills 101: A Behavior-Management Program for Young Students.* New York:LRP

Zeitlin M, Megawangi R, Kramer E, Colletta N, Babatunde E, and Garman G (1995) *Strengthening the family – Implications for international development.* United Nations University Press

Zweig, C and Abrams J (1990) Introduction: the shadow side in everyday life. In C Zweig and J Abrams (eds) *Meeting the shadow: the hidden power of the dark side of human nature.* NY: Madison

Index

achievement 2, 124, 134
African history 19,
American Psychological Association (APA) 21
Autism 89-99

behaviourism 154
bilingualism/multilingualism 22, 101-111
black history 169
black psychologists 17, 23, 24, 27, 28
black psychology 20-22, 71, 76, 153, 155
black self-concept 154-162
black women *see* women
British Psychological Society (BPS) 1, 4, 34-35
BPS Standing Committee for Equal Opportunities 23

Child and Adolescent Mental Health Service 10, 81
childbirth 10
clinical psychology 1, 3, 83, 86
cognitive behavioural therapy (CBT) 70
cognitive psychology 156
colour-blindness 12, 31
community education 119, 121
community psychology 80, 87
counselling 142
cultural awareness 16, 160
cultural competence 20, 31, 34-35, 99, 103, 183

discourse analysis 30
drugs 159
English as an additional language (EAL) 102, 107, 160 *see also* bilingualism
educational psychologists (EPs) 20, 63-64, 133
Educational Psychology Service 27
equal opportunities 22
ethics 11, 30, 34-35, 91
Every Child Matters 102, 153
evidence-based practice 10
exclusions 21
existential psychology 156
existential therapy 159-160

families 2, 3, 88 *see also* parents
family worker 82-83
fear 10, 40 65
forensic psychologist 30-31, 33-34
Further and Higher Education 47-53

homophobia 177, 183-190
humanistic psychology 154-155, 158-159

identity 18
immigrants 36, 81, 182
inclusion 101, 103, 165
inclusion manager 106-107
institutional racism 17, 23, 31, 50, 75 *see also* racism
interpreters 13
Johari Window 156-158

Jung, C 135, 141, 143
Justice System, Juvenile 29-35
kin networks 35, 93, 125-126

Learning Difficulties and Disabilities (LDD) 101, 107, 160

marginalisation 175
masculinity 115-119, 133, 136, 138, 140, 143
Mental Health Act 32
mothers 78-87 *see also* parents

non-verbal communication (NVC) 13, 109
Nursing and Midwifery Council (NMC) 10

Obama, Barack 53
Ofsted 101, 179
organisational culture 15

parenting programmes 82, 84
parents 57-67, 79-88, 89-99
pedagogy 41, 121
pluralism 22
positive discrimination 42
practitioners 23, 34-35, 37-42
prejudice 123
Project 2000 10
projection 72, 92
psychiatric diagnosis 91, 99
 – DSM-V 90
 – ICD-10 90

psychiatrists 31
psychodynamic theory 62, 92

Race Equality Impact
   Assessments (REQUIAs)
   39
Race Equality SWOT
   Analysis 42
racism 12, 20, 29, 30, 31,
   176, 177
Rastafarianism 32
reflexivity 91, 94, 99

schools 21, 25-26, 43, 65-66,
   81, 104, 118-119, 132
scientific racism 30
self-acceptance 160
self-concept 167
self-determination theory 156
self-development 16, 40-41,
   44
self-esteem 167
SEN 58-59, 90, 101
SENCo 104-106
Slavery 137
sociology 155, 166
spirituality 83, 92, 98
stereotypes 1, 2, 30, 32, 32
Systemic Theory 38, 92

testing 20-21, 33-35
Triad of Impairments 90

user involvement 145

violence *see* domestic abuse

West Africa 11, 93
women 165-181 *see also*
   parents
World view 34
   – African 21, 93-99
   – Eurocentric 20, 21